MBA Admissions Strategy

★★★★★ Amazon.com reviews for the first edition:

Amazingly good

"This book is incredible. I'm in the process of applying. If you've got the time to devote to doing apps 'right', this book will guide you through a surprisingly rigorous, insightful, and valuable process to decide on and write your essays. Particularly if you're of an analytical mindset, it will help you apply very helpful, intuitive frameworks to thinking about your app. Buy this book."

Great book, great value

"This book was very informative and a quick read. This was my first attempt at getting into grad school. I've been out for over 15 years and I had no idea where to begin. The book outlines section by section what adcom is looking for and gave me some ideas as to how to minimize any weaknesses I had on my application. . . . I have been accepted to one of the top 20 schools in the nation. I only applied to one school! So excited."

This book helped me get into INSEAD

"If you buy only one book about how to apply to a top 20 MBA, make it this book!

Easy to read, straight to the point, very practical, it makes you take the customer's (MBA admissions committee) viewpoint on your application with lots of insights into what happens with your application after you send it in . . . By luck I stumbled across this book and I would say it helped me tremendously to get into INSEAD (ranked No. 5 worldwide in latest FT ranking)."

Best book on the subject

"MUST HAVE BOOK. By far the best book on the subject.

Even if you have already purchased Richard Montauk book or any other MBA consulting book, I still advise that you buy and read this book.

If you have not purchased any book yet, I strongly recommend you to start with this book.

If you are targeting top 15 MBA programs, reading this book will be the best thing you could do to improve your chances.

Pros –

1) Very structured approach. It begins with helping you profile yourself.
2) No nonsense material. Very brief, succinct and to the point.
3) It leaves the obvious clutter out. Author does not repeat himself. I think this is the biggest plus of this book. There are many top sellers (no names), which are too thick at the expense of being repetitive.
4) Comprehensive.
5) Refined. Polished."

I couldn't agree more

"I have bought a LOT of MBA books, pretty much everything you can think about, but I have never written a review for any one of them. I honestly felt guilty not to write one for this book. That should just give you an idea of how good this book is. This is the book that you WANT to read. Most people who give reviews don't mention what I consider the single most important part of this book: Whoever you are or whatever you have done, if you want to go to b-school, you can."

★★★★★ Amazon.co.uk reviews for the first edition:

Well worth the money

"This is a succinct and at the same time comprehensive guide for anyone targeting the top schools. Reading the book in the beginning of the application process will save a lot of time later on. I found it especially helpful at the brainstorming stage and in developing themes and positioning. Tips on essay writing are invaluable."

Well written and full of insights

"The book is dedicated towards tackling essays which is an area which many (including me) struggle with. The book repeatedly emphasises the importance of marketing oneself through the application campaign. It does an excellent job in this respect as it is filled with insights such as personality profiling, extracting themes and mapping these themes into the essays . . . Full of useful self-marketing tips such as creating your own memorable labels to insert into the essays.

I wish I had read the book earlier! This book certainly stands out among the crowd of books on the subject."

Fantastic. Well-written and very helpful

"I highly recommend this book. It is one of the newest MBA admissions strategy offerings, so I figure the info is up-to-date. The 22 specific attributes, and the way they fall on the diagram of 4 general attributes have been very helpful to me in writing my essays. Also the essay archetypes saved a lot of time. The real surprise though is that this book is enjoyable to read. I have reread some sections several times, the advice is logical and nuanced."

It'll make the difference between good and great

"A great GMAT score on its own won't get you into a top business school, an average one makes it even harder (but not impossible) – your essays make all the difference!

I really enjoyed this book and its practical advice and guidance really helped. I'm off to an Ivy League school in the States this year, down in no small part to essays written after reading this book:

BUY IT!"

MBA Admissions Strategy

From profile building to essay writing

2nd Edition

Avi Gordon

Open University Press

Open University Press
McGraw-Hill Education
McGraw-Hill House
Shoppenhangers Road
Maidenhead
Berkshire
England
SL6 2QL

email: enquiries@openup.co.uk
world wide web: www.openup.co.uk

and Two Penn Plaza, New York, NY 10121-2289, USA

First published 2010

Copyright © Avi Gordon 2010

All rights reserved. Except for the quotation of short passages for the purposes of
criticism and review, no part of this publication may be reproduced, stored in a
retrieval system, or transmitted, in any form or by any means, electronic,
mechanical, photocopying, recording or otherwise, without the prior written
permission of the publisher or a licence from the Copyright Licensing Agency
Limited. Details of such licences (for reprographic reproduction) may be obtained
from the Copyright Licensing Agency Ltd of Saffron House, 6–10 Kirby Street,
London, EC1N 8TS.

A catalogue record of this book is available from the British Library

ISBN-13: 978-0-33-524117-0
ISBN-10: 0-33-524118-7

Library of Congress Cataloging-in-Publication Data
CIP data applied for

Typeset by RefineCatch Limited, Bungay, Suffolk
Printed in the UK by Bell and Bain Ltd, Glasgow

Fictitious names of companies, products, people, characters and/or data that may
be used herein (in case studies or in examples) are not intended to represent any
real individual, company, product or event.

Mixed Sources
Product group from well-managed
forests and other controlled sources
www.fsc.org Cert no. TT-COC-002769
© 1996 Forest Stewardship Council

The McGraw·Hill Companies

Contents

Preface to the second edition   vii

Acknowledgments   ix

Introduction   1

PART ONE
Admissions Fundamentals   5

  1 **Marketing to Adcom**   7
  2 **Attributes that count**   15
  3 **Admissions fundamentals**   28
  4 **Investigating schools and managing social
      media resources**   42
  5 **What goes on after you hand in your application**   51

PART TWO
Profile-Building Tools and Techniques   61

  6 **The profiling project**   63
  7 **Personal profile analysis**   72
  8 **Professional profile analysis**   79
  9 **Positioning, messaging, and mapping**   85

PART THREE
Essay and Interview Management   95

10 **The MBA essay question archetypes (part 1)**   97
11 **The MBA essay question archetypes (part 2)**   117
12 **The MBA essay question archetypes (part 3)**   131
13 **Essay approaches and content mapping**   146
14 **The interview**   153

PART FOUR
Writing Tools and Methods   169

15 **Managing the reader's experience**   171
16 **Idea discipline, structure, and outlines**   182
17 **Improving expression: word and sentence strategies**   199

Conclusion 208

    Notes 211
    Appendix: essay revision checklist 213
    Index 215

Preface to the second edition

The first edition of *MBA Admissions Strategy* has been critically and commercially well received. Most gratifying of all has been the reader response from its core target readership—MBA applicants—particularly the many who have written reader reviews on Amazon.com or Amazon.co.uk reader to say how much the book helped them. I too have learned a lot in the intervening years from my clients, from other admissions coaches, and from the business schools themselves, so this new edition gives me the opportunity to add this in.

Also, trends move fast in MBA Admissions, demanding an updating and refinement of the methods of the book. While written essays remain the core of the communication between applicant and admissions committee, and this won't change anytime soon, there are clear trends to augmenting written essays with "alternative" submissions: presentations, multimedia essays, and so on. This gets more play here. Further, driven by the same trends towards visual and talk-based communication, the MBA interview is becoming ever more important. In this edition the interview gets a whole chapter. Other trends are affecting the MBA Admissions field. Social media, for example, has changed how schools communicate and how applicants do their due diligence. Business scandals and "business ethics" have changed corporate practice. All these are increasingly reflected in MBA admissions and therefore considered at greater length here.

On the other hand, many of the fundamentals remain the same. There is still no substitute for understanding what makes you, the applicant, singularly valuable to the business school, and packaging and communicating your value message successfully. This is what this book is fundamentally about. So, while sections have been added, care has been taken to keep the book "lean and mean," around this fundamental principle, just as in the first edition.

As before, I have specifically *not* tried to write an encyclopedia of the MBA admissions process, because others have done this (and almost all the information at this level is easily available on the Web.) I have stuck to what's hard for MBA applicants to find: the what-I-wish-they'd-told-me insights that come from having worked with thousands of successful applications to top b-schools schools. This is a guide specifically aiming to get you past the sweet-talk and give you what you need to know so you don't go in with your eyes closed. At the top level, MBA admissions is astoundingly competitive and unforgiving. This is not a "try hard and wish you well" book. It's a streetfighter's guide.

This book brings together, to this point, the best of my skills and insights into successfully managing the elite MBA admissions process. For ongoing updated commentary and advice, please see my website at http://mbastudio.net.

Acknowledgments

No book comes into being without considerable assistance from many outside sources. Melanie Havelock, the book's principal at McGraw Hill-Open University Press has helped me constantly from 2005 to 2009, including championing this second edition. Under her guidance, various MBA admissions industry reviewers (who remained anonymous to me) suggested many great improvements for this edition, and I would like to acknowledge and thank them. Since then, Katherine Morton has brought this edition into existence, most ably filling Melanie's shoes. I would also like to thank the many clients of the *MBA Admissions Studio* (http:// mbastudio.net) who have enthusiastically adopted and enacted the principles suggested in this book and therein not only corroborated its approach with their many high-level admissions successes, but also taught me where I need to sharpen my game. Finally I'd also like to acknowledge the Association of Graduate Admissions Consultants (AIGAC), of which I am a member, which provides an expert community and resource base for graduate admissions advisors, and which upholds standards and ethics in the field.

Avi Gordon,
April 2010

Introduction

Get wise! Admissions is the final exam

You can get an MBA a thousand ways, but graduates from the top-20 or so brand-name business schools start higher, progress faster, and have more senior and interesting careers. Whatever the degree costs, those coming from the better institutions reap the investment with interest in their lifetimes. It's dumb not to aim as high as possible. Of course, everyone else knows this too, which is why admissions at the top level are so competitive.

The other thing to know right upfront is that nobody fails business school. Every year, in every program, everyone graduates, save a few extreme cases where students have serious adjustment or disciplinary problems (and they are excluded early.) In other words, every candidate who is admitted will graduate *because* they were admitted. In fact, the better the school's reputation, the less grades or exams seem to matter. If you were good enough to get in, you're good enough, period.

But, of course, only a tiny percentage of applicants are admitted to competitive admission MBA programs. Figures go up and down with the economic cycle, but on average 5–15 percent of applicants are admitted to exclusive institutions. In other words, *application failure* is the norm. What this means is that the MBA application is, for all practical purposes, the final exam. Admission is the only hurdle between the candidate and a top MBA, and all the fast-track career good fortune it brings.

But real people pass it

Part of business school culture, one quickly learns, is that the MBA is *not* an "academic" degree. Smart people are required, of course, but you will repeatedly hear how the most intelligent don't always make the best managers and business leaders. This explains why seats are often refused to brilliant academicians and those with 750+ GMATs, and offered instead to candidates with diverse experience, personality, talent, and drive. Admissions committees (Adcoms) constantly reward dynamic, efficient people with a track record of real-world success, particularly if they appear easily recruitable on MBA-exit, and have interesting, worthwhile plans for the future.

This means that anyone (of appropriate age, with respectable undergraduate results and test scores, and a good professional record) has a realistic chance of getting into the finest business schools . . . assuming they have the strategic and competitive understanding of *what* in their background is valuable to the Adcom and the communications ability to make their case powerfully. Yes, the top business schools are populated with air force pilots and Senators' daughters, but every year many thousands of apparently very ordinary people are accepted too, because they applied well. That is, they found and compellingly communicated the valuable attributes in their background and connected them closely to the needs of business school admissions officers. Getting in is a little bit about pure intelligence and a lot about procedural and organizational smarts. This is to say, the tools and techniques of admissions matter enormously. You don't need to be a superstar. You just need to be competitive and apply well. Or better still, apply "smart."

By applying "smart"

This book is about how to apply smart. It is written to be the word of experience in your ear as you assemble your application to competitive business schools so that you can do it better than your competitors. It is a tactical guide to turning a good application that will get you only so far into an exceptional one that will get you where you want to go. But, please note, it does not offer a "mystery key" to unlock the admissions gate. There is no such key. Getting in is the result of successfully identifying, maximizing, and communicating your value, and combining this with knowledge of the admissions system and preferences. No more, and no less.

Nor is this book an admissions "pep talk," of the kind that unfortunately plagues these sort of guides both on- and off-line. Here we don't offer nice-sounding advice like "develop your essay theme", or "play to your strengths," or "show integrity." We provide step-by-step methods for *how* to do it, including analytic tools, diagnostic exercises, and practical to-do's and don'ts.

Guide to the guide

The book is divided into four parts: admissions fundamentals, profile development, essay and interview management and interviewing, and writing techniques.

Part One discusses the players, practices, and culture of the MBA admissions process and how to promote yourself in this context. It describes the attributes schools seek in applicants and the various considerations they have in admitting or rejecting applicants. It considers not only how the process works from the point of view of the Adcom, but also who it works for and how the needs of the committee's stakeholder base play out in various stages of the admissions process. Insight is provided into many practical areas, including researching and choosing schools, understanding school rankings, timing the application, managing the GMAT, strategizing recommendations and preparing recommenders, and managing the MBA resume.

Part Two shifts the focus from the admissions process to the candidate's own profile. It offers profile diagnostic tools to analyze both personal and professional profile strengths, weaknesses, and distinguishing factors. This is followed by techniques to identify and extract the most important and persuasive parts—the key areas of competitive value—and consolidate them into presentable, coherent, application themes, and guidelines for developing these themes into a strategic positioning and a compelling message.

Parts Three and Four show how the profiling work done in the previous parts is carried forward and applied to the essay and interview requirements—how to know what to say where, and how to say it well. Part Three deals with the problem of understanding the essay questions and fitting a profile and application message to them. The 10 MBA question "archetypes" are revealed, which provides the basis for recognizing each question, and therefore understanding what answer information is relevant, what might be additional, and what is superfluous. A consolidated approach to mapping an application profile message to the essay questions is provided, along with a worked example. Following that, the interview process is discussed in similar terms, and a step-by-step guide to interviewing well is provided.

Part Four is about how to write the essays, from first draft to final revision. It examines the tools and techniques for attracting and retaining readers and promoting message absorption, beginning with targeting the admissions officer with important and relevant information. Solutions for organizing and structuring essays are addressed, and templates for organizing specific essays are suggested. Various principles of better writing, including developing stories, using imagery, creating emotive effect, and managing tone, are provided. Common essay pitfalls are identified and fixes suggested. The part ends with strategies for a first essay draft and seeing it through the revision process, including tips for improving expression, sentence construction, and word choice. An essay revision checklist is provided at the back of the book.

PART ONE
Admissions Fundamentals

1 Marketing to Adcom

Marketing yourself

MBA admissions turns on the simplest and oldest rule in communications strategy: to win, you need to connect your objectives with those of your audience. You need to understand what they need or are ready to hear, and increase the overlap between that and what you have to say. If you are better than the next applicant at demonstrating the common ground between your objectives and the objectives of the MBA program's admissions committee (Adcom), you will be accepted.

Conveying a sense of fit between an item and its target audience is, of course, nothing other than marketing. Your application to business school is a marketing campaign. You have to introduce and sell a product (you) to a consumer/client (the admissions committee) under competitive conditions. You have to understand the needs, wants, and desires of your clients in detail so you know what they value and why they value it, and how to pitch your product within this value system.

Just as Colgate Palmolive researches your toothpaste preferences, creates a desired product, and sells it by telling you how it correlates with your needs, so you too must research your "buyer" preferences, shape yourself into an attractive and necessary product, and coordinate various methods of communication (essays, interviews, recommendations) to get the committee to pick you ahead of the rest. You have to create a coordinated campaign to influence the admissions officers' buying decision, and manage this campaign as it unrolls over weeks or months.

Or getting elected

Another, similar way to look at the process is to think of yourself as campaigning for elected office. You are the politician, the b-school Adcom members are the voters. Every other applicant is also standing for office. You each have your platform: what you stand for, what you will bring, what you will do if elected, and what you have done in the past that proves this intent. You each get opportunities to make your case. Your job is to understand your voters' needs and wants better that the others, and to find, champion, and communicate the parts of you that fit with their agenda.

Understanding your admissions task in these terms should turn your application world upside down: it's not just "about you." It's about your *fit* with them. Companies don't make products and then try to sell them. They study the market, determine needs, and produce accordingly. Politicians are influenced enormously by voter sentiment and are led by the polls. (Perhaps this is unfortunate, but it works.) If you know what the admissions committee is looking for and listening for, you can almost always find things in your profile to hit the right notes.

But staying true to you.

There is an important, immediate caveat. Nothing about this market-driven approach implies that you should try to bend yourself into the mold of what you think the ideal business school applicant is. There is no one MBA applicant success "type." In fact, paradoxically, trying to be the stereotypical candidate puts you right outside your target because they want a spread of different, diverse individuals, not stereotyped generality. Therefore, your marketing and electioneering task is always to be highly individualized and absolutely true to yourself—but also savvy about which parts of yourself happen to overlap best with Adcom's needs and preferences, and alert to ways of communicating that overlap. Your application task is one of judicious profile selection and framing, not self-compromise.

Pursuing a two-way fit

When a school has more good candidates than places, the Adcom will not just be choosing the best candidates and the best class balance. They will also have the luxury of selecting those whose profile, contribution, and aspirations match—in the short and in the long term—the educational offerings and culture of their business school. The questions the committee will be asking are not just whether this candidate is impressive and interesting. They will also ask: Does he fit with us? How does she add value to our community? Will her style of work mesh with our school and its way of doing things? Will he interact well with the kinds of people we have here and the kind of programs we offer? Will he be recruitable by the kinds of firms that come to this campus? Remember one key thing. You are not just applying for a seat in a classroom. You are applying for membership of a select community, for the duration of the degree and for life.

This means that you have to provide a specific argument not just why you are a good candidate for *any* program, but why you are the right candidate for the particular program and its community. They want you to show the overlap between your goals and the school's distinguishing attributes, and explain why their program and their community, rather than any other, is exactly the right one to help you meet your MBA and post-MBA aspirations.

How to do it

Market positioning, brand characteristics, and reputation—the mix of place, values, reputation, attitudes, and faculty strengths that it projects—all serve to distinguish the school and keep its attractiveness to top students, top faculty, Fortune 100 recruiters, and major donors focused. You will *not* be able to gain insight to institutions at this level by reading their glossy promotion brochures, because schools inevitably all claim to be strong all-round. You will only begin to understand a school when you get underneath all the surface chatter and general promotional claptrap about it, and find what really underpins its brand identity.

You will be able to glean this in such items as press releases on new initiatives for the program, or by seeing what type and level of faculty are being hired (and which types are moving on), or what conferences are being held on campus, or co-sponsored by the university and certain (which?) corporations, and so on. Among the best resources for this are blogs of current students and faculty, who sometimes are ready to tell things as they are, warts and all. Understanding what a school is really about requires a bit of skepticism and some hard-nosed investigation to get behind the institutional spin. It won't be given to you on a plate. More about how to research programs is offered in Chapter 4.

But general requirements trump specifics every time

As you begin to understand what exactly each school stands for and what it is aspiring to stand for, and therefore what drives Adcom's choices at this deeper level, it will become clearer how choosing you (or not) fits with the school's broader aspirations, and you will be in a better position to understand what about you might be a more or less valuable contribution. This understanding can then find its way into your essays as you position yourself as a reliable vehicle for the continuance of their brand and their culture and the expansion of the school's "mission."

However, the specificity looked for by each institution is almost always *the smaller* part of what they are looking for. Look across any entry or graduation class and you would be hard pressed to say that accepted students are prototypes of the school's brand. Yes, many will clearly be a fit with one or other part of it, but class diversity and balance remain the dominant force. Why? Because business school education is not a pre-packaged set of skills that you are going to be "spoon fed," but thousands of learning events, co-created between faculty and students, and between the students themselves. The diversity of the student group makes a huge difference to the quality of the program. Therefore, they can't just admit "the best." They have to balance the incoming cohort in terms of abilities and experiences, in order to provide the best overall learning for all. So all Adcoms are looking for class balance, not class prototype, which means the type of candidate sought by the top business schools *in general* is more important in admissions than what "type" any specific school allegedly wants. As discussed further in the next chapter, they all want more or less the same thing.

Seeing the world through Adcom's eyes

So what does Adcom want? To find and exploit the overlap between you and the Adcom, you need to step into their shoes and understand their point of view: what they are looking for, what persuades them, what's most important about you to them, who they will choose, who they will reject, and why. If you know this, you will be able to think through any MBA application as an admissions officer would, and know why—if you were in their position—you would say "yes" or "no" to your application.

Part of this to get straight exactly who you are talking to. This doesn't mean you should be looking to target or "game" your essays in a narrow sense. But getting your head around who is on the other end is a crucial part of your role in creating effective communication and thereby getting admitted. Allowing for minor variations according to the specific school and its management philosophy, the following are the main categories of people processing your file:

- current (2nd year) MBA students working in the admissions office;
- adjunct application "readers;"
- alumni interviewers;
- academic faculty;
- career services representatives;
- professional admissions staff.

At some schools, particularly in the US, current students have a role in selecting future students. They may do simple "back-office" processing of files, but they may also be doing "first-reads" of essays, and sometimes even conducting on-campus interviews. At Wharton, for example, current students play a huge role. Other schools don't use students but may employ adjunct outside readers to do early-stage assessment. The main purpose of these inputs is to do initial screening and weeding out of clear "non-starters." The current students have considerable say in determining the first cut but don't have the final say in who gets an offer of a place.

Alumni interviewers are also satellites in the process, providing external evaluation of candidates, particularly of those who live or work far from the campus. The admissions committee also may contain the dean or members of academic faculty (rotating). For university political reasons, admissions is often set up so academics can—should they choose to—wield influence and have the final say. But be sure that the non-research, non-publishing, non-teaching work of admissions is very far from the primary concern of most academics. Their bias is, generally, to have the smartest students, from interesting, diverse backgrounds, but they have, at best, a mild supervisory stake in the process.

Career services officers are often on the committee too. Their interest is that the Adcom offers places to students who (on exiting with an MBA) will be desirable in the marketplace. They represent the interests of the school brand that does not benefit from having unemployed graduates hanging around. Their bias in admissions is obviously applicants with great work experience and a history of professional success and promotion.

Just who are professional admissions staff?

The real force in the admissions office is the corps of professional admissions officers. These are not academics and usually not MBAs either. With some exceptions, they will have little specialist knowledge of engineering, technology, or business. Although statistical processes augment admissions decision-making, it is very unlikely that there will be any genuine quantitatively oriented people in the admissions office. They are, in fact, mostly career human resources professionals, typically with a strong background and prior professional experience in the human and social sciences and training in areas such as human resources management, organizational behavior, psychology, or education. They often have a mixed background with many experiences.

For example, here is a *Business Week* extract on the background of the current (at time of writing) UCLA-Anderson Director of MBA Admissions:

> The assistant dean and director of MBA Admissions at the UCLA Anderson School of Management, says she ended up an admissions officer the way most people do—unintentionally. She went to Russia to teach public policy, but was assigned to teach negotiations at a business school at the last minute. After two years, she wanted to continue her Eastern European stay and almost took a job teaching in Kazakhstan. Her graduate school loans, however, forced her back to the U.S. There [her] international and business-school experience eventually led her into the admissions department at Anderson.[1]

This is not an extreme profile. It is the everyday profile of an Adcom member. Every admissions officer is of course different. But it appears in most cases that becoming an admissions officer is not a direct career path. Most come to it "sideways." They have lived life in more than one industry and often more than one country. They typically have broad interests, are people-focused, and are good communicators.

So here's the news: the professional admissions officer is a *completely different person* to the average MBA applicant. They have different personal and professional interests and they are on a different career track. They do not live life to create positive free-cash-flows or to take companies public, or other things that MBAs live for.

The road to Adcom's heart

Good marketing people know you get people to buy stuff through offering psychological fulfillment. You can cut prices and add freebies, but this mostly provides an "excuse" for a purchase. The real reason people pick products or services is because it makes them *feel* something, or feel that they *are* something.

As marketeer Jerry Bader puts it:

> Cosmetics make women feel attractive or sexy, while cars make men feel they've achieved some level of status. Even services make people feel important, as in "I've got a guy, who does that for me." Finding the psychological hot spot in your marketing, and promoting the hell out of it consistently and continually should be your primary marketing goal.[2]

The implications of all this are paramount. If you are to persuade a human resources professional working of your value as a candidate, you need to make the effort to anticipate and engage *their* psychological fulfillment and talk to *their* language of motivation. You need to reach *their* hot spot. What is that? Why do they do their job in the first place? They are in admissions because they are the kind of people who are interested in:

1. People, their lives, their motivations, their challenges and their choices.
2. Groups and organizations, and how people come together and function to achieve larger goals.
3. Education and skills development, and the advancement of knowledge resources and human capital.

Their professional challenge, their joy and triumph, is to apply their superior people skills and organizational insight to select the best candidates for admission, and to construct a balance of abilities, experiences, and attributes across the class intake.

This means they will be most readily engaged by your lucid, insightful, carefully motivated human resources-friendly self-analysis and life-path analysis, complete with a well-developed understanding of your organizational and leadership profile. No matter what the particular business or technical thrust of your application, you need to frame it and yourself adequately in such human "behavioral" terms.

Reflective writing for "people people"

I know of no better example of Adcom's call for the behavioral side of your candidacy than this (2004) guidance to applicants from Stanford's admissions office:

> Our goal is to gain insight into the person behind the resume. We encourage you to share with us your influences, motivations, passions, values, interests, and aspirations. Although there are no "right answers" here, the most effective essays emphasize the "who" and "why" as well as the "what." We believe each applicant has a set of unique experiences and perspectives to bring to the Business School community. This is your opportunity to share what you consider to be most important: treat your essays as "conversations on paper." Tell us your story, and tell it in a natural and honest way.[3]

Here is Stanford essay advice from 2009:

> The best examples of Essay 1 reflect the process of self-examination that you have undertaken to write them. They give us a vivid and genuine image of who you are—and they also convey how you became the person you are. They do not focus merely on what you've done or accomplished. Instead, they share with us the values, experiences, and lessons that have shaped your perspectives. They are written from the heart and address not only a person, situation, or event, but also how that person, situation, or event has influenced your life.[4]

As you can see, little has changed in five years, and you can be sure there is nothing unique to Stanford in this. All the top schools would endorse this advice.

Taking this on board makes the MBA applicant interview and essay writing job both harder and easier. It's easier to engage an interesting person. Almost any topic you raise will be valid material in their eyes. But it's harder if all your stories are highly technical, or closely work-oriented, or if you don't have the skills to analyze your actions and choices. If your life experience or perspective is limited, and thus your ability to reflect deeply and persuasively on your life and career path is therefore also limited, you're not going to impress someone with broad life and people experience.

The pressure-reward system for admissions officers

There is more. If you are to fully understand the motivations and choices of the Adcom, you must also understand the systemic network of responsibilities, rewards, and censures that admissions officers operate inside of. Adcoms are, in fact, directly and indirectly responsible to a broad set of stakeholders (Figure 1.1.)

In other words, in choosing between you and the next candidate, they have to be satisfied that you will make the grade:

- *For the other students*: to provide them with the smartest, most talented, most diverse and most experienced class.
- *For recruiters*: to provide them with quality candidates who are valuable and recruitable on exit from the program.
- *For alumni*: to provide them with a continued high-value, high-achiever network in the future, to maintain the exclusivity and value of the alumni network.
- *For the faculty*: to provide them with brightest, most interesting, most challenging students.
- *For the school*: to provide it with another excellent, lifetime ambassador who will reflect well on the institution wherever he or she goes. (Ideally, also someone who makes lots of money and donates handsomely to the school.)

Note that these stakeholders' concerns mature over different time horizons. The needs of fellow students, and faculty are immediate. Recruiters' needs are a year or two away, while the interests of the alumni and the university are five or more years off. This explains why the Adcom examines you both as a short-term asset who can

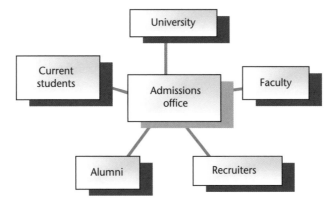

Figure 1.1   The five stakeholder sets an MBA admissions committee has responsibilities to

contribute immediately (due to experience, intelligence, team skills, personality, diversity, and so on) and as a long-term asset who will mature into a senior business position in years to come (as suggested by leadership potential, management capabilities, ambition, etc.).

So don't forget that, while the process is competitive for you, it is competitive for them too. For admissions officers to best serve each of their stakeholder communities, they must compete furiously against other schools to choose a class of the finest candidates, to satisfy their various stakeholders. Even for the top programs, getting "the best" is not something they take for granted. Most invest many hundreds of thousands of dollars in expensive marketing to attract quality applicants, and they take the business of screening them very seriously. They rigorously process many thousands of applications, normally under quite tight deadlines, to separate out the best ones. And, as we have seen, it is not only about selecting the best. The pressure is on them to shape a balanced and diverse class from the applications they get.

Communicating your value

If you understand that the admissions office is answerable to each of these stakeholders, you understand the risk that each offer of a place implies for the admissions officer. In accepting a candidate, they are betting on that candidate fulfilling the needs of the school's various stakeholders better than every one of the rejected applicants. It is a risk which can and does backfire from time to time—as students bomb out, drop out, cheat, disrupt teams, upset faculty, or annoy recruiters. If you position yourself as the candidate who will help the admissions officers to most comprehensively and reliably serve their various stakeholders, they will be inclined to take a risk on you and make you an offer. If you look like you might embarrass them with regard to all or some of these stakeholders, you will be too high-risk and you will be rejected.

The better you are able to help them satisfy the demands of this competitive situation on them, the more likely you are to move through the system towards admission. Don't expect them to mine your application for its value. It is up to you to understand what is valuable, and for you to frame yourself broadly in those terms. Chapter 2 elaborates what Adcoms are looking for.

2 Attributes that count

What satisfies the admissions committee?

We saw in the previous chapter that each business school's internal culture and market position are slightly different. Each program has a slightly different "signature" in terms of curriculum, type of students, faculty interest, clubs and extramurals, internship-recruitment opportunities, alumni network. Part of your task in seeking admissions is definitely to show that you understand what each school's "signature" is and why you fit with it, and it with you.

But it is important not to overplay this. If you cruise the Web, you will see soundbites of advice, saying that "Kellogg seeks team players," or "Ross looks for immersion learners" or "Harvard looks for leaders," and so on. These are clichés. Kellogg is not just about teamwork, Wharton is not just about finance, Chicago-Booth is not only for quants, and so on. Harvard looks for every quality, as does Ross-Michigan, as do all schools. If you look across the programs, you will see that they are far more similar to each other than they are different, and all schools are looking for students way beyond their (alleged) core type.

This is the first reason that any school-specific criteria count less than overall criteria in any admissions decision. The second reason is because, as we saw in the previous chapter, schools are required to provide a varied and balanced cohort, which absolutely mandates a wide diversity of intake. To indulge their own stereotype would be to do so at the cost of class variety and balance.

So, yes, they will want to see that there is a fit between you and the program—particularly that they can offer you the training and opportunities for development that you specifically need. And, yes, they do want to know that you will fit in with their program style and emphasis. But this does not imply that they want you to be in any way their "stereotype" cookie-cutter student. Look at the profiles of accepted students at every top-tier program and you'll see that it's a wide variety of backgrounds and a wider still range of personal and professional experiences. The bottom line, anything you are (as long as it's impressive on its own terms) is a valid basis for admission. You do not need to be, or contort yourself to be, a bearer of a school's (alleged) type to get in.

So programs all apply very similar criteria, with similar weightings, asking the same kinds of questions, making the same demands, and competing for candidates with similar demonstrated skills. These are the 22 attributes that all programs look for:

1. *Intellectual ability*: A candidate who is smart and easily able to handle the demands of the schoolwork and, ultimately, the business world. This is assessed by academic record (GPA or equivalent) and GMAT score, although other postgraduate and non-degree score may be considered. The GPA and GMAT are particularly valuable in that they allow the committee to compare applicants from different backgrounds. Academic results from a previous Master's level postgraduate degree may count, but they will count less than your more-easily compared undergraduate record. The quality of undergraduate institution attended (that is, the competition you beat out to be admitted to college) is also weighed.

2. *Quantitative orientation*: A candidate who can "do" numbers. Business school does not require any advanced math but a basic quantitative orientation is important to handle the coursework at a day-to-day level. If you have years of engineering or finance behind you, Adcom will ask no more questions. If you are coming from a non-quantitative background, the math score in your GMAT will be a crucial piece of your application. Any quantitative course you have, or can acquire (and get an A in) before applying, will help you. Most schools run a "math camp," that is, a module for accepted candidates in the weeks before school starts, but this will not get you admitted in the first place.

3. *Analytical mindset*: A candidate who is able to think critically and tolerate complex, open-ended problems. This is different from intellectual ability or quantitative ability in the raw: it is the ability to cut through a mass of data and extract the critical variables, to sort and connect relevant ideas, and to see patterns and develop optimal solutions from them. Analytical skills are heavily demanded by the case method and are the basis of solving the case "exams" that consulting and other firms use for recruitment.

4. *Success record*: A candidate with a proven track record of personal and professional success. It matters less what you succeeded at than that you have achieved in good company (which suggests likely future success in whatever you choose to do, that is, you have professional promise post-MBA). Faced with equivalently good candidates, admissions officers put their faith in the old maxim "success breeds success." This is why top schools routinely select Olympic athletes, Air Force pilots, and prominent young achievers in the arts and sciences. Your claim to success will be more compelling if it can be verified by awards, trophies, or job promotions. The quality of the challenge also counts: making "Associate" at McKinsey means more than making Associate at the local consulting shop.

5. *Maturity, professionalism, and good judgment*: A candidate who looks, talks, and acts "like a grown-up." Through your essays and interview Adcom will get a good sense of whether you have the personal maturity, diplomacy, self-awareness, and professional polish necessary to succeed at school, in recruiting, and in life. Are you poised under pressure? Are you diplomatic under fire? Can you handle responsibility? Do you have "senior presence," or do you come across as a brash kid? Immaturity will be signaled by giveaways such as whining about past failure, recriminating about circumstances beyond your control, blaming others for your bad calls, showing an inability to see your own weaknesses, and poor self-restraint, particularly when dealing with others.

6. *Leadership*: A candidate who has created value by being at the helm in group-based activities and is comfortable in this role. Leaders are able to operate both independently and collaboratively as necessary. Their actions demonstrate evidence of insight into people and situations and significant self-knowledge. Beware that management and leadership are often confused, because very often the two functions are present in the same person and the same job. Management refers to the processes of direction and coordination that senior jobs require. Leadership is something else: it is the unquantifiable mix of stature, assurance, and charisma that evokes greatness and gets the best out of others. It is the mysterious mix of factors that makes up the person that other people will "naturally" follow, and who will make the difference between success and failure.

7. *Ambition and motivation*: A candidate who is aiming for big things and planning to play in the senior league. It matters less exactly what you plan to do than that you plan to do something grand (but specific,) and that you have the will and the focus and sense of purpose to achieve it. The MBA-based career path is not for wallflowers. It is for those who will search out and seize opportunities and challenges. Adcom seeks people with big career dreams and deep resources of motivation and self-reliance to achieve them.

8. *Career potential*: A candidate who has what it takes to go to the top. Ambition is a prerequisite, but the committee will also ask itself whether you have "the right stuff" to actualize your ambition and your potential. Wanting it is one thing, the ability to get it is another. They will look at how you have strategized and built your career so far, and the validity and wisdom of the career goals you desire for yourself. The committee wants to have picked the person who's not just a dreamer, but who is going to "make it;" whose picture one day is going to be on the cover of *Fortune* magazine.

9. *Perseverance and mental toughness*: A candidate with evidence of the gritty staying power and self-reliance needed to overcome adversity. Successful managers and leaders are the people who come to the fore when times are tough, profits are down, and obstacles are seemingly insurmountable. They have the drive and focus to keep going when others fall, take whatever tough decisions are necessary, and bring their companies out ahead no matter what the obstacles. The committee will respond well to evidence of single-minded determination and tenacity in your approach (as long as personal and organizational ethics were maintained).

10. *A strong, extrovert personality*: A candidate who likes people and who is professionally (if not naturally) gregarious. Being thoughtful and shy isn't a crime, but management often rises or falls on the power of personality: the ability of key people to motivate, to exhort, to mentor, to be visible and vibrant, and passionate. The Adcom will be on the lookout for optimism and enthusiasm and an engaging, "can-do" approach. This doesn't mean being "a loudmouth," but it does mean having high social self-confidence and strong interpersonal skills.

11. *Active orientation and initiative*: A candidate with a bias to energy, action, and getting things done. There's nothing wrong with being an observer, thinker, and planner, but there soon comes a time in the life of a successful company when it is

necessary to act. Adcom looks for people who can make that transition; who know when to measure a risk and when to take the plunge for better or worse. They don't want the bystanders of the world. They are looking for people who, after demonstrating the skills of analysis, have the stomach to seize the opportunity boldly and "win by doing."

12. *Killer instinct*: A candidate who is not afraid of winning and seeing others lose. No matter what they tell you, all business schools are competitive places, as is the business world out there. Adcom must select those most ready for competitive situations and competitive careers, who have an affinity for the cut-and-thrust realities of beating competitors and making money, and who thrive in high-pressure environments and head-to-head situations. They will be weeding out those otherwise-excellent people who are temperamentally better suited to careers in inventing, teaching, caring, designing, etc.

13. *Personal integrity and honesty*: A candidate with good interpersonal values and a clear moral compass. This is very much back in fashion, since energy companies, auditing firms and Wall Street brokerages have been among the many that have shamed themselves with out-and-out thievery in the last decade, and leaders of investment banks paid themselves untold millions of dollars in bonuses only to run to the Treasury for a handout in the "credit crunch." The admissions office knows that if you go to a top school, very soon you will be in charge of a lot of people, a lot of money, and many powerful technologies. They will want to know how genuinely you care about people other than yourself and your immediate circle. Nobody expects you to enter the priesthood, but they want you to play clean with others. They like to think they are choosing people who will do the right thing—even when nobody is looking.

14. *Social welfare and broader community orientation*: A candidate who demonstrates responsibility to the community, society, and the environment, and who has an integrated, sustainable view of the role of business in the world. Adcom particularly wants to see evidence of your involvement in your own community, however you choose to define that, and some active (non-financial) contribution to social welfare, suggesting your good intentions. They want "givers" not "takers." Again, you don't have to save the world, but a lack of clear willingness to "give back" to the institutions and resources that sustain you will be missed.

15. *Collaborative team member*: A candidate who works well with others and who operates smoothly and constructively in collaborative situations. From day one at business school and throughout your business career, you will work on projects that require group-based productivity. Generally, if you have individualist, perfectionist, style you will be rejected by an admissions committee that holds it more important that students can and will collaborate with their classmates to solve messy problems and manage difficult conversations. Team skills are easy to claim— who, after all, will say they are *not* a good team player? (And we all know many who are not.) So, rather than a self-congratulatory assertion of your faith in teamwork, the committee is looking for evidence of your willingness and ability to engage in diverse teams, and some sophistication in your understanding of the dynamics of the groups you have been in, and your own role in them. They also want to see

evidence of valuing collaborative success—you and others help each other to succeed as a group—rather than individualistic success.

16. *Diversity contribution*: A candidate who brings interesting attributes, experiences, and depth of background to the group. Diversity can come in standard ways, such as race, and foreign country of origin, or it can be more subtle—a unique experience, a particular skill, a reason to see the world differently in some way. Diversity is, of course, not the value in and of itself. It is a proxy for the ability to contribute life experience and extracurricular knowledge to the peer-to-peer business school learning experience. The question the Adcom asks is: What additional or unique perspective or expertise does this candidate bring that will be valuable to others?

17. *Intercultural experience and tolerance*: A candidate who has demonstrated a real sense of others and tolerance for diversity in people and cultures. This is not the same as being "diverse"—this is openness to the diversity in others. The question is whether and how you have demonstrated an ability to get along with people who are not like you in looks, diction, gender, dress, culture, language, sexual orientation, or any other axis of difference. Adcom will regard your ability to mix comfortably with all sorts, and one day to hire and promote without prejudice, as key to being a successful manager and leader.

18. *Creativity and innovation*: A candidate who is comfortable with change and ready to use it creatively. As technology moves forward, and societies and markets change, the skills of savvy adaptation are an ever more fundamental part of management. Chances are, before long, you as an MBA graduate will be asked to take part or all of a company in a direction for which there is no roadmap. An innovative mindset, curiosity, and tolerance of uncertainty will be required. An open disposition to change, a demonstrated ability to initiate new ideas and to develop original solutions, and any past activity in the creative arts or sciences, will be an asset to your application.

19. *Communication ability*: A candidate who can write, speak, and organize ideas well. Financial and technical skills are important, but the single key skill in senior management is communication: the ability to frame, transmit, and negotiate ideas in meetings with clients, staff, investors, regulators, lawyers, industry partners, and other stakeholders. Note that, generally in business organizations, the quantitative analysis is done by those at lower levels in the organization, in service of those in the C-suite and at Board level who spend almost all of their time *talking*. So Adcoms will be looking hard at how well you organize and communicate concepts and ideas, thinking down the line to when you are going to be interviewing in front of an employer, and on and on through your career, representing yourself, your company, and the school. Your communication abilities are assessed in your verbal GMAT and analytical writing assessment (AWA) scores, as well as in your essays and interview.

20. *All-rounder*: A candidate who is more than a "suit," and who has an array of interests and passions in things other than work. "Balance" is valued. Adcom will ask: "Does this person do significant things other than work? What moves him? What's her passion?" It sounds dated to talk about your "hobbies," but

you must be able to show reasonable time commitment to non-work activities, excluding TV and your "significant other." They like people who have experienced "what it's like to live." These are the things that will develop the committee's interest in you. Business schools don't need any more one-dimensional, workaholic, millionaires-in-training.

21. *Recruitability*: When you are offered a place in an MBA program you step on a treadmill. That treadmill will take you through courses, projects, and exams and then back out into the professional world via the job-search process managed by the school's Career Services office. Adcom is concerned that you will move on easily and seamlessly—that you will be a desirable professional prospect once you have their degree added to your previous skills and experience, and they will find this in attractive pre-MBA skills, proven job performance, and promotions. If your profile (including the MBA) appears as if it will be not-particularly attractive to the type of MBA recruiters that come to that campus, it is less likely that you will be admitted. Note that this attribute is more keenly applied in recessionary times.

22. *Likeability and enthusiasm*: A candidate whom people enjoy having around. All else being equal, people always choose people they *like* as colleagues and co-workers. If you are the otherwise perfect candidate, but sound like you are arrogant, or emotionally unavailable, or an egotist, or antisocial, or ready to trample everyone else with a win-at-all-cost attitude, your application will stall. Business school is an intense 16-hours-a-day kind of place. Adcom prefers people who are easy to live with and who will be easy for the other students, faculty, and recruiters to live with. It's just human nature that an Adcom will be reluctant to turn down someone they like (so far, on paper). Don't underestimate this one.

Obviously, many of these categories overlap, but they are individually listed here so you can consider them closely. Note that Adcom will not have "a list" like this and mechanically check your profile off against it. Nobody, not even MBA Adcoms, can score personality in an Excel spreadsheet. However, they will be looking and listening for these attributes in general. Finding them is the way for the Adcom to ask the single basic question they need an answer to: what is the likelihood you will succeed on campus (inside and outside the classroom), and in recruiting, and in your career, such that you will satisfy the multiple stakeholders they are responsible to? Are you are a successful person who is likely to *continue to be so* for all concerned, *including them*?

Cross-cutting principles

Making a difference
There are many principles of selection that cut across these categories, drawing from many of them. One that one often hears is: "We are looking for people *who will make a difference* in the world." What is important about this is it says nothing about business. Obviously business school is about business and management, but b-schools interpret their mandate as broadly as possible. Truth is they are happy to train anyone for any senior position in any for-profit, non-profit, or government sector—assuming seniority implies management skills are required.

But the intention to "make a difference" in the world is crucial. You don't have to feed the starving: it almost matters not what the difference is, just that you will impact the world positively and uniquely. If you're just going to be another banker or another consultant or another PE portfolio manager, or even just another venture capitalist or entrepreneur, that's *not* making a difference in the world. You can be any of these things, or something else, but the question is: how will this applicant, given their MBA, leave a better world behind them?

Seizing opportunities

If you get into an elite MBA program you are being given a huge opportunity in life. No surprise then that Adcoms look to see whether and how you have maximized the opportunities and advantages you have had so far. Part of this is to represent why you made the decisions that you did—about situating yourself for opportunities to succeed and to grow as a leader and as a human being. They are looking to see that you have moved and grown in a way that made sense for you uniquely, and in a way that suggests you are looking long term and preparing yourself for big things.

The value of soft skills

Oftentimes what sets a candidate apart is so-called "soft skills," the mix of interpersonal skills and charm that will be evident in categories such as likeability, communications ability, team player, integrity. B-school is a "hard-skill" environment to a point, but Adcom will absolutely definitely want to see soft skills coming through your essays and, particularly, the interview process. Soft skills are leadership skills.

"The rankings" and admissions

The unspoken "elephant in the room" of desirable applicant attributes is the business school rankings—the frequent top-10 or top-100 lists put out by various business media platforms such as *Business Week* and the *Financial Times*. Officially, of course, Adcoms don't pay any heed to the rankings in choosing students. Yeah. Right. If you're ever at a cocktail party with a business school staffer you'll find it won't be long before they are muttering and moaning about the extreme demands of the rankings organization—endless rounds of data required and forms to fill in—and how they "have to" comply with them. Many schools hire full-time staff just to manage this function.

In other words, make no mistake, for schools, the rankings really count. What goes into the ranking algorithm are many things to do with faculty, research, school facilities, and so on, but a decent chunk of it is made up of student-related metrics such as average GMAT of accepted student, percentage of students with job offers on graduation, and average starting salary. The pressure is on Adcom to get these numbers up. If you drive up their GMAT-accepted number or look like you will boost their career-continuation numbers, that's going to work in your favor for admission. Issues in school rankings and how to think critically about them are developed in the Chapter 4.

The four attribute dimensions

An alternative way to grasp what schools are looking for is to understand that each of the 22 key attributes named above can be viewed as part of one of four attribute sets: academic, professional, interpersonal, and personal.

Academic

All things being equal, admissions committees will offer places to candidates with higher undergraduate GPA and GMATs. Generally, you need a GPA in the high 3s and a GMAT at least the high 600s—and not obviously low in either Math or Verbal—to be considered at the better institutions. On the other hand, schools generally have quite a broad range for the GMAT and do not stipulate their minimums. They leave themselves some wiggle-room to take a candidate with shaky scores who is otherwise exceptional. More on the GMAT and managing low academic scores is in Chapter 3.

Professional

This set incorporates attributes that relate to work profile, professional skills and experience, and career potential. The committee wants candidates who have demonstrated early professional mettle and who therefore have the most to contribute to classroom peer-to-peer learning. Any high-level experience, specialist technical or methodological skills, or experience in unusual industries is a bonus, particularly if you can explain exactly why this skill or experience is relevant to the learning of other students. For example, a "veteran" of high-level procurement negotiations could persuasively suggest that experience with her company's negotiation pre-planning methodology will add special value in the Negotiation ("Nego") elective.

As they evaluate your professional trajectory, Adcom considers your success history, your stated career goals and your anticipated trajectory. They match this against the potential they and others (your recommenders and interviewers) see in you in assessing your potential for high-flying career continuation. Even though they know your career aspiration will change while you are at school, they prefer those who have clear and ambitious goals and huge reservoirs of motivation to achieve them. They don't look for particular goals as much as the impression that you are the type who sets goals and reaches them. More on goals and goals essays is presented in Chapter 10.

Communal (interpersonal and team)

This attribute set tells the committee about you in relation to others: as a member of groups, teams, communities, and society at large. Adcom knows that whatever you choose to do and whatever industry you are in, a huge slice of your time will be spent in teams, on committees, and in groups of all kinds. Therefore, your profile as a social and communal person and your ability to add value to teams are critical.

They want to know how you interact with others, how you collaborate, and how productively you manage multi-cultural situations.

Proof of your interpersonal skills may be clear from your record at work, or in extramural or community service projects. On a broader scale, Adcom looks for some evidence of your positive relationship with society at large. They don't mind what it is you choose to do, but the fact of doing it is telling evidence of your commitment and broader cooperative value set. They also like you to take an active service role in community organizations because it tells them good things not just about your values, but about your collaborative intent.

Personal

This set of attributes covers who you are as a person, your values, beliefs, and motivations. Adcom is interested in what kind of family background you come from and the other significant features in your personal and social background—national, ethnic, religious, immigrant origin, minority—which have created you and continue to shape your choices.

The committee particularly wants to get behind your record to better understand your perspectives and insights. They want to know what is important to you personally and why; what personal choices you make in pressure situations and why. As we will see in the essay section, this "inward" look at yourself demands the ability to reflect honestly and openly.

In the personal dimension there is no right and wrong. Any background is fine, as long as it is dynamic and shows a reasonable standard of personal integrity and values. Values and ethics questions always touch on personal beliefs. Any steps you have taken in self-development classes, spirituality, or introspection generally plays well. Beyond that, any personal free-time pursuit is also fine, as long as *you* are active in it (not watching someone else, for example, NBA stars, be active). A sure way to chill your reader is to be so bland as to have no obvious non-work pursuits.

These four dimensions of attributes—academic, professional, interpersonal, and personal—interlock to form a balanced competitive profile (Figure 2.1). Key to a good application and good essays is being able to claim enough of the key attributes, spread across *all four dimensions*, in your application. This is what will give your profile the necessary balance.

Summary: a CEO-in-waiting

It is also no accident that the above 22 attributes, taken together, are more or less the essential qualities of a successful chief executive officer or other senior business leader. The more you have of these attributes, the more you will seem like a CEO-in-waiting. This also points to a fundamental insight in application strategy: to create the right kind of impression, you should apply *the way a chief executive would*. Imagine that, for some reason, a CEO had to apply to business school. How would he do it? What would be her essay strategy? How would he approach the interviews? How would she manage her recommendations? If you can imagine yourself into that position, you will generate the kind of "senior presence" that sets your application apart. (Whatever you plan to do in your career, you should

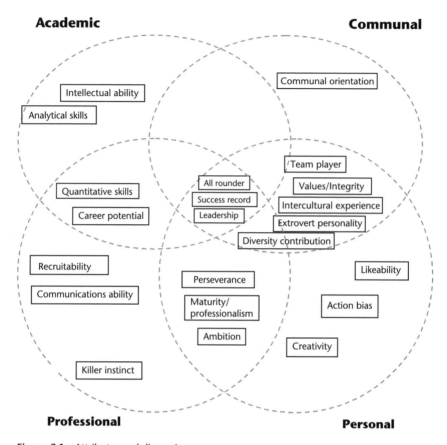

Figure 2.1 Attributes and dimensions map
The sets that represent the four attribute dimensions overlap because many of the attributes play a role in more than one of the dimensions.

strive to create the impression that you are the chief-executive-to-be. Even if your goal is to be an entrepreneur or finance or technical professional—not a general manager—you should still create the impression of wanting to be the senior player and decision-maker in your organization.)

Managing weaknesses and red flags

When you apply, it stands to reason that your essays, interview, recommendations, etc., should highlight your profile strengths and mitigate weaknesses. We have so far highlighted attributes that an Adcom looks for because they are markers of applicant value and "admit" indicators. The flip side, of course, is these are the markers they look for in order to weed out less attractive applicants. There are also further specific markers of weakness, factors that cause Adcoms to raise their eyebrows and ultimately to waitlist or outright ding candidates. Applicants get sidelined for many reasons, often specific to the candidate, but there are identifiable common weaknesses or red flags that push an applicant into ding territory. The following are 20 of them. You are in "red flag" zone if:

- You are under 23 or older than 29 at the time of application (for a full-time MBA); or under 30 or over 45 (for an executive MBA).
- You are currently or have been previously self-employed; or there have been breaks in your career.
- You have been with your present company for under a year, or you have been employed by three or more companies.
- You are or have been unemployed in the last three years.
- Your background is very common, e.g. banking, consulting.
- You have no volunteer or community service experience.
- You come from a high applicant country—the US, India, China, etc.
- Your undergraduate academic record, GPA or equivalent, is sketchy.
- You have not been promoted in your job (or your previous job).
- You do not have recommenders who will praise you unconditionally.
- Your GMAT is below 680 (for a top-20 program).
- You are underpaid considering your level of seniority and responsibility.
- You are not sure what you want to do with your MBA.
- You have no clear team experience, or don't know your team player profile.
- You have an arts or social studies background (hello, you're a "poet").
- You were dinged last year from a business school.
- You have another Master's degree, or a PhD.
- You don't have some math or stats in your background.
- You are short of international or intercultural contact experience.
- You don't think you have any weaknesses.

Note that many of these can be successfully justified. The point is to highlight what causes Adcom worry, that will need mitigating. How to do this varies from situation to situation: sometimes it's better to say nothing and not draw attention to a problem area, and sometimes the best policy is to create countering information. If you are underpaid for your level, explain how your compensation comes in other forms; if you don't get team experience at work, explain how much you got at college, and so on. More on dealing with weaknesses and failures is presented in Chapter 10.

But now for the good news . . .

All these demands may seem overwhelming. And to cap it all, Adcom is not going to be satisfied with your *claims* to have plenty of the good attributes and few of bad ones. As we will see in the essay and interview sections, your claims must come with proof, via awards, promotions, recognition, verifiable anecdotes, and so forth, or they are worthless. But there are reasons to be optimistic and not to get too thrown by any particular weakness or omission in your profile, or lack of evidence thereof. There are many ways to make a good application despite all kinds of failings and there are various ways to make the admissions process work for you, as detailed in the following sections. But for now consider these general admissions forces that work in your favor:

Nobody has it all, and you're not meant to

First, be aware that nobody has all of the attributes. It is unrealistic (and therefore an admissions mistake) to try to have them all. You are not a CEO. Your are, more or less, at the beginning of your management career. It is fine and expected that you are not a master of all the attributes mentioned above. As long as the general picture is good and you can show a few areas of remarkable strength, it is okay to have blemishes—which, by the way, is clearly the case with most successful chief executives. Adcom knows that business school is where you will develop many of your management and interpersonal skills, and work on your weaknesses. So what they are looking for is some clear areas of excellence, and the associated implication that you have kind of the raw materials for developing missing attributes.

School due diligence counts big

Think dating—how predisposed you are to someone who wants you so badly they have taken time to really notice who you are and what you like—and you'll know what's at stake here. Like everyone else, schools are seduced by a genuine interest in them, their program, their distinguishing features and attributes. They want to know you have been "pursuing them," meeting students or alums or Adcom members, or otherwise showing willing. If you do this and can pick out what makes them special—if there is evidence that you've really thought about why they are better for you than anywhere else, why you'd gain from the community, that you have taken the trouble to work out the "personality" of the school, they will warm to you. Note this does not mean you should trot out blandishments in your essay praising the school generically for its fabulous faculty or great amenities. That's the route to being dumped.

A campus visit is still the holy grail of showing intent, but these days there are myriad ways to connect, from participating in live chats to attending Adcom or student-hosted events in cities worldwide. Due diligence of this sort can make up for a lot of weaknesses.

Class balance works in favor of the smart

As we have seen, while looking at each candidate individually and choosing the best, the Adcom is required to balance the class as a whole, in terms of professional backgrounds, cultures, nationalities, ages, interests, skills, and career aspirations —in order to maximize the richness of peer-to-peer learning. So, they want everything from oil engineers to dance choreographers, with no one profile type overrepresented. The challenge of shaping a balanced class as a whole makes the challenge of *selection* not quite the same thing as the process of *evaluation*. You may be evaluated as an "admit" but not be admitted because you are part of a profile that is overrepresented. But the corollary is clear: if you can wiggle your way via smart choice of themes and highlighting, into a less oversubscribed category, then you can turn the balance imperative in your favor. More about class balance in Chapter 3.

It's your future not your past that counts: Jam tomorrow!

Note that, while the key attributes look to your past for evidence, they are all, also, fundamentally questions about your future. Getting into business school is not a reward for past achievement. You do not get admitted because you were a successful youngster who got As and won awards, or *were* a superstar in some area. You will be admitted because your future looks bright, and you will likely be a superstar soon, and that will reflect well on the school and all concerned. In this sense, getting an offer of a place is a benefit advanced to you on the expectation of future achievement. A successful past obviously helps make your case for this and part of your job in your essays is to make a compelling link between your past and future success, but the future *cannot be examined* by Adcom. It is a blank slate for you to pitch yourself into. Within reason, and with backup, you can make any promise—the bigger and more interesting, the better—about your future success.

3 Admissions fundamentals

In the previous chapter we isolated the elements that Adcom values in applicants, explained why these attributes and attribute-groups count across all schools, and began a discussion about how to isolate positive factors and mitigate negatives. This discussion is continued throughout the essays and interview-preparation sections of this book. In this chapter we look more broadly at strategy and tactics of managing other parts of the application process, from the GMAT to recommenders to the MBA resume.

The key principle that cuts across all of the MBA application deliverables is this: each item, from the GMAT to recommendations to essays to interview to resume, tests the applicant in a different way. Each exists because it offers a different window into the aptitude and potential of the applicant. So a big part of managing each item is to get clarity on what it particularly tests. Of course, all the deliverables have to work together, offering an overarching and integrated picture too.

Managing the GMAT

The GMAT is a fundamental part of an applicant's profile. It has two basic uses. First, it tells Adcom about the applicant's intellectual and cognitive (math and verbal) skills. It is not an exact measure of course—these things are always controversial—but it is taken to roughly measure "who's who" in terms of cognitive smarts (including the ability to crack standardized tests.) The second fundamental benefit of the GMAT to Adcom, is that it allows easy comparison of students across institutions and undergraduate majors, and across countries and cultures.

For these reasons, the GMAT score is the key way that Adcom judges your academic ability and potential. They will factor in your college GPA and other academic results you may have achieved along the way, but the GMAT is the number that counts most. Every 10-point gain adds to the applicant's admissions prospects, and a move of 30 or so fundamentally changes which b-schools one can legitimately hope to get into.[1]

But, crucially, this is true only up to a point. A threshold is reached at around the 700 level (depending on GPA results and other variables, including the accepted-GMAT average the school seeks to achieve,) at which point Adcom can safely put a check mark next to your academic ability, and move on to see what else you offer. If you are too far below the school's average GMAT, nothing else you are, do, or say will count. After you achieve the threshold—once it is clear that you are intelligent and numerate enough—the Adcom will start looking for other attributes. So the value of even higher standardized test scores quickly has diminishing returns. A higher GMAT won't check any other box than "cognitively capable" and once it is checked, it's checked.

"Geek" scores and the myth of the 800 GMAT

The GMAT is nominally out of 800. It would be natural to assume that the higher you score the better, and GMAT test prep firms certainly have a vested interest in perpetuating this perception. But, as explained above, the higher your score, the better, up to the threshold, beyond which you exhibit rapidly diminishing marginal returns. Moreover, beyond 750, the marginal returns can be negative, that is further rises in GMAT score can potentially—believe it or not—harm your chances.

There are two reasons. First, although the MBA is a postgraduate university degree, it is primarily a professional education. Its fundamental task is to prepare and place people in business management positions, not academic positions. Managers need to be smart but, as everyone knows, the cleverest people don't necessarily make the best managers, nor best entrepreneurs, or bankers, or consultants. Jack Welch, Herb Kelleher, George Soros, Ted Turner, etc., are smart enough. But they are not Einsteins. MBA Adcoms are not looking for brainiacs.

Scoring in the superbracket (750+) means that you are, by definition, in the 99th percentile. People who score like that are often better pure scientists or philosophers, than managers. It's a stereotype, and perhaps a poor one, but the absentminded professor is commonly associated with being a poor people-person and a poor manager. If you get a very high score, Adcom will be absolutely sure to thoroughly check and almost disbelieve that you are also a leader and team player and can manage adversity and do all the practical and sometimes routine things you need to get done in a business day. Maybe you can and do. But an extra burden of proof falls on you in this regard if you are in the GMAT superbracket.

The second, related, problem is that applicants who obsess with studying extensively to hit a 750+ GMAT (or improve an already 700+ GMAT) are, almost certainly, taking time and effort away from improving the rest of their admissions profile. A superscore is not going to help you if your recommendations are so-so, your essays are undeveloped, and you stumble in your interview. A wellbacked up 700 will beat a stand-alone 750. Adcom prefers "balanced excellent" to "unbalanced geek."

When to rewrite the GMAT

B-schools generally don't publish the minimum GMAT score they accept because the minimum is a guideline not a rule. In fact, looking at Harvard's acceptance data, which they publish via their admissions director's blog,[2] they take candidates with GMATs in the 500s (but not many) as do other top schools. Schools publish the average GMAT of accepted applicants, or median 80 percent, but not the minimum, because they don't want candidates with an otherwise excellent application "failing themselves" where, in fact, they might have had a real chance. Admissions officers know that test scores are often a misleading guide to presence or absence of intelligence, and intelligence is just one of the demands that will be made of successful business executives.

Traditionally, 670 has been the guideline minimum for top schools, and about 600 for second-tier good schools. But GMAT score "inflation" has put these figures on the upward march. Anecdotally, it appears that 700 is becoming the new bar for a top-10 program, but this assumes the candidate doesn't have anything else compelling. Note again that schools take applicants in the 500s when they want to.

Generally, there is more malleability in the system than most candidates realize. If the rest of your application is good and your undergraduate record is in the right range, you can be up to 40 or 50 points below the school's GMAT average of accepted candidates (providing you are not too lopsidedly low in the math or verbal.) Obviously, the program's published average tells you that half of the scores are below that mark. The AWA score is less important, but doing conspicuously well in it might push a weaker GMAT over the bar, while doing badly may flag an English disability.

Therefore, overall, it makes sense to be concerned with your GMAT until it is within the guidelines for your target program, and then forget about it and spend time on other aspects of your application. Only consider rewriting it if your score is clearly below the average or 80 percent median of accepted GMATs for your target program, or if your verbal and math results are seriously unbalanced—more than 25 percentage points apart—particularly if it is the math that is low. Bear in mind also that all your GMAT scores appear on the report ETS sends to the school. Generally, schools ignore previous lower scores, but it starts to look dodgy if you take the test repeatedly and potentially obsessively.

Mitigating a low GMAT or GPA

A lot of very smart, very capable people with extremely high career potential cannot get their standardized test scores into the 700 range. If you find yourself in this situation, take heart. As described above, Adcom knows the problem. That's why they give you the opportunity to offset a low GMAT (or GPA) in various ways. As always, put yourself in their shoes and ask: What is the GMAT telling them? What are they looking for here? What they really want is reassurance about my academic ability. So, can I tell them another way?

The first way would be to show skills and results in the kind of things the GMAT is testing for. For example, if you are a published writer, you can point to this to show Verbal-side skills. If your job requires you to develop and manage complex statistical analyses of property portfolio returns, you can use this to show Quant-side skills. Another way to mitigate doubts about your academic ability is by taking supplementary college-level courses and doing well in them, providing a so-called "alternative transcript." Good grades in courses in accountancy, statistics, and microeconomics will demonstrate a willingness and ability to manage quantitative requirements that are just as good as a rise in GMAT score.

Further, you can sometimes demonstrate how you have been recognized academically, via awards, scholarships, published papers in refereed journals. Also keep in mind that admissions committees are duty-bound, in the search to balance the cohort, to value diversity of academic experiences, so if you have unique attributes in your academic experience—you mastered Japanese, for example—or other brain-taxing experiences such as being a competitive chess player—this kind of thing can mitigate a GMAT that is not quite enough. For GMAT and GPA guidance for international candidates, see below.

The GMAT vs. the GRE

There is a trend in MBA Admissions to accept the GRE as a GMAT equivalent. This has to do with corporate politics and big money in the standardized test-taking industry that don't overly concern us here. The point is more schools are taking the GRE, but everything that has been said about the role and use of the GMAT in MBA admissions will be true of the GRE too. Where schools accept either test, as is increasingly the case, business schools are saying that they see them and treat them as equivalent for MBA admissions purposes.

Managing the MBA resume

Many b-schools ask for a resume as part of the applicant's package. It is professional school and they want to see your professional record and make a judgment about your professional future, just as an employer would. If there is a careers office person on the admissions committee, as there often is, that person will look hardest at your resume and its implied potential (including an MBA from their school.) Careers does not want to be "stuck" with you on graduation day. Further, Adcom knows that fairly early in your degree you will be starting to get together your resume for internships and then recruitment. They will coach you in this, but how you present a resume on application still alerts them as to how you will present it later on. Giving the committee a polished, power-packed resume is indicative of your ability to be professionally appealing to recruiters all the way through your career.

Much is identical in a standard resume and an MBA admissions resume, so you should start by getting your resume as good as it can be as per conventional requirements. There are thousands of guides to this, many free on the Web. Be certain to take note of at least these basic points.

A resume should:

- be in reverse chronological order, education last;
- contain tight clauses rather than full sentences, and not use the first person singular;
- start with perfect-tense verbs: "Managed a team of . . ."; "Assigned priority to . . .";
- contain evidence, particularly quantitative amounts of budget managed or people supervised, etc.;
- not contain obvious age, gender, race, or other similar bio-data (more latitude is allowed in Europe);
- be easy on the eye (text at readable point size; layout not too dense);
- be absolutely, completely error-free.

These are the basics. And this is first base for Adcom too. They want to see you can do this common business communications task effectively. Once you have that, then it's time to adapt it to the needs of MBA admissions particularly. Good resume builders will always advise you to show as much experience relevant to the job you are *applying for* as you can. This it true of an MBA admissions resume too, only doubly so, because doing an MBA implies that you will be transitioning to or accelerating quickly along a management path. It implies a leap in career and often a change of industry.

Look to your next job

The mistake that many make in their resume is to proudly present their past experiences and achievements, which are very often technical or specific to the field they are leaving. Success is always good, but MBA Adcoms don't really care whether you cracked a complex software conundrum or isolated a biological compound, or developed prefabricated housing units. What they care about is whether you will make a good manager or leader, that is, the management portion that was there (or is implied) in what you did.

So that is what you should focus on: on the management, leadership, organizational (teamwork, negotiation, liaison), innovation, or communications implications of your past experience. Don't say: "Developed molecular compound BN6R in three months using BitPro Software Analytics." Say: "Was part of team that developed unique molecular compound; led interim reports and presentation to the Board; liaised with company PR in media announcement."

The other key part of making your resume an MBA admissions resume is to work carefully with the knowledge that, unlike a typical employer, Adcom has various overlapping sources of information about you—not least all your file and short-question data. So you want to augment that rather than simply repeating it. The holy grail of admissions is to get all your admissions communications to elegantly dovetail and reinforce each other, not simply overlap.

Obviously, your resume must not leave out the basic resume attributes: dates, places, company names, and so on, even if this is already in your file data. But there are often ways to cut out repeating subsidiary information—names of products or service units—that often just clog up a resume. This should leave space to say more on quantitative evidence of experiences and successes. In fact, putting as much quantitative data in the resume as realistically possible can, in turn, free up the essays to be more discursive and reflective.

Managing recommendations and recommenders

Selecting and briefing recommenders is an important piece of your strategy. Once again, put yourself in Adcom's shoes and ask: What are they looking for? What questions do they really need answered that only the recommender can answer? What information can they not get any other way?

Put this way, it becomes simple. What they specifically need from the recommendation (the "reco" in admissions speak,) is to know that there are serious, relatively senior or proven people *in the working world* ready to go on the record and vouch for you. Just as Adcom relies almost exclusively on the GPA and GMAT to judge you academically, they rely on your recommenders to judge your professional performance and potential. In fact, they have almost no other way to judge you professionally. So while it is nice if your recommendation says good things about you as a person, the essential point of the reference for Adcom is the recommender's judgment of you at work: your work style, work values and characteristics, strengths, and weaknesses. Getting this opinion from the working world spreads the risk and helps safeguard the committee against accepting the nice-sounding candidates who are not good working professionals, or better suited to artistic or intellectual or other alternative career paths.

Who to pick as a recommender

Given the clear professional demand on your recommendations, it is obvious that they should come primarily if not exclusively from the workplace. The ideal recommender is someone at your company who has supervised your work and knows you well enough to rate your professional qualities and performance. The person should be able to speak closely about your accomplishments, your ability to work in or lead teams, and can convincingly testify to your professional promise and the fact that your ambitious goals are in fact realistic.

In other words, as first option, the recommender should be your current work supervisor. If not, the committee will be asking themselves "why not?" and you will probably need to use the extra essay to explain. It happens fairly often that an applicant cannot tell their current boss or anyone at their current company that they are planning to do an MBA, for fear of being fired. Schools specifically understand this and will allow you to go to a previous supervisor or previous senior work associate. What counts is if they are in a position to judge you at work on a day-to-day basis, from a position of seniority. Occasionally a school will ask for a peer review, in which case the condition of seniority to you is relaxed, but the peer should still be a professional colleague. Anyone you choose should, obviously, also be an enthusiastic supporter of your candidacy. This shows that you are high-quality, but also that you have the professional skills to form real bonds with senior workplace professionals.

This is one of the places in the MBA application where if you duck the requirement it will be obvious. If you go to a friend of your parents, or your old swim coach, or Uncle Bob, it will seriously hurt you. It is not problematic to have all recommenders from the workplace, but it is a grave problem not to have any from the workplace. (If you are asked for three recommenders, the *third* one can be the coach or some other soft-touch character testimony.)

It is very tempting, especially if you are relatively fresh out of college (and nobody at your office particularly notices you or really knows you,) to go back to your favorite college professor. Don't do it. All that says is that you haven't impressed anyone since college. Also, an MBA does not lead to an academic career, so there is a limit to how effectively an academic recommender can judge your potential. You do not need any testimonials to your academic merit beyond your GPA and GMAT score or extra-transcript representations as discussed above.

Resist the temptation to seek a reference from the most well-known person you know, or the one with the highest sounding title. If you get a reference from the president of the Accor Group, or your father's friend who is on the Board of Citibank, the alarm bells will ring and the committee will ask: How well does this person really know you or your work? But if this person really does interact with you often enough (for example, to competently answer the detailed questions on the recommender form), then there is no problem and their ultra-seniority works in your favor.

If you are self-employed, or in a family business, the recommendations give you a ticklish problem. You can't exactly write it yourself or go to your parents. In this case you are expected to go to professional associates, particularly longstanding clients. It is less good to go to suppliers because they may have a conflict of interest—motivation to be nice to you.

Learning from the recommendation guide form

Many schools ask (effectively demand) that the recommender fill out a guided recommendation form. One way to know who to pick as a recommender and what he or she should say, is to carefully consider the guided recommendation forms, whether or not your particular target school demands them. These forms look for very specific information and if your chosen person can adequately and independently answer the questions, they are probably the right choice.

Further, the guided forms show what Adcoms want recommenders to focus on. Example 1, from Columbia, the specifics of which may be slightly out of date by the time you read this, is nevertheless typical of the forms schools use and clearly shows their main concerns. You can "reverse-engineer" it to see the kinds of questions your recommender should be addressing.

Recommendation form Example 1: Columbia

1. *What is your relationship to, and how long have you known the applicant? Is this person still employed by your organization? (Yes/No) If "No," when did he/she depart? (e.g., August 1999)*
The recommender must confirm how well he or she knows you. This tells Adcom how heavily to weigh the opinion that follows.

2. *Provide a short list of adjectives which describe the applicant's strengths.*
The recommender should underline your strength and value as a candidate. These should be strengths relevant to an MBA and post-MBA career. They should dovetail with what you said about yourself in the essays.

3. *How does the applicant's performance compare with that of his or her peers?*
The recommender must make a comparative judgment. Not just that you are good, but that you are better than most.

4. *How has the applicant grown during his/her employment with you? Please comment on the applicant's maturity.*
They must address your professional growth and likelihood of a successful future trajectory, and how ready you are for an MBA at this point.

5. *Comment on the applicant's ability to work with others, including superiors, peers and subordinates. If the tables were reversed, would you enjoy working for the applicant?*
They must address your team and group skills, and likeability.

6. *In what ways could the applicant improve professionally? How does he/she accept constructive criticism?*
The recommender must include and deal with your weaknesses and career needs. The faults and lacks should broadly be the kind that an MBA will help to fix.

7. *How well has the applicant made use of available opportunities? Consider his or her initiative, curiosity, and motivation.*
The recommender should talk about your initiative, drive, and ability to be a self-starter. He or she should also talk about ability to weather obstacles.

8. *Comment on your observations of the applicant's ethical behavior.*
The recommender must explicitly endorse your professional ethics and values.

9. *What do you think motivates the candidate's application to the MBA program at Columbia Business School? Do you feel the applicant is realistic in his/her professional ambitions?*
The recommender should comment on your goals and, therein, reasons for doing an MBA. They must judge that it is likely that you will achieve the goal(s), and that an MBA will specifically and directly help this.

10. *Are there any other matters which you feel we should know about the applicant?*
Here they should use this space to sing any praises that did not fit into a prior question.

Here is another set, from MIT-Sloan, which shows a similar and overlapping pattern, even though the questions themselves are different.

Recommendation form Example 2: MIT-Sloan

1. *How long and in what capacity have you known the applicant?*
   As in the case above, the recommender must say how well he or she knows you. This tells Adcom how heavily to weigh the opinion that follows.

2. *How does the applicant stand out from others in a similar capacity?*
   Similar to questions 2 and 3 from Columbia. The recommender should underline your strength and value as a candidate, with a particular emphasis on why you are unique. These should be strengths and uniqueness relevant to an MBA and post-MBA career and should dovetail with what you said about yourself in the essays.

3. *Please provide an example of the applicant's impact on a person, group or organization.*
   Adcom is seeking the recommender's corroboration of the fact that you are the kind of person who "makes a difference."

4. *Please provide a representative example of how the applicant interacts with other people.*
   Similar to 5 from Columbia. The recommender needs to address your interpersonal, group, and team skills, using examples.

5. *Which of the applicant's personal or professional characteristics would you change?*
   Similar to 6 from Columbia. The recommender must deal with your weaknesses and career needs. The faults and lacks should broadly be the kind that an MBA will help fix.

6. *Please tell us anything else you think we should know about this applicant.*
   Similar to 10 from Columbia.

In other words, taken together, the reference questions posed by various programs reveal Adcom's agenda for references in general. Even if the reference *does not* ask a particular question, or does not ask any questions at all (allows a "free" letter format,) the recommender should still follow these tracks and signposts. You should guide your recommender to covering all these bases.

Overall, your recommendation should:

- be congruent with your profile, positioning, and goals, as stated in other parts of your application;
- augment your candidacy and reinforce your positioning by endorsing your claims to ability or experience, with proof;
- enthusiastically anticipate your potential and endorse the validity and achievability of your career goals;

- avoid generalities and platitudes, and be as specific and detailed as possible, giving examples;
- anticipate and comment favorably on any apparent weakness or area where the committee may have unanswered questions;
- include at least one criticism or cautionary point (the best kind of weakness is one that a good MBA experience will fix).

Priming recommenders

You are not allowed to write your own recommendation. But that doesn't mean you can only ask your recommender to write it and that's that. You are allowed to, and expected to brief your recommenders fully. Set up an appointment time and use it to carefully define the terrain you want covered (described above) and particular issues or attributes you want highlighted, to create congruence between what the recommender says about you and what you say about yourself in the essays. Give your recommender a copy of your essays, resume, and any other relevant information so that they can write something that dovetails with the thrust of your application. Talk to them about why you are interesting in going to business school, and why you are interested in going to a particular institution, so that they can bring that out in their text. Have them review past performance appraisals of you.

You don't want your recommenders to parrot out your application message. In fact, as discussed below, you get value from an alternative view of you. But you do need their take on you to be broadly consistent with your application themes. If your essays sing a song about your move to microfinance in the Caucasus, and your recommender writes about your continued maturing as a BCG consultant and exciting prospects at the firm, alarm bells will ring. Either your essays are unreliable, or you haven't been straight with your recommender, or your recommender hardly knows you.

The techniques of compelling communication—discussed in later sections—are as important in recommendations as anywhere else. As the applicant, you will suffer if your recommender writes in lazy generalities and banalities. Not only will he or she lose the reader's interest on your behalf, but you will appear no different to every other candidate and, worst of all, it may seem that the recommender doesn't really know you well enough to make a detailed case in your favor. Push your recommender as hard as is diplomatically possible to write using specific, interesting, detailed, concrete observations and stories about you that prove your attributes (as you will likewise do in your essays).

This means *you* will have to feed them the details and put the stories in the front of their mind. You want him to remember to say: "There was one time when a major client showed up in the hotel bar after his laptop had been stolen and (how you saved the day, etc.)" Specific details drive proof which drives both impact and believability. Without specifics, Adcom won't fully appreciate the virtues the recommender cites, or won't believe him.

Recommender fatigue

Recommenders are busy people and many will wave you away and tell you to do your own "first draft" or say "Just write it yourself and I'll sign it." This is *not* a good idea. First, Adcom can tell. They have read thousands of MBA applicant recommendations so there is a strong chance they will be able to tell. Also, your writing in your essays will have a certain character and you would need to be a truly professional writer not to reproduce this same writing signature in the recommendation. This is incredibly dangerous to your application for obvious reasons.

So, tricky as it might seem, and it often is, the task is to convince the recommender that the new and different angle on you is what is most valuable. An alternative perspective on you and why you have interesting and valuable potential will bring out alternative examples and points of value you may not have thought of or would sound odd coming from you. For these reason, a fresh, different perspective is truly more valuable than what you as the applicant could ever write. So if your recommender wants you to dummy up more of the same as in your essays they are in fact doing you a disservice compared with other applicants who get a real recommendation. Tell them that.

We should not be naïve either. Recommenders are busy and, as seen above, schools each have their own dedicated forms, with their own specific questions and checkboxes to be filled in. Each school insists recommenders use the dedicated form—it focuses their attention on the specific questions Adcom wants answered and makes comparing candidates easier. This requirement will inevitably get you into an awkward situation with your recommenders who obviously prefer to write one letter for you and send it to all concerned. There is no simple way out of this headache. You will have to judge how many times you can ask them to go the extra mile before tolerance wears thin—which will come out in how enthusiastically they support you. Recommender fatigue is probably the single biggest limitation to the number of schools you can apply to.

Managing international applications

Being a foreign applicant to US schools brings its own set of advantages and disadvantages. On the plus side, you are exotic. You don't have to work too hard to explain how you add diversity and experience to the program. The kinds of things you have done, the cultural differences you bring, the foreign places you have worked, and the languages you speak will work in your favor, particularly if you link them to the program in specific ways, for example: "My experience working in Brussels on EU agribusiness regulatory issues will be relevant to my fellow students at McDonough because . . ." There are, however, other obstacles to negotiate:

GPA

If your college degree were from Michigan State, Adcom would easily know what to read into that and would draw conclusions (rightly or wrongly.) But if it is from the University of Balamand, Lebanon, chances are they won't have a clue how that rates, and you could get the benefit of the doubt. Or not. Programs generally have experts that "translate" foreign transcripts into the American GPA system, factoring in both the prestige of the school, the difficulty of the class, and the grading system. Do not attempt to do it yourself. There is rapid grade inflation in US colleges and so you'll most likely just short-change yourself. Alternatively, ask your college for a transcript addendum that gives your rank in class (first, second, third, etc.) or rank in percentage terms (top 5 percent, top 10 percent, etc.) By the way, don't ever call yourself a "topper," a term used only in India.

GMAT
As mentioned above, part of the reason why the GMAT is so important to the Adcom is that, while colleges vary wildly, the GMAT is a national and international standard for assessing the academic potential of all comers. For this reason, the GMAT carries even more weight in an international file because the value of the foreign GPA and other parts of a foreigner's scholastic background are harder to assess. If you crack the GMAT, pretty much all of the other "indecipherable" parts of your academic past will be forgiven.

English ability
One aspect of a foreigner's application that always attracts special attention is English ability. Don't think the MBA program is all about numbers—spoken and written English is critical to managing the reading and academic workload and also to functioning in teams and extramurally. English ability will continue to be a key component of success in recruitment and in your professional life. Therefore the TOEFL, the GMAT verbal score, the analytical writing assessment, and your essays, will all be scrutinized by the committee looking for reassurance on this matter.

Do not underestimate the negative effect that incorrect or clunky English has on your application. Your readers are almost all mother-tongue English speakers. Many of them will have an active interest in people, writing, communications, language, and literature. They can tell the subtleties of good language use from bad, and they care about it. It may not be fair, but admission readers don't have the time or the patience to decide whether a mistake is non-native phrasing or whether it is carelessness or stupidity. Anything less than fluent will give the perception that you are not as good as the next person.

Even foreign applicants with English as their mother tongue cannot take their communications for granted. Americans, particularly those in the business world, live in a culture with high expectations of self-expression and a cultural preference for blunt messages and sound-bites. If you sound quaintly "Oxford donnish," for example, in your application, it could harm you.

Distinguishing between schools
Foreign students normally have to work harder to appreciate the subtle differences between different US programs. Applying to an "American" MBA is not enough. The schools want to know why you chose them particularly and in detail. It takes carefully focused research *plus* the acquisition of significant cultural knowledge for the, say, Chilean applicant to be able to distinguish between Chicago-Booth and Kellogg. For locals, this knowledge will not only be easier to get, but it will be more immediately culturally comprehensible.

Understanding competitiveness

Without cultural experience of the US, foreigners don't always appreciate the career and life-changing difference implied in getting into a good business school. Therefore, they don't understand the immense competitiveness they face nor the ability of the admissions committee to make extraordinary demands and expect candidates to "jump" to fulfill them to the letter. Americans are culturally more used to the bitterly competitive, tightrope-walking nature of the application process: one foot wrong and you are in the ravine.

US applicants to foreign schools

American candidates going abroad face a different spectrum of issues. While the status of their undergraduate program or command of English will not be factors, other problems arise. Foreign programs almost all value international experience highly and will look for this, and also look carefully at the ability of the American applicant to operate outside of his or her language and cultural milieu.

Rule number one is to show commitment to an international career. Don't make it seem like America is the only place where people know how to do business, raising the suspicion that the only reason you are thinking of coming over to London is that you were rejected from Columbia last year. Show a willingness to take other cultures, manners, education systems, institutions, and workplaces as seriously as you do your own, because they are, in fact, just as good and sometimes better than those you are familiar with. Foreign languages are a significant demonstration of positive intent.

Managing age: what to do if you are "too young" or "too old"

Historically it took at least five years of work experience before applicants became eligible for a full-time MBA. It was designed to prepare people for a managerial role more or less at the point where they would be transitioning to it, somewhere around age 30. But the trend is for applicants to want to do an MBA at a younger age, and for the top schools to allow this. Current records show that institutions such as the Harvard Business School and Stanford GSB see age 25 as more or less the sweet spot, and many are being drawn into this trend to a greater or lesser extent.

All schools value candidates with good work and life experience. Experience translates into more mature students who bring more to the classroom and their study teams. So why are they increasingly letting in early-career applicants? Once again, think how they are thinking, and you will see there are various reasons for this.

First, admissions is as competitive for them as it is for you. They are competing for the best applicants. Prospective MBA candidates generally want to go as soon as possible, to accelerate their careers. So once some key schools break ranks and start offering them early places, they are effectively selecting the cream and the other schools are forced into the game.

The other reasons are all follow-ons from this. MBA programs have always tried to create a cohort of more-or-less same-age matriculants who will therefore bond more closely on campus and also form a stronger alumni cohort. Once they start offering places to younger applicants, logic says they have to take the whole cohort in that direction. Partly as a rationalization of all this, schools are now trumpeting the "formative" role of the MBA experience. That is, that the role of the MBA is to fundamentally shape you (rather than rounding you out). Whatever the merits of this, and whether it is real or "spin," the implication is the earlier they get candidates, the more formative they can be. So they take younger candidates. Finally, once the cohort is younger, then that attracts different types of recruiters. The companies coming to campus are often no longer looking to hire a 32-year-old executive, but rather a 27-year-old analyst.

Solutions for older applicants

In today's MBA market, if you are 29 or older on MBA entry, you are in the older-applicant category. How should you handle this? There are two core strategies. The first is to show and prove how you are bringing more to the program due to your greater experience and greater seniority. You should be able to show work experiences and experiences in challenging environments that a 24-year-old just can't match.

The other angle is to show how and why you are recruitable despite (or because of) your age. If their main worry is that the on-campus recruitment roadshow will look past you, you have to show how why they won't, or how you will be able to conduct an independent job search and why it will work. This will rest heavily on special pre-MBA skills you have, or special relationships you have developed, or both. If you look obviously recruitable, a lot of the downside of age will be removed from your candidacy.

Solutions for younger applicants

You are an early-career candidate if you have two years or less of work experience. The trend is undoubtedly with you now that many top programs have cut their work experience requirement. Still, assuming your essays and interview, and everything else in your application is good, and you stand on the cusp of being admitted, the question Adcom will be considering most intensely about you is whether you have enough work and life experience to manage yourself in the program and be valuable to your cohort.

As you can't point to years here and years there, your play is to show the *quality* of the experience you have. Some people do an immense amount in two years, which is more valuable than 10 years of doing the same tasks again and again. The other thing you need to focus on is a really careful argument as to "why now," that is, why it is the right time in your life to do the degree. If you are 30, that's more or less a no-brainer, but at 23 it requires careful thinking and argument. If you can make your argument for an early-stage MBA convincing, you greatly improve your application.

4 Investigating schools and managing social media resources

So far we have dealt with understanding the needs and preferences of Adcoms and how to manage your application in their terms so that they choose you. We will return to this in the next chapter when we look at what goes on after you put in your application to a typical elite-level business school. Before that, in this chapter, we discuss how to manage the main choice you have, which is where you apply to. Choosing the right institution is important in terms of what you learn inside and outside the classroom, for your post-MBA recruitment and progress, and ongoing career network building and career identification. In short, it is a big deal.

As emphasized in previous chapters, b-schools are all the same, and they have more commonalities than differences. That's why schools look for all types of applicants. But the reverse doesn't apply. You are not looking for all types of schools. You will do only one MBA in your life and the more closely it meets your needs, the better off you will be.

Researching and choosing programs

Choosing which business school to apply to requires detailed, hands-on research about each institution, culture, curriculum emphasis, extramural activities, and recruitment opportunities. The key parameters along which to judge programs against each other are detailed below. But first, above all, judge them against your needs.

Obviously, you greatly increase your chances if you apply to programs to which your profile and interests are already aligned, and where your aspirations fit naturally. It's almost impossible to falsify a fit, so don't bother trying. Not only will the "false you" be a pale shadow of the real you, and therefore much less likely to get in, but even if you do get in, you will only succeed in putting yourself at an institution where you are unhappy. So, first carefully analyze your own motivations, needs, desires, and preferences for getting an MBA, and work out clearly what *you* want from the school you go to. Then search for the right place. You are paying the fees: it is your graduate education and your life. If you don't define your needs and preferences at the start, you will soon be blown off course by what the schools want you to look like and what they want you to aspire to.

Part Two of this book delves further into profile analysis and developing your competitive positioning in order to prepare your essays. What you do here will be a preliminary to that. Take a sheet of paper and write short answers to the following questions:

- Why do you want to go to business school? Why do you need an MBA?
- What are you hoping to learn? What general things and what specific things?
- What sort of learning environment and culture are you looking for?
- What are your career goals?
- What are your personal goals?
- What skill or background do you have that is unique, that will make you attractive?

These are just starter questions to get you thinking. Add your own. You may also consider duration, location, cost, and any other factors that shape your preferences. When you have finished brainstorming, spend some time getting your answers to the questions into a few key points. You should be able to write a mission-statement paragraph that goes something along the lines of:

- I'm applying to do an MBA because . . .
- The kind of program I want to go to is . . .
- Given my particular goals, I need an MBA program that gives me . . .

This document is your anchor in the application storm. Paste it in front of you on your desk. Refer to it when you feel you are being run ragged by the demands and preferences of the schools.

Bear in mind that schools will likely have both a general reputation and a focus on certain specialties. Sometimes the specialty focus is more important than the general one. For example, going to the Johnson School, Cornell, may be a better place than Stanford if you intend a career in hotel management. (Overall the general reputation is more important, Stanford would be good for you no matter what you plan to do.) The point is, general reputation will never measure how well a business school meets your specific goals. It will be more rewarding to go somewhere where you have some intrinsic congruence with the culture of the school, faculty, and fellow students, and where your profile and aspirations fit the curriculum and the alumni network.

This is true not just for your own happiness. Choosing the right school helps strategically in admissions—the fit between you and the school will be more convincing. So certainly orient yourself to the better schools, but pick the right school for you. Also, if possible, try not to have your heart set on any one. Even if your dad went to Harvard, and you've been expected to go there since you were three years old, remember that all business schools in the same tier will, ultimately, give you an equivalent professional boost. And, even if you are an ace applicant, and your chances of getting into an elite program are strong overall, the odds on you getting into any one specific school are never strong. There's just too much competition.

Evaluating business schools

The following is a list of key ways that programs differ, therefore providing a basis for you to assess them against your own needs.

1. Rankings and real reputations

The reputation or brand of a school is everything. Alright, almost everything. The top schools attract the best students, the best faculty, the most lucrative industry partnerships and internship placements, and the top recruiters offering the best jobs—and have therefore, in a virtuous cycle, the most powerful and best-connected alumni networks. Also, the prestige of the school and hence its ability to be selective—and therefore your achievement in having got in—will be an important legacy of your business education.

Note that reputation is *not* the same as the popular annual rankings published by business periodicals. The rankings are a sort-of and often misleading guide to reputation. It is true that an enormous amount of genuine research, and data collection and processing goes into the rankings each year, but the problem with the rankings is they are not primarily there to help you, the candidate. They are there to sell more copies of the publications that publish them and the advertising that goes with it.

This leads to a fundamental conflict of interest, for example, a repeat of the same number-one school every year is bad for magazine sales. That's why the rankers have to suddenly "find" that schools "climb rapidly" or "drop unexpectedly," or whatever it takes to grab magazine headlines. Do not be concerned that your dream school has suddenly dropped three places. Next year it will be back up, amid magazine headline hoopla.

In reality, the reputation that a school has in the marketplace and among recruiters is consistent year in and year out. Here's the news. The top schools (in alphabetical order) are: Chicago-Booth, Columbia, Dartmouth, Harvard, INSEAD, Kellogg, LBS, MIT-Sloan, Stanford, and Wharton—with Darden, Duke-Fuqua, Esade, Haas, IMD, IESE, Cambridge-Judge, Cornell Johnson, Michigan Ross, Oxford-Said, and NYU-Stern also there or thereabouts. Little or nothing will have changed by the time you read this or in five years from now. As you proceed to the next tier down, beyond the top-25 or so, what counts the most is to what extent the MBA has been accredited by the world's three business school accreditation bodies: EQUIS, AACSB, and AMBA. Also the top school in any country, no matter how insignificant, will always carry some graduate kudos.

If you are in any doubt as to what a program's reputation is, check out the data. Every school publishes a list of companies that come recruiting and how many graduates they hire, overall placement rates, and average starting salaries. The grade of hiring company and average starting salary are a much better guide to a program's real prestige than any ranking you'll find in a magazine. (However, when considering starting salaries between schools, make sure to compare the same year, as MBA starting salaries look quite different in booms and busts. Also bear in mind that the monetary value of salaries outside the US is generally lower, but non-US jobs often include better vacation allowance and other benefits of a saner work–life balance.)

Therefore, forget ranking turbulence that will not alter your career prospects in any way and concern yourself with the overall long-term reputation of the school, the kind of faculty it attracts, and the recruitment company it keeps. The real question to ask is: Which band is the school in—is it consistently a top-3 or top-10 or top-25 ranked program, or not? Schools tend to move between the bands very slowly or not at all.

2. Location

Location is the other major determinant of MBA program quality and character, and greatly affects your options and future prospects. Other than fees and cost of living variance, and visa headaches, location affects you in the following ways.

Education, extramurals, and speakers

Where you are in the world strongly determines the industry orientation of the school, the type of faculty who gather there, and what is on the menu both inside and outside the classroom. At NYU-Stern, a short walk from Wall Street, you will have dramatically different options than you will in Palo-Alto. Not necessarily better, just different.

One particular aspect of this is what type of guest speaker will be on campus and how often. This may seem trivial, but one of the big pluses of going to a good business school is to see and hear industry idols, often in relaxed off-the-cuff mode, and be able to ask them questions. In a major center like New York or London, you will get a veritable global business glitterati passing through. Further off the beaten track, in Hanover, NH, or New Haven, CT, for example, you can wait longer between speakers of note.

Internships and recruitment

A school's location (as well as its reputation, and specializations) strongly influences which companies recruit there. Every school publishes a list of companies that come to campus and if you look through these you will see how different—not necessarily better or worse—your exit opportunities will be in Chicago vs. Houston vs. Oxford, UK. You will have more chance of making your big start in media-entertainment management coming out of UCLA than out of Michigan. Your career in Europe will be launched better from LBS than from Kellogg. Having said that, generally, the candidates of top-branded schools have a much wider recruitment basin—around the US and around the world. Smaller or less well-known schools usually have strong links with the companies in their local region.

The pros and cons of locations can sometimes be mitigated by the opportunity to do part of your MBA as an exchange student at another business school.

3. Electives and extracurricular options

Mostly, the core curriculum is identical everywhere and, from a strictly educational point of view, it doesn't matter too much where you do it. Electives, however, differ significantly from school to school, according to faculty interest and expertise, and location. Also, faculty with common expertise tends to congregate together. In this way, schools become known for one or a number of specialties. For example, Wharton is considered to be the place for specialist finance and real-estate concentrations, Stern, NYU, for media management, MIT-Sloan for technology management.

In addition to classes, programs often provide experiential learning opportunities, exchange opportunities, internships, and consulting projects with industry partners, as well as regional, national, or international "treks" (networking and jobseeking tours). Programs also offer different and numerous opportunities to join and run clubs and societies, and to organize conferences. Judicious selection of these opportunities will help you align your MBA program to your goals and create more of a track record in your chosen field by the time recruiters come to campus.

Many schools offer joint degrees with other parts of the university: law, international relations, urban planning. Joint degrees will take longer but will give your MBA a clearer industry focus. This is more important if your career path has not been narrowly defined before your MBA, or if you are too young to have had much career definition.

4. Profile of the participants

Most people will tell you that the make-or-break of your experience at business school will be the fellow-students you meet and the friends you make. They will become, of course, your alumni network, and this network will be a lifelong resource. Make the effort to understand the subtle differences in the type of person each school attracts—their age, educational background, industry orientation, international exposure, amount and type of prior work experience, and so on. This may be subtle. There will be more in common in student profiles between, say, Chicago Booth and Georgetown-McDonough but there will also be clear differences. This is true everywhere. Go somewhere where you will more easily fit in and you will be a lot happier and productive.

Location overlaps with a school's culture, history, reputation, educational method, and faculty specialization in determining the kind of students who you will study with. Big-city campuses generally have student populations that are more ethnically and globally diverse. The same will be true of the faculty. At the main European schools, the student body and faculty will be genuinely multilingual and multinational.

American schools will have more women in the program (about 40 percent) than foreign schools do (about 20–25 percent). Certain schools take older students (in their 30s) more readily than others. Almost anywhere in the world the curriculum will be significantly oriented to American business issues (most of the cases are written by US professors and published by US schools, particularly Harvard), but in the US an American orientation will obviously be more pronounced.

5. Length, structure, and curriculum flexibility

The time it takes to get an MBA can vary from 10 months to two years (more for a part-time program). This affects both the cost and how long you will be out of the workforce. Longer programs offer more electives, exchange programs, and other forms of enrichment, including the opportunity to do a full summer internship. If you are younger (in MBA terms, that is 25 or less on MBA entry), chances are you need the time to figure out what you want to do, and you'll benefit by getting good internships on your resume. If you are older, you may need speed of completion more than anything.

Shorter programs cut the opportunity cost—and "the waffle"—to a minimum. Some programs only allow you into their accelerated program if you have advanced candidacy in business or a specialist technology. Generally, shorter programs are better for:

- older, more experienced candidates;
- candidates with a prior Master's degree or PhD;
- candidates planning to return to a familiar industry (moving from a technical to a management function).

Executive MBAs (EMBA) are done by older candidates, usually with 10 or more years of work experience. Typically, students in these programs have been sponsored by their employers, although this trend is on the wane. Executive MBA programs are seen to be easier to get into—therefore, the prestige of having got in is lower and the relative career boost is, on average, also lower.

EMBAs, like part-time programs in general, are structured to allow for educational "contact" and "distance" modules (time back in the office), offering the key benefit of allowing students to apply what they are learning to their ongoing work life, and create studies and projects based on real problems. Most view this as the key benefit students bring to and get from the EMBA or part-time MBA experience. In economic downturns, more students use these options because they are less inclined to give up their jobs.

How many schools to apply to?

There's some simple real-life economics in deciding how many applications to make—the more you do, the more you spread your risk of missing out entirely, but the thinner you spread your time and attention, not to mention the patience of your recommenders as mentioned in Chapter 3. Obviously, you and they can recycle a lot of information, so it gets easier each time, but there are many aspects of an application that just can't be compressed.

Even if you are an excellent candidate, it is impossible to be sure you will get into any one institution. You need portfolio effects to work for you, so apply to at least three or four. For most people, the physical and psychological limit is about six. Apply to at least one "reach" (dream) school. On the flip side, also apply to a "safety" school, that is somewhere less competitive where you have an outstanding chance of getting in—and would still be happy to go to—if all else fails. If you are on the younger end of the spectrum and could reapply in the following year at little career cost, then you don't need a safety school.

Doing due diligence on the school and "the fit"

From the above you should have a good sense of the ways in which MBA programs that may look similar are in fact different, and be able to identify the elements that chime with your needs. This should be the basis for your selection. Once you've made your choice, the process of learning about a program is not over. In fact, it has just begun because a big part of application success is showing Adcom why a particular program fits with who you are and what you want from an MBA. No good school thinks of itself as just offering you an MBA. Rightly or wrongly, they see their MBA in specific, differentiated terms. To argue your fit with them closely and passionately, you need to know a lot about your target institution. This requires detailed, hands-on research about each prospective business school and its particular culture, curriculum emphasis, and extramural activities, and opportunities.

There is a lot of information about MBA institutions available—everything from the schools' self-promotion brochures and Web resources to thousands of other websites, articles, and social media options. Your task is to select and use these judiciously to advance your application. The following section discusses how to do it.

Dig behind the websites and glossy brochures

A lot of information about business school is easy to come by, not least because the schools are pushing it at you in the bid to get you to apply. School "push" media is the fastest way to find out the basics on any program. But you won't get much past the basics of what you need to argue your close fit with the program by looking at the glossy brochure or the school's glamor website. That won't make you enough of an "insider." What you get will be generalized and so well known as to be effectively useless for competitive applications where you will only impress with fresh, specific, accurate, detailed information that is relevant to your situation and your goals.

The information you want goes beyond what is commonly known, so when you use it in your essays, it will show that you have really done independent homework on the school in question rather than just downloading from the Web. The only way to know enough about a program in this way is to get inside it for a while—by interacting with people who are there, or visiting the campus and talking to people who are there.

The best quality sources of information on any program are current students and recent alumni. They will know the way a school really operates, what's important, what areas of study are currently "hot," and generally how the culture really manifests itself. They will have learned how the system works and how to work it. Students can also describe the ins and outs of your options, both academic and extramural, and help you to understand which societies will suit you and the contribution you could make while on campus. That's the stuff you need to hear.

Generally, schools are quite happy to put you in touch with students. If you have trouble getting to students, approach them under the banner of a common interest. If you are a rugby player, call the head of the rugby club; if you are a stock market buff, call the secretary of the equities club; if you are a Spaniard, call the European club. Within minutes you can move the conversation to your more general school-research questions.

The campus visit

You should plan to visit the schools that are within a reasonable distance. You will get a more rounded picture of the institution and its culture and may get specific things to talk about in your essay. Also, if the campus is reasonably close to you, eyebrows will be raised if you have not taken the trouble to visit.

But it is hardly worth doing if you just sniff the air and pick up the glossy literature. Your campus visit will only be worth it if you engage the staff and current students in conversation and ask leading questions. If the school doesn't arrange its own introductions, go to the cafeteria and hang out with people, and come away with a picture of your target institution that contains some unique impressions and is specifically oriented to your interests and goals. Again, this both helps you directly in making your assessment about the place, and will play well in your essays if you apply.

Don't put too much store on the meeting you may have with the admissions officer. When your application file comes up, she will as likely as not have forgotten you among thousands of others. Also, the fact of having visited the campus will *never* formally benefit you in admissions: Adcom is careful to be fair to applicants in other states and around the world who cannot visit. What's important is that your actual application shows you are enthusiastic enough about the program to be fully and intelligently informed about it.

Social media makes itself felt

The social media revolution has significantly altered how business schools communicate with and promote themselves to applicants. At the time of writing, schools are figuring out how to integrate their presence across *Twitter*, *Facebook*, online discussion forums, webinars, podcasts, Adcom officer blogs, or student blogs. What is clear is that the "broadcast" model—where they launch information at potential applicants in a top-down way is being eroded in favor of a more interactive approach. This opens up opportunities for engagement with admissions staff or current students.

Adcom blogs, where these exist, are being used differently by different schools, reflecting the personalities of those who run them as much as any coherent strategy. Some are very much one-way traffic, announcing upcoming deadlines and offering general do's and don'ts. Others have absolutely broken new ground in being personable and offering a transparent, and relatively honest behind-the-scenes view into the admissions process, almost proving that Adcom is made up of human beings. You can follow, interact, and absorb the school's culture in this way. (Be appropriate. Don't, for example, use a blog comment facility to ask about your own personal application.)

Some schools sponsor student-based chat with prospective applicants. Wharton's *Student-2-Student* discussion forum is the best known among these—allowing students to pass on school and admissions insights. While keeping one eye on potential brand risk, most schools are happy to facilitate the emergence of student bloggers and support their role in painting a worm's-eye view of the student day-to-day life. MBA students being what they are, these blogs are often on the cutting edge of technology, including *YouTube* video, "Second Life."

You can connect with or "follow" current students or clubs via their blogs or tweets, or their identities on *Facebook, LinkedIn*. If there is a Stanford club entertaining Steve Jobs, it will be on someone's blog. If Wharton students are on a trek, someone will have uploaded video to *YouTube*. Following this assiduously and interacting (politely) where appropriate will give you a window into the nature and culture of the program you are targeting in a way that just was impossible to imagine a few years ago. Beware, quality is mixed, to say the least. You will get many perspectives from parties with vested interests that are not necessarily aligned with yours. Use them wisely. But overall this is the way to go.

The downside

Clearly, social media allows for the cultivation of relationships that would not have existed a few years ago. But the downside to social media for MBA applicants is: If you can find and know them in this way, they can find you. Be careful about what you say online and what you have said. I'm not saying that Adcoms Google an applicant or routinely look them up on identity sites to find out more about them or corroborate what they put down on the forms. They probably don't. But they very well might.

Expect Adcom to treat you in some ways like a potential employee or client. It's well known that these days prospective employers or clients, or anyone who wants to look you up on the Web, can and will do so. And when they do, they may find that beery and not-altogether-clean bachelor party photo on *MySpace*. Or they may find *Doostang* profile that doesn't adequately match what you've told them. And it's quite hard, once something is out there on the Web, to take it back.

So be smart about it. Use social networking to get inside a program to research and develop your "fit" argument. Be scrupulous about what is out there under your name, make it consistent with your application platform, and try to remove unprofessional material where you can.

5 What goes on after you hand in your application

Inside the admissions process

The required elements of your application—biographical and file information, academic transcripts, GMAT score, recommendations, and essays—are standard for all schools. There is some variation. Some schools ask for more recommendations or a peer recommendation, some interview routinely, others interview only selectively. Some ask for additional biographical summary items such as resumes and cover letters.

Whatever a particular program requires, the Adcom will wait for all elements of it to arrive before proceeding with your case. As with college applications, the various elements usually come separately from different places. You can expect the admissions department to have a reasonably well-organized system for collating the parts of your application, and to know which items they are waiting for. You may get periodic mail or email notices telling you what has and hasn't arrived.

Once everything is complete, and they are ready to proceed, everything gets printed out. This may change in the future as online collaborative working systems improve, but now everything is printed out, primarily so it can be easily shared around the office. Note that *everything* is printed out. That is, everything, including your written correspondence, emails, extra material. This means every single time you communicated with Adcom is up for inspection. They are asking themselves: how does that look? Was it professional? Was it appropriate in style and content? Here's some hardball advice: if there is something that you are really unsure of committing to paper then don't. Use the phone. The Adcom member may note it into your file in writing, but they may not. But if you interact with them in writing it always becomes part of your application.

Managing first impressions

There's a book called *Blink*, by *New Yorker* writer and celebrity author Malcolm Gladwell,[1] which is about first impressions, the first few seconds during which we appraise information and make instant judgments. Gladwell says these conclusions oftentimes produce better, more accurate, conclusions than those made by way of exhaustive analysis. Michael LeGault came out with a rebuttal—*Think!: Why Crucial Decisions Can't Be Made in the Blink of an Eye*,[2] and the jury is certainly out on whether "Blinking" provides a better basis for decision-making than formal analysis. But the point is it certainly provides, in every situation, an ever-present *alternative* basis for decision-making (whether the decision-maker is aware of it or not). When people talk about "love at first sight," or say "you never get a second chance to make a first impression," they are talking about the Blink factor.

The implication for MBA admissions is that, while b-school Adcoms everywhere would assert that they rigorously analyze the strengths and weaknesses of each candidate, there is also considerable Blink involved in how they choose one over the other. Note that Adcom essay readers and committee members are not seeking to make an impressionistic judgment. In fact, the opposite is true. They aspire to neutrality and rigor. But they will be picking up impressions at every turn. After all, they have to make a big decision, fairly quickly, about a complex situation (you and your future prospects) and they don't actually have that much formal stuff to go on.

So the Blink factor counts for a lot in MBA admissions, and before Adcom even gets to fully considering an applicant's grades and scores, performance metrics, and work history, they will have formed an impression from the first things they see. It's hard to know what they will see first of course, but very often it will be the file data or resume or cover letter. (As mentioned in Chapter 14, the interviewer will have formed her own Blink impression in the interview, which will be reflected in her report.) As they look over your stuff, an impression or "instinct" will form almost immediately, and they will continue to absorb first impressions about each part; the essays, particularly their organization and erudition; the tone and warmth of recommendations, making Blink judgments of your personality, motivation, determination, charisma, team orientation, and overall prospects. These impressions "battle" with rational analysis in the mind of the reader, becoming reinforced or eroded by evidence. You can make a poor first impression and slowly win them over with reasons to admit you. But better to get the Blink factor on your side to start with.

The best way to deal with Blink is to realize it is there, and always will be, and provide ways for admissions officers to use this mode in judging you. Expecting snap judgments about your motivation, take care that everything you submit is carefully checked and complete. Expecting snap judgments about your pre-MBA work experience as a 23-year-old, take care to get the highlights of it high up in your essay. Expecting snap judgments about your professionalism, take care that any correspondence you enter into (by phone or email) is scrupulously professional. In general you should play to the impression mode first, and follow this with data and detail that corroborate the impression.

The first read

The application then goes for a "first read." In many US schools, current 2nd year students (working for tuition reduction or a stipend) may be involved in the initial reading, evaluation, and sorting. Sometimes external, trusted, external readers (who may be "alumni" of the admissions office) are hired. If your file is rejected at the first round, chances are it will be either of these types of readers who were primarily responsible.

Typically, your file will be read by two people. The readers will make notes, which may or may not be part of what the second reader sees (if not, the aim is that they come to the file without prejudice). Either way, a series of notes gets built up in your file. Where everyone is coming to more or less the same kinds of conclusions, your file moves fairly rapidly to be dinged or towards the Adcom meeting.

Where there is less clarity of opinion, more extended, multiple readings are called for and these will be done by professional admissions staff, with senior admissions staff or designated faculty reading in the event of a question or dispute about the merits of the file or (very occasionally) where specialist technical or financial input is needed to judge an applicant's claims. These may just be referred to specific sections or essays for comment.

Readers are normally free to approach the file in their own way. There will be guidelines as to what to look for and how to weigh the elements, but it varies from one reader to the next what they look at first and how they progress through the application. However, most commonly, the reader will take the following route:

1. A survey of your basic information
    Your age; nationality; profession; amount, nature of and place of work experience; salary level; languages; special competencies; certifications; and educational and professional awards and promotions will be gleaned from the answers you provide to questions on the application form. This quick tour through your biographical and employment history will provide the main coordinates of your candidacy.

    Candidates with biographical success and decorations will start to distinguish themselves, even at this first stage. The most common way candidates fail at this point is if they are too young (not enough work experience) or too old (better suited to an executive MBA) or if they don't have a primary college degree or some other basic requirement.

2. Academic assessment
    The reader will then review your academic claim to a place, including status of college attended, courses and course loads undertaken, chosen major, GPA achieved, graduate degrees or diplomas if applicable, and GMAT score. A weak academic profile or any hint that you will not cope intellectually will result in rejection. The reader may mentally raise your GPA up a bit to compensate for harder college courses, a prior graduate degree or any explanatory factors that you have mentioned. She may even view a low GPA with some leniency if grades were on a solid upward trend, or shrug off a few Bs and Cs in the light of significant extramural activities and successes. Of course, a subsequent reader may view your extenuating circumstances differently and apply a different personal judgment.

    Readers will look kindly on good grades in post-college courses taken at any credible institution—the so-called "alternative transcript." Readers will definitely check for evidence of quantitative or business-related courses, and poor grades here are a serious handicap, probably worse even than being completely untested in this area—where at least you retain the benefit of the doubt. The flip side is that alternative transcript courses in quantitative subjects are considered particularly favorably, if you do well.

3. Essay assessment
    The readers will then read your essays. They will get an impression on two levels. First, they want to see that the essays have been done competently and diligently and that the questions have been answered. If you are just waffling, they might try to determine whether this is simply due to poor communications skills or whether it is something more nefarious, such as lifting from another essay set, which is an automatic ding. They will want to see that points are clearly made and well organized. They will notice how thorough you have been—spelling, punctuation, or typographic mistakes will cost you dearly. Adcom's "favorite" mistake is catching the name of a rival school in the essay set. Any lurking feeling that the application is not conscientiously done will provide them with an excuse to reject it.

    Readers will also judge the vision, argument, motivation, and passion in your essays. They will be looking for clear, appropriate, and well-thought-out career goals, and a workable plan to achieve those goals—a plan that includes needing what an MBA and their specific program offers. They will evaluate the benefits you claim to be bringing to the program and the relevance of those benefits to the classroom and extra-mural experience. Readers also look for leadership potential, as well as maturity, independence, professionalism, and the other attributes that were mentioned in Chapter 2.

4. Recommendation and interview assessment
    Once the reader has a picture of your profile, experience, and intentions, she will turn to the judgments others have made about you—the letters of recommendation. As mentioned in Chapter 3, the "recos" are the way that Adcom evaluates you as a workplace professional. Your application reader will look to see who is recommending you—evaluating your judgment in who you chose for this—and then look to what they have said for independent corroboration of the professional merits you claim, and of the assessments he has made while reading the file. If the recommenders do not endorse your potential and unequivocally support your candidacy, you will be in trouble. If significant and credible people stand up for you, and can provide concrete details to support their own argument, and if their assessment chimes with your application message and the reader's own positive impression of you, your application will go forward.

5. Interview invitation
    Some schools interview everyone. Others who interview selectively will, at this point, make a judgment on all they have seen so far and decide whether to interview you. Where interviews are not mandatory, this is because they are resource intensive—they require lots of admissions officer or alumni time and goodwill. They don't want to waste their time, so if they think you are not up to much, they will pass. Alternatively if you appear borderline, but have something that has piqued their interest, an interview call will be put out.

    Where interviews are discretionary, usually not more than about a quarter of total applicants get an invitation, so getting one is a very good sign. Some offer an on-campus day package (interview + campus tour + class experience + introduction to students), which is further indication that they think you are worth spending some time on. At interview-by-invitation schools, applicant acceptance rates post-interview are generally about five times a school's overall acceptance rate. If you are not invited for an interview, you are dinged.

Whether the school interview everyone, or interview only after a first cull, it is very unlikely these days that anyone will get admitted to a top-25 level program without an interview. Some schools use only on-campus admissions staff, others use only alumni, while most offer a mix of the two. However they work it, the face-to-face check is a fundamental part of Adcom's due-diligence and usually the last chance for information about you before making their decision. Therefore they take it very seriously. For more on the interview and how to manage it, see Chapter 14. After your interview, your interviewer will write up an interview report, based on the school's standard interview-report form, which becomes part of your file.

6. The committee meeting
    If the application fails at the reading or interviewing stage, it is cut. There may be cases where a number of people read the file, are unsure, and then a senior admissions officer looks at the file and decides to reject it. In all, you should not underestimate how many times your file gets read. It will be more times than you think. Files that make it past these hurdles move forward to the committee stage.

    At the committee-meeting stage, again there are common practices but also mild variation. Some schools favor a small committee made up of just the core professional Adcom staff. This will be about 4–7 people. Others use a larger committee, which includes a broader base including Career Services (job recruitment) personnel, and sometimes the Dean or other school representatives or stakeholders. Either way, the committee, chaired by the Director of Admissions, will review each case again in full and decide whether to make an offer, waitlist, or reject. Different committees each have their own preferred method: a common one is to get the chief reader proposing the candidate (the "sponsor" or "champion") to go through the candidate's profile and to explain its merits and drawbacks. The others will then agree or not. One way or another, each application is discussed thoroughly. If there is a weakness or a fudge, they will find it. Usually a consensus decision will be made. If consensus cannot be reached, the director will make the final call.

The imperative to balance the class

Remember, the committee is making a decision about you at two levels. First, are you good enough to merit a place, that is, in the top 20 percent (roughly speaking) of the applicant group in terms of overall merit; and, second, do you add something interesting, of unique value that broadens the class base and balances it?

Every business school thinks of itself as a "team-based, collaborative, environment." They are picking a team. If you were picking a team—say, a soccer team—you wouldn't just pick all center backs, or all wings or all goalkeepers. You need a balance of skills and aptitudes. Likewise for Adcom in picking the team in each admissions year. They will handpick every person to play a role in the cohort and they will be sure to balance skills and experience as widely as possible.

This has an important corollary: you are not up against everyone for admission—you are up against the people whose profile is similar to yours, the other goalkeepers or the other wingers. No matter who you are, or how well you present yourself, you will be competing for admission first in the overall terms and then in your "position."

For the purposes of class balance, Adcom will reduce your profile to a few key factors. You might be the Chinese Ministry of Defense woman, or the 23-year-old Chicago agribusiness futures trader, or the Booz Allen Hamilton tax consultant, or the Washington DC radio journalist. The Chinese woman will be in a sub-competition with all the other Chinese candidates or other military types. The trader will be compared with the other traders and all the younger candidates. The Booz Allen consultant will be compared with the other applicants from Booz Allen and all the applicants with a tax consulting background. The radio journalist will be compared with media professionals and all the candidates with non-business backgrounds (the "poets").

It is highly unlikely that there will be official quotas for any background or skill, but you can be perfectly certain that the admissions committee will keep tabs on how many offers have gone out to people with more common profiles, and such offers will be more competitive and dry up sooner in the admissions cycle. Given this state of affairs, your strategy is to define yourself as far as possible into categories that are less competitive. Any atypical parts of your personal or professional background will allow you to do this. This is discussed further in the diversity essay, in Chapter 11.

The most common professional profiles are usually banking, consulting, information technology, and engineering. Competitive nationalities are usually Indian, Chinese, and American. There are, on average, more male than female applicants (three times as many in Europe), so getting in is, on average, harder for men.

Application timing issues: When to apply?

Timing your application can have important consequences. Whether the school has continuous "rolling" admissions or a series of discrete deadlines (typically in October, January, and March), early on in the cycle there are lots of places and by March–April there are none. Schools with unusual start dates will have different schedules, but the same general rule applies.

Common and absolutely correct wisdom is to submit your application when it is at its best. A carefully considered and well-worked Round 2 application will have much better prospects of success than if it was rushed to make the Round 1 deadline.

Having said that, it's worth keeping a weather eye on how the deadlines work. Generally, about 40 percent will be admitted at the first round, and again at the second round, and the remaining few places will be filled up in the third round or subsequent rounds. Some schools divide more equally between these three rounds, but this is not the norm. The key principle is that each round is its own separate mini-competition: candidates not accepted or waitlisted do *not* go forward to the next round and may not apply until the following year. The school will make definite offers to the candidates it chooses, up to the quota of seats it has for that round (plus some for candidates who will decline a place); it will waitlist some and it will reject the rest. Part of the reason for this is that accepted or rejected candidates who apply early get a definite answer early—early enough to be able to plan for the school move, or follow their "B" strategy.

It has become very common for schools to waitlist first-round applicants they are in any way not sure about, effectively saying "we like you" but we want to see who else applies before we commit. If you know your options theory, you will recognize this as a call option—they are giving themselves the right but not the obligation to "buy" while they wait to see what else is out there. Once the second round is in, or all the rounds are in, they will feel in a better position to decide. Adcom's downside risk in writing themselves call options is that good applicant may be accepted at another good school in Round 1, and they will lose that person.

In the first round, the field is wide open. Every part of the class profile, every nationality, every background, every skill set and every previous employer is, by definition, under-represented. Here schools traditionally select the best, with little or no regard to the class mix. The second round is where the business of balancing the class begins in earnest. By this deadline the school has almost all the serious applications it is going to get, and sets about sorting the best and balancing those under consideration with the candidates who have accepted offers from the first round.

By the third or fourth round, there are a relative handful of places left, which are given to the late or wild-card applicants who bring some amazing and unique attribute: the school keeps these places back so it has the power to make an offer to a truly exceptional candidate who pops up at the last minute. It much harder to get in at this stage—you may be the best banker in the entire group, but if they already have enough bankers who have had and have accepted offers, you're out of luck.

The risk of waiting, if you are a conventional candidate, is that the unofficial quota for your professional profile will already be full before the second round, or full enough to lower the odds of success. So it is generally advisable to submit as early as possible, that is, in Round 1. This is particularly true if you are both a strong and traditional candidate (from a common and possibly oversubscribed background such as banking or consulting), and you meet all the academic number requirements. If you have lower numbers and/or you come from a more unique background, it is generally better to apply in Round 2, when the committee is looking for candidates that provide depth and variation to the class. Note that schools generally get the biggest application numbers in Round 2. Schools usually re-review all Round 1 waitlisted applicants for possible admission in each subsequent round, so the advantage of using Round 1 is if you are waitlisted you buy yourself the prospect of being reconsidered along with the Round 2 pool at no extra cost to you. You may also be reconsidered for scholarships.

For foreign students applying to US schools, an important consideration is that being accepted at any deadline after January may not leave enough time to get a student visa, particularly if you are not a citizen of a G20 nation. Don't underestimate the obstacles the US Department of Homeland Security will put in your path and don't forget that Europe has absolutely fantastic business schools too.

Deadline flexibility?

In determining whether you will make a particular deadline or should postpone to the next, note that there is no flexibility in you getting your material in on time, but a fair degree of flexibility for your recommenders and for transcripts and GMAT reports to trickle in. Mostly schools have a 5pm deadline in the time zone in which the school itself resides. Be aware that their servers get very slow at around deadline time. If you get within four hours of the deadline you may be in for a frustrating time. But as long as all parts of your side of your application are uploaded by cut-off time, you are in the running. Schools will accept recommendations a few days or even a week or two beyond the deadline. Similarly with transcripts or test scores, where you have self-reported your "unofficial" score, the verification is allowed to trickle in from the official agencies over days or weeks. Many school don't bother with verifications until later in the process, that is, they only verify the applicants who get offers.

Note also that they will not start processing any applications until after the deadline. Once the deadline has passed Adcom will start to print and distribute material to readers. Early submissions will not be processed faster.

Waitlist and multiple-admit strategy

It's quite common in a competitive process to get a "waitlist" notice, particularly if you apply at Round 1. As mentioned above, they are giving themselves an option on you while they wait to see who else is coming to the party. How should you manage this? First, you do have some status. They have looked at you and liked you, just not enough to make an offer yet. The best way to deal with this is on a school-by-school basis, because all are different, and many are highly touchy about being "bugged" by waitlistees.

There is no harm in asking them politely if there is anything you can add or any particular issue (that may be holding you back) that you might address. As mentioned, every last scrap of your interaction with Adcom is printed out and goes in your file, so ask politely once and don't make a nuisance of yourself. If they offer you the opportunity to add something, do so promptly and stick scrupulously to the topic or issue. The second area where it is legitimate to add something to your file is if you have retaken the GMAT, or if there is a *significant* change (of advantage to you) in your professional life. If you have been given an award or a promotion or a clear new professional opportunity that suggests you will bring in new skills and experiences, it is fair to want to add that while you fate hangs in the balance. But do not assume they will allow it. Call or email to explain what the new factor will be and ask if they will allow it to be added. If they say no, then too bad. Usually they will say yes because their motivation is to make the right decision not just to be ogres for the fun of it.

Further, if you have an offer from another school, particularly a top school, tell them. They will recognize that you will have to make a decision about that other school and put down a deposit, and this is likely to light a fire under them to clarify their decision one way or the other. Also it is human nature to want people that other people want. It works well in your favor.

PART TWO
Profile-Building Tools and Techniques

6 The profiling project

Getting admitted under competitive conditions requires you to present the most compelling portrait of yourself possible—situating yourself in the niche where you are most competitive and tightly arguing the fit between you and the program you want to be admitted to. Part One dealt with the fit primarily from the business school's point of view: understanding what its needs are and therefore what the Adcom looks for in candidates and how this plays out in various aspects and stages of the admissions process. We now turn to the other part of the fit: you. This section offers diagnostic tools you can use to investigate and understand your profile, as well as techniques for recognizing and extracting the most important, valuable, persuasive aspects of it, and consolidating this into application themes and an overall application message.

The benefits of profiling

Some people think you have to have a certain type of profile to get into a top program. As described in Chapter 1, you don't. Schools need people of all profiles for class balance. But whatever profile you have, you do have to fully bring it out. You have to demonstrate acute self-knowledge and knowledge of why you are valuable to a quality MBA program. The self-analysis you do here in the profiling stage will provide the basis for persuasively demonstrating self-understanding in your essays, interviews, and across the rest of your application. By now you will have decided which schools to target and you are moving into the phase of creating the best case to put forward to them. It is time to deepen the self-analysis and to formally consider your abilities, preferences, and experiences, and strategically select from among them.

The aims of profiling are to create enough useful and detailed raw material, and to present enough stories about you to provide (a) the direction and (b) the richness of detail that will allow you to focus your strategy and build your case for admission. In the first phase, you explore your background for its richness, strength, and key themes; in the second, you select, concentrate, and consolidate your message. You will be able to explain to the reader not just what your formative choices and experiences have been, but why they make you a valuable candidate.

Profiling involves putting the time and effort to explore the further reaches of your personality and your past, including mining for self-knowledge and insight you might not even know you have, or have forgotten. It requires self-work and, by definition, this can be uncomfortable to those not used to challenging themselves in this way. Furthermore, not all of the work will find its way into the essays. So it's tempting to leave this stage out and just get going with answering the essay questions. Resist that temptation. The work you put in here will be tapped again and again for each school you apply to, in each essay you write and each interview you do. You can only get out what you put in. Also, if profiling is done properly, it will not only enhance your essays, it will significantly shorten your essay writing and rewriting time. You won't need to rack your brains each time—the material will be there in front of you.

Getting to, and telling your own story

Part of the holy grail in MBA admissions is "telling your own story." Schools ask for this all the time, in various ways: "Tell us something that is unique to you." "What are your motivations and passions?" "Don't tell us what you think we want to hear, tell us your own story." In other words, self-awareness and telling your own story are not an extra, but fundamental: the MBA application demands a compelling inward look at yourself. As discussed further in the essay section, the essays have to interpret you to Adcom, reveal your personality, and capture what's interesting and valuable and compelling about you by sharing telling anecdotes and providing personal insights that matter. You want then to find you unique and engaging, a "must meet" or "must admit," and the only way this will happen is by engaging them person-to-person with your life as an evolving story. Adcom are not gossip-mongers—once they have closed your file, they couldn't care less what you actually said. They are judging whether you have the insight and maturity to be able to self-evaluate in this way. This balances the action-oriented "just-do-it" mentality that they are also looking for.

Also, "telling your own story" sounds simplistic, childish even, but this is the most dramatic distinguishing factor that any applicant can present. Most applicants cannot get beyond the cookie-cutter values, generic personality traits, common interests, and standard aspirations. Therefore they will not distinguish themselves in competitive company. The best way to distinguish yourself is to find your unique base of life experiences and motivations, and the parts of your life and career journey that are singular to you. The only way you can get to this—to find your own story and get it clear in your own mind—is to look inward and ask yourself probing reflective questions in a structured way, that is, through quality profiling.

Creating an alternative basis for essay responses

A second crucial advantage of profiling is that it allows you to create your application platform—your value points, themes, and overall message—without the pressure or bias of any particular essay or interview questions. You make an *a priori* profile of yourself that gives you an independent basis for deciding what to say, which you then take forward to the essay and interview questions. You decide what's important to communicate and how and where you will do it, rather than letting the school's agenda define your responses. You then are in control of the agenda. When it comes to talking about you, you will be communicating what you think is most important—via whatever questions you face. By contrast, if you allow your agenda to be defined by the questions, you will find it difficult to create an integrated, centered profile and your message will come out in confused bits, if at all.

You must, of course, *also* take care to closely answer the questions in essays or interviews. Being off-topic is one of the cardinal sins of admissions essays and Adcom will not hesitate to penalize you for it. But if you know what you want to say upfront, you will almost always be able to adapt it to the terms of a given question. The key is to know what you want to say.

Preparing for behavioral questioning

The third key reason for doing intensive self-assessment work is to prepare yourself for the exploratory, open-ended, reflective, behavioral nature of the essay and interview questions you will face and the demands of answering them satisfactorily. The questions you get from competitive-admission schools won't ask for simple information. They will probe your motivations and patterns of behavior—the "why's" of your actions rather than the "who, what, where, and when factoids," although the fact and details are necessary support. This means, you won't just get, "What are your career goals?" but "What about these goals that motivates you?" You won't just get: "When have you led an organization?" but "What is your leadership style? How does this reflect who you are?" This is as much true of the interview as the essays, and managing behavioral questions in interviews is discussed further in Chapter 14.

Behavioral questions delve behind your actions to get to the behaviors, preferences, and motivations. They search for the nature of the individual behind the actions. They don't seek to know what you did in any situation, but why you did it; not how you responded, but what caused that response; not which choice you made, but why you chose it and what that says about you. Behavioral questions probe not just what your behavior pattern is, but how well you understand it. Navigating such questions requires that you know yourself very well: not just the details of your life, but the fabric of motivations and intentions that drive you and explain you.

Profile brainstorming

If you follow the profiling method suggested below, you will go through two separate profile brainstorming exercises—the first concentrating on your personal profile, the second on your professional profile. Brainstorming is the process of generating a free flow of ideas on a given topic. It can be done in various ways, but the general principle is the same: to provide a "safe" space to stimulate ideas, temporarily holding back from editing or analysis.

Your profile brainstorming should surface all kinds of memories, thoughts, ideas, events, experiences, and insights. It will be messy. Don't hold back. Don't try to order it. The goal is to get a lot of thoughts and ideas out on the table. There will be plenty of time to clean up later. For speed and economy, it's best just to jot down the minimum keyword that relates to any one thought or event—just enough so that it makes sense to you if and when you need to flesh out the idea to use it in your application.

The more openly and honestly you do this, the more self-knowledge you will gain and the more resources you will have for communicating this knowledge to others. Getting to the self-knowledge is entirely separate from the strategic choices you will make in deciding whether and how to communicate it. You do not need to communicate everything. In fact, you will hold most of it back. So be honest with yourself. At least some of your work should be personal enough that you would not just leave it lying around for anyone to see and would think twice before you showed it to anyone but your nearest and dearest.

Methodology

Take a blank sheet of paper. Turn it sideways (landscape) and draw two vertical lines down the page, dividing the paper into three equal vertical columns. You can do this in spreadsheet software too, of course. Across the top, label column 1 "Points," column 2 "Stories," and column 3 "Analysis" (Figure 6.1).

1. *Points*. In this column, put down personality traits, qualities, events, and influences that surface in response to the questions in each section. This is the column where you tag your memories and associations as they come up.

2. *Stories*. In the second column, write down keywords for the stories that demonstrate one or more of your points in column 1. Stories can be any anecdotes or vignettes of things that happened to you. They will give substance to what you have listed in column 1 and bring it to life.

3. *Analysis*. In the third column, draw out the analysis. Considering your attributes in column 1, and the stories that demonstrate them in column 2, extract the juice and write what this means to you. What does any experience or event or preference or attribute or quality or goal really say about you? How do your stories elaborate who you are? How might attributes and events you have surfaced come together in an overarching insight? What are the implications of this?

Figure 6.1 The profile development table

Shadowing the essay process

Taking your profiling through these three stages of inquiry—attribute, story, and analysis—is not a random process. It exactly anticipates the path of self-exposition you will need to achieve high performance in your essays. In the essays, you will repeatedly go through the process of:

- making a point about yourself or identifying an attribute in yourself (that is relevant to the school and its admissions criteria);
- sharing a story that demonstrates and effectively "proves" the point you are making, or attribute or value you claim to have;
- extracting the lessons and implications: developing insight from your attributes and stories in ways that show the validity and competitiveness of your candidacy.

In all that you do, you will be claiming your value, demonstrating it and proving it, and extracting implications that show why you will be a valuable candidate.

Finding and developing stories

The profiling method suggested here is heavily oriented to finding and developing stories. It is excellent advice to "tell stories," in your MBA application. You tell stories (anecdotes) in your application essays and interviews for two reasons:

> *Raising reader interest*: Narrative brings facts and attributes to life. Most people hate to read theory or conceptual copy but they love to read stories, particularly stories about people in difficult situations. They get sucked in and they want to find out what happened and how it turned out. Not only are stories engaging, but they are also memorable. People remember narrative more vividly and for longer than they do interpretation or bald data. Further discussion about stories from the perspective of how to write them well to capture and raise reader interest, is dealt with in Chapter 15.

Proving points or attributes: While your application process as a whole, and your essay writing in particular, are meant to be self-reflective, there is also a great focus on your results and successes. The MBA admissions communication is not a nice whimsical "waft," it is a an exercise in persuasion—persuading them to admit you. To make your reflections stand up to critical scrutiny, you need to provide evidence for what you say and what you claim. Particularly your claim to some or other great personal attribute means zilch unless you can back it up. Obviously the most direct way is to provide evidence of recognition in the form of an award or a promotion, but this is not always possible. The alternative is to illustrate and prove the attribute in the retelling of an event.

For example, you may say you are "cool under pressure," but what makes it more than mere hot air is when you tell the story of how you landed a Cessna on Route 505 when the pilot passed out. Claiming your "team spirit" is one thing; telling the story of being stuck in the elevator in Taiwan with six fellow McKinsey associates at 4 in the morning, when you were taking a break and trying to find an all-night pizza parlor, is more compelling.

Tips for thinking of good stories

Search for events, moments, and insights that were turning points in your life. Any time you can say "that changed me," you are dealing with a situation where events led to a fundamental development of character, and this is likely to be a moment that speaks powerfully of you. For this reason, it will likely make for a story that can be milked for personal analysis and insight. Other considerations in selecting a story are:

- Is it memorable, dramatic, or somehow likely to stick in the mind of the reader?
- Does it have interesting and lasting imagery? Does it create scenes and pictures that stick?
- Does it have action and some imperative moving events forward, making the reader curious?

Be unfaithful to time and scale

To find and develop your story properly, it is helpful to break with the unconscious habit of representing events and experiences in your past in the order in which they happened, or being bound by the relative time prominence they assumed. Length of time in an essay does not have to be faithful to length of time in life. Prominence of a story in life does not have to be faithful to prominence of a story in your essays. Liberate yourself to move freely through your past, looking for the things that have the most personal and emotional prominence, or which provide the basis for glimpses of self-insight. Develop stories around those moments and exclude everything else.

For example, say you spent ten years in hockey training, tournaments, and hockey camp, and one day, through a series of accidents, you took part in a ballet class warm-up—and that totally changed your perspective. You are perfectly within your rights to talk about that one day. Similarly, you can have spent six years at General Motors and you could choose to talk only about a single late-night conversation you had with the janitor.

Part Three of this book deals further with writing techniques that will help you focus on what's interesting and relevant, lengthen "interesting time," and cut the rest that drags your essay down.

Small is beautiful too

In searching for stories, don't confine yourself to fantastic and memorable events: the time you saved the lives of ten people stranded by a forest fire and won a bravery medal, for example. The best stories are sometimes about simple, everyday incidents: Locking your keys in the car. Written in an engaging way, they can provide memorable insight into your values, motivations, fears, and personal philosophy.

Formative stories are valuable

Most stories are demonstrative: they show you demonstrating an attribute. But a story can also be a tale about the *formation* of an attribute. An example could be how your grandfather peppered you with spelling bee questions every time he came to the house and would give you 5 cents for every one you got right. Soon you were first in your class in English, and that's where your passion for languages started . . .

Subjective reality is a safe space

In picking meaningful moments that are worthy of consideration, recognize the difference between subjective and objective reality: what happened versus what it meant to you. Something or someone can objectively be a tiny part of your life, but subjectively be enormous. It is ethically compromised to claim an experience was objectively more that it actually was—that is, to falsify information. You should not claim that you were on the team that won the national high school athletics 4×400m, when in fact you won a local school meet. But you are absolutely entitled to say that your win was the most important event of your adolescence and the turning point of your life, or magnify the importance it held for you, or express any other subjective association you choose to. Adcom is interested in your personality and subjectivity. You are invited to blow a molehill of an event up into a big-rock-candy mountain of an experience, as long as you clearly represent it as your subjective experience.

Going deeper in reflection and insight

The profiling questions for personal and professional self-insight are given in the following chapters. There are some further tools and techniques that you can use while you are doing this particularly for life and career goals (and how these express core values) which many MBA applicants struggle with. Here are two: a retirement visualization and "the Maslow challenge."

The retirement visualization

Picture yourself at your retirement function in 50+ years from now. You are at an age where you have had many experiences, seen many things, learned many things. But above all, you have achieved what you set out to do in your career and your life. Assuming it all goes according to plan, or better than planned, what have you done? What have you achieved? And even more important, why does this make you feel fulfilled and satisfied? Who is around you at the function? Why do they value you? What have you taught them? You may think of this in terms of a retirement speech, or a radio interview, or a letter to your grandchildren or whatever format strikes up your muse, but be specific and fresh in your insights. If it could be anyone's letter or anyone's retirement speech, that's not specific and personal enough.

The Maslow challenge

Psychologist Abraham Maslow created a five-level theory of human motivation,[1] in which he proposed that people's needs and satisfaction move "upwards" through a common structure that he called a "hierarchy of needs." Once lower needs of sustenance and safety are met, we aspire to fulfill social, self-esteem, and self-actualization needs. The triangle of Maslow's hierarchy of needs is shown in Figure 6.2.

The model made Maslow world famous. The structure of the pyramid itself has been tinkered with over time, for example by Manfred Max-Neef, who sees levels of: subsistence, protection, affection, understanding, participation, leisure, creation, identity, and freedom. But the core insight remains: once more basic levels of fulfillment are achieved, and as long as they remain achieved, humans moves up the hierarchy in search of fulfillment.

You can use the Maslow pyramid to push your profiling deeper. Too often applicants dwell in and around levels 2 and 3, thinking of themselves and their future in terms of security and quality of employment, taking care of their family (including elderly or immigrant parents) and developing friendship and contact networks (including alumni networks), career progress, and so on.

This is all important. But there will be more to life and career journey than this, and Maslow shows the way to developing your thinking about it. Where is the

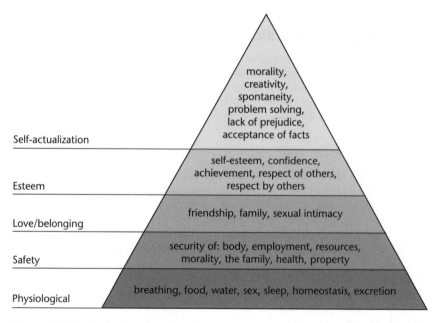

Figure 6.2   Maslow's Hierarchy of Needs
Source: http://en.wikipedia.org/wiki/Maslow%27s_hierarchy_of_needs, viewed December, 2009.

rest of your motivation going to come from in your life: how will you achieve further self-esteem, self-respect, and the respect of others? What will you create? What will put you, personally, on the higher plane of self-actualization? A good career and family security are great things to want. But what else is there? What comes after that? You don't need to aspire to be Nelson Mandela or Mother Teresa, but you do need to reach into yourself and ask: "My levels 4 and 5—what are they, for me? What would actualizing myself at these levels look like? And how will an MBA be part of what takes me there?"

7 Personal profile analysis

Look back at Figure 6.1 on p. 66 and make keyword lists responding to the following questions, and further questions you think of to ask yourself, along the lines of this sample:

Points	Stories	Analysis
PERSONAL FEATURES – Independent – More driven than most – Self = hard to please – Thrive on recognition – Big picture guy	– Time when Cedric asked me to be best man at his wedding but I refused. – Website publishing fiasco events and my intervention.	– Shows the ability to take a principled stand. Also good interpersonal diplomacy. – Cool head under pressure. Also a certain tendency to shoot my mouth off, which I am working on. Better at getting things done than dealing with organizational politics.
ACTIVITIES – Music gigs – Outdoor expeditions – Read two daily papers – Foster care centre visits – Leaders' tour to Cuba	– Papers: How I got to be current affairs analyst for high school newspaper.	
ACHIEVEMENTS – Leadership award – Made associate – Helped little Barry cope with deafness		

Figure 7.1   Example of a profile development table

1. Personal features and attributes

Points: In the first column, list the words you use when you describe yourself. What are your defining personality traits? What are your key characteristics and qualities? Are you a thinker or a doer? Collaborative or self-reliant? Intense? Focused? Competitive? Analytical? Creative? What words would your friends use to characterize you?

Stories: In column two, think of stories related to your characteristics. What events in your life corroborate the characteristics you have written in column one?

Analysis: In the third column, draw out the juice from your list of characteristics and associated stories. What do they say about you?

If you are community-minded and you have a story about volunteering at an elderly persons home once a month, what would this tell someone about you? If you are a "techie" and your illuminating story is how you once wrote your own applet to get your cell phone to interact with your garage door, what does that say about you?

2. Activities

Points: Actions speak louder than words. Again in column one, make a list of your most important regular activities—large and small. What do you do for fun? What do you do at the weekends? What gets you up early and/or makes you stay up late? What do you hate to do? What activities could you not give up? Perhaps you play in a hip-hop band, or you go off on archaeological digs in your vacation time. Also, consider any activities that place you in a community—which community? Maybe you lead activities at a youth chess camp in Bologna every summer, or do pro-bono legal consulting, for example. How are you active for a cause other than yourself?

Stories: In column two, again think of stories related to your activities. How at that chess camp, for example, you held a little boy's hand as he threw a tantrum and you slowly taught him the importance of losing with dignity.

Analysis: In the final column, once again draw out the juice from your lists of activities and associated stories. Why are you motivated to take part in these activities? Why do you do what you do and not something else with your free time? How do your activities show who you are, or how might they develop your (or someone else's) understanding of who you are?

3. Accomplishments and achievements

Points: Consider your achievements in the academic, communal, and personal realms. (Professional activities will be considered in professional profiling, see Chapter 8.) What are your major accomplishments? Have you overcome unusual obstacles? Where have you excelled? What have you done that makes you really proud? Does any achievement distinguish you from everyone else? When have you struggled hard for something and succeeded? Remember that sometimes a minor personal achievement says far more about you than a major award. Do you have a personal success that hardly anyone knows about? Do you have a small daily triumph?

Stories: Stories should come easily here—behind each success worth having will be a tale of struggle and overcoming worth telling.

Analysis: Why do you consider your achievements to be achievements? What about your accomplishments fits with your motivations and aspirations? How have your achievements so far brought you closer to being the person you aspire to be? Why?

4. Skills and strengths

Points: Behind every achievement lies one or more strengths. Your achievements listed in (3) above will be based on strengths of ability or character. What are these? What is behind your accomplishments that made them possible? List them in column one. Think what other people who know you well might consider your strengths to be.

Stories: The stories that tell of your strengths may be very similar to the stories of your accomplishments—but there may be others. Note down any event that would demonstrate to an outsider what your special abilities are.

Analysis: Consider the implications of your strengths. How do they shape your profile and your sense of self? How have they affected your choices in the past and how will they shape them in the future? How do they affect your personal aspirations?

5. Difficulties, failures, and weaknesses

Points: When and how have you messed up in your non-working life? Have you ever worked and struggled for something and still not got it? What has been the time of greatest adversity? What is your most painful memory of failing yourself, or someone you love or respect, or a group? List the failures and the weaknesses that underlie your failures. Nobody finds it easy to think about their weaknesses and failures. For a more extended discussion of managing failures, see Chapter 3, and the discussion of the weakness-failure essay in Chapter 11. The short story is, if you can't see or can't put up your hand to admit your failures and weaknesses, you are not ready to hold a responsible position in a company, and therefore you are not ready for admission to an MBA. Adcoms will be far less interested in your specific failures than whether you have the maturity to recognize and address them.

Stories: What are the stories of your failures? Face them and write them down.

Analysis: What part have you played in your failures (the part that was not bad luck or a quirk of circumstances)? Are there patterns of weaknesses that consistently get you into trouble? What have you done to work on this? How might you do things differently next time? How have you responded to adversity? What positive learning has come out of your experience? How have your actions or perspectives changed as a result?

6. Leadership

Points: Consider times when you have been in a leadership position in any circumstances other than work. (Professional leadership is dealt with in Chapter 8.) Note the key leadership opportunities you have had. Think of occasions when you have been responsible for coordinating, influencing, or motivating a group, or when you have been directly responsible for the outcome of a group effort. Remember that leadership *always* involves other people, and is *always* in the public domain.

Stories: What are the anecdotes you can tell about your leadership experiences? What went right? What went wrong? How did it turn out?

Analysis: What have you learned about leadership? What have your leadership experiences taught you about your approach to leadership or your own leadership style? How do you influence, how do you motivate, how do you solve problems? What does this say about the kind of person you are?

7. Major influences: People

Points: List the people who have influenced you in your life. Who have you looked up to in the past and who do you look up to now? Who are your mentors, idols, and role models?

Stories: What are the stories behind your relationships with your role models? What impressive interactions have you had that makes you think of them in this way? Can you bring the "quality time" spent with a mentor to life through an anecdote?

Analysis: Why are these people your idols and mentors—what is it about them that you admire? What are the qualities in them that you aspire to? How have they influenced your life or your decisions?

8. Major influences: Culture, art, books, movies

Points: What are your favorite books, movies, works of art, music, or other profound media influences that have shaped your perspective in a meaningful way? Which influences were once powerful but no longer are?

Stories: Do you have stories that tell of your relationship with these shaping forces? Perhaps you stayed up all night when you were 10, reading *Tom Sawyer*; or when you were a student in Illinois you saw an aerobatics display that changed your life. Take us there.

Analysis: Why were, or are, your significant influences so compelling to you?

What did you or do you get from them? What does this say about your personality and preferences? How have you moved on from certain influences to others? What does this say about your development? Be frank with yourself about your influences. If you'd like your main influence to be Winston Churchill's speeches, but it is in fact *The Simpsons*, don't kid yourself. (Learn that you are probably a bit cynical, ironic, and irreverent—that can also play well in an essay.)

9. Life-changing events and experiences

Points: List the major events that have changed your life—things that influenced you so profoundly that you were not the same afterwards, or you couldn't think about yourself in the same way again. These could be such momentous experiences as becoming a parent, emigrating, losing a family member, or nearly drowning. Or they could be more experiential, such as living abroad, getting your movie script optioned by Paramount, or being the first member of your family to go to college—anything that fundamentally changed your situation or your outlook. Identify the major crossroads you have come to in your life, decisions you have wrestled with, and the choices you made.

Stories: These events, experiences, and decisions are all going to be stories in themselves—list them as story possibilities.

Analysis: How have major events in your life changed you? How are you different now? How are you the same? When you had hard choices to make, why did you choose the path you did? Would you do the same again, and why or why not? How have you grown? How are you different to who you used to be?

How far back?

Considering life-changing experiences brings up a topic that crosses all profiling content, that is, how far back you should reach in your life when preparing to make your case in the MBA essay questions? Generally, essays are weakened by a focus on childhood and adolescence, which is often seen as backward-looking and possibly avoiding adult issues or having nothing new to point to. Therefore the basic rule is to keep to stories from the last five years. However, momentous life-changing events, which may well be in the distant past, may remain current and poignant, and deeply relevant to your adult choices and perceptions, and to your post-MBA future, and are therefore valid for use in your essays.

10. Diversity and contribution

Points: List the set of skills, experiences, and qualities that distinguish you from everyone else. What about you and the mix of forces and circumstances in your background is unique? Which unusual qualities and experiences can you contribute to the school, your class, and your group? If you were to get a letter from the Adcom saying they had admitted you solely because you bring one super-special quality, skill, or experience to the class, what would that one thing be?

Stories: What are the stories and events associated with your unique individual features or attributes? How did you come to develop a unique skill? How have your distinguishing elements played out in a real-life situation?

Analysis: How does this difference affect you? How does it enrich the lives of those around you? How has it added to or affected your personal interactions and relationships? How has it shaped your perceptions? How does it affect your life goals?

11. Values and philosophy

Points: What are your most important principles and values? If you could change the world, what would you do first? Have you experienced moments of clarity and insight into yourself and your role in the world? What were they? Have the lessons you have learned in your life come together in a set of personal principles? What would you want written on your tombstone? What do you concretely do that speaks of your values? Which causes do you support financially or as a volunteer?

Stories: What are the stories that demonstrate your values in action? Which events tell of how you developed your values or personal philosophy? Perhaps your aunt took you to an Indian reservation when you were a teenager. Or, maybe you have spent the last year unemployed. What significant things have happened to you that have reaffirmed or challenged your values—and how did you respond?

Analysis: What do your values and the changes in your values over time say about you? How do your principles or your outlook on life affect the way you manage yourself in your day-to-day life? How do they affect how you interact with other people? How does that change what you do with your time and who you do it with?

12. Personal goals

Points: What are your non-professional aspirations? (Professional goals are dealt with in Chapter 8.) If you could pursue any dream right now, regardless of skill, money, or other restrictions, what would it be? What do you want to be remembered for? When you look back on your life in 50 years, what would it take for you to consider it a success? Connect your goals to the MBA: Why do you want to spend two years getting an MBA? What role does the qualification play in the fulfillment of these goals? Apart from financial and career success, how will your MBA meet your emotional, social, and family needs?

If you are really stuck determining your goals, try the following exercise. On a sheet of paper or a blank screen, write the heading "20 July 2061" and write "Note to my biographer." Underneath review your life, starting with what happened right after business school, what that led to and what came after. Write it as you would most dearly like to see it unfold. What you get will be your personal (and professional) aspirations.

Stories: What events have happened to you that developed your aspirations and made you see your goals more clearly?

Analysis: What do your goals tell you about yourself? Why are these your goals rather than others? What, if anything, has happened along the way to change your aspirations or make some more important than others? What does that say about where you want to focus your life's energy and purpose?

8   Professional profile analysis

This chapter allows you to explore and understand your professional profile, asking similar questions to those you have just considered in developing your personal profile. It is important to make a distinction between personal and professional. While they do overlap (you take your personal self to work, and no doubt you bring your work home), considering the professional on its own terms allows you to create the same richness of motivational material in this sphere as you did in the personal where self-interrogation may seem more natural. There's no-hard-and-fast rule, but a standard MBA essay set and standard MBA interview should be about two-thirds oriented to professional matters.

Once again, take a sheet of paper and draw two vertical lines down the page, dividing the paper into three columns. Across the top, label column one "Features and attributes," column two "Stories" and column three "Analysis." Starting on the left, make keyword lists, responding to the following questions or further questions you think of, on the following topics:

1. Characteristics and qualities

Points: List your professional characteristics and qualities. Which words would you use to describe yourself at work, or in work-like situations? What are you like in the office? Are you good in groups? Are you a patient planner or "do-and-see" type? Do you promote change or stability? Do you chafe under supervision? Do you prefer to be left alone to do what you need to do, or do you enjoy constant interaction? What words would your work colleagues use to characterize you?

Stories: In the second column, think of anecdotes that demonstrate the professional qualities you claim. What events in the workplace have led you to develop your professional persona? What occurrences have demonstrated your valuable attributes?

Analysis: Are your various attributes concentrated in certain areas, for example, organizational skills, creative skills, or strategy skills? What are the implications of this? Why do you choose to adopt these particular professional characteristics and qualities in work situations? What does that say about the way you like to work, or the kinds of work situations you promote, or the kinds of people you like to work with?

2. Activities

Points: Think of your work day—either at your current job or previous full-time or part-time jobs that you have enjoyed. List your most important daily activities. How do you spend your time when you have a choice? Are you in meetings? Are you in front of customers? Do you do site visits or are you mostly behind a desk? Which activities do you hate to do? Which could you not give up? For what, other than money, would you happily get to the office early and stay late?

Stories: What "war stories" do you have related to your work life? Was there a time when you stared down the boss? What about the all-nighters you have pulled, or the laughs you have shared? What are the stories worth telling?

Analysis: In the third column, consider the implications of your activities at work (bearing in mind that you very often don't get to do what you want to at work, particularly when you are junior or new in a company). Nevertheless, it is likely that some part of what you have done has been your choice. Perhaps you spent a lot of time doing financial spreadsheets and that precision of analysis was gratifying to you. Perhaps you got to travel a lot and your work paid for you to learn Portuguese, and that was meaningful. Why did "what worked for you" work for you? What does this say about you and the kind of professional activities you will want to be involved with in the future?

3. Accomplishments

Points: Consider your professional achievements so far. What are your major accomplishments? Where have you overcome unusual obstacles? Where have you excelled? What have you done that makes you really proud? Remember that sometimes a small achievement says far more about you than a major award. Do you have a professional success that has not been recognized but is still important to you?

Stories: Tell the story that you love to tell: your finest hour in the workplace, how you read the situation right, made the right moves, and aced it—and got a bonus or a promotion.

Analysis: Why do you value these specific achievements? What does this say about your professional motivations and your future aspirations? How and why have your achievements so far brought you closer to the career you want, and to being the career professional you want to be?

4. Skills and strengths

Points: Your professional achievements will point to a set of skills and strengths that underlie them, without which you achievements would never have happened. List these strengths. Also write down what other people who know you well in the office would say your strengths are.

Stories: Think of workplace stories that prove you have the abilities you claim. If you are the meticulous attention-to-detail type, which events in your work history show this? If you are a charismatic motivator, what story proves it? The stories that tell of your professional strengths may be very similar to the stories of your accomplishments, but don't let that stop you looking for others.

Analysis: Consider the implications of your workplace strengths. How do they shape your professional profile and your sense of yourself at work? How have they affected your choices in the past and how will they shape them in the future? How do they affect your career aspirations? How do your strengths come together in such a way to be useful to an MBA class and to an employer?

5. Difficulties, mistakes, and failures

Points: Think of times when you had professional difficulties or failed in a work context. When and how have you messed up? Have you ever been expected to master some task or new skill and failed at it? Have you worked towards a job, or a promotion, and missed out? Have you failed others who were counting on you, or whose work success was riding on yours?

Stories: What are the stories of your work failures? Face them and be ready to tell them without ducking the blame or pointing fingers.

Analysis: What part have you played in your failures? What are the weaknesses that your failures expose? What have you done to correct this? How have you responded to adversity? What does this say about your attitude to failure? On the positive side, what good learning has come out of your experience? How might you do things differently next time? How has your perspective on work or life changed as a result? You, like everyone else, will learn more from failure than from success. Through your mistakes, and your scramble to correct them at the time—and your longer-term willingness to address the cause of the error—what have you learned about yourself or about the world of work?

6. Weaknesses and inexperience

Points: Failures that are not attributable to bad luck or others' mistakes will point to weaknesses or inexperience in your profile. Neither weaknesses nor inexperience are bad: the MBA is there to fix them—if you were perfect, you wouldn't be applying, and you certainly wouldn't be accepted. So, what are the factors that caused your project to go down? What is the weakness that regularly gets you into trouble?

Stories: Your stories of professional weaknesses will go hand-in-glove with stories of failure. There may also be stories of where you were able to forestall failure because you were alive to your weaknesses and compensated early enough.

Analysis: Do your weaknesses give insight into you? Perhaps they point to preferences, fears, or ingrained compensating mechanisms? Does this speak of territory you have learned to avoid, or where you have learned to get help, or to cope in some other way? How have weaknesses affected what you chose to do in the past, and how might they shape what you choose to do and what you will be sure to avoid doing in your future career? How might an MBA help you overcome weaknesses?

7. Leadership

Points: What leadership opportunities have you had in your professional life so far? Remember, often leadership is disguised and comes without a title or perks. Think of the occasions when you have directed the outcome of a project or part of a project, or have been responsible for coordinating or motivating others.

Stories: What are the anecdotes you can tell about your leadership experiences? What were the times that worked the best, or the worst, or taught you the most?

Analysis: What have you learned about leadership in the workplace? Bearing in mind that leadership is something you will spend your whole life learning, what have you yet to learn (that an MBA could teach you, perhaps)? What have your early investigations in leadership taught you about the kind of leader you are becoming? Are there patterns to the ways you motivate and influence others, and how do these reflect your personality? Is this as you would wish it, or would you want to redirect yourself using different leadership skills?

8. Influences

Points: List the people you have met in professional situations who have influenced your career and your career choices. Who do you look up to? Who do you aspire to be like? Do you admire your boss? If so, why? If not, why not? Are there any other strong influences in your professional life—books or other resources?

Stories: What are the stories behind your relationships with your professional mentors and role models? What events come to mind when you think of how they have affected you? What experiences have you shared that make you think of them positively?

Analysis: Why are these people your idols and mentors—what is it about them that you respect? What are the qualities you aspire to? How has their influence led you to becoming what you are today? How will it continue to influence your life and choices? How does your opinion of your mentor suggest the kind of mentor you aspire to be one day?

9. Change and growth experiences

Points: List the key events that have shaped your professional life to date. What are the major crossroads you have come to in your career since college? What decisions in particular have you had to wrestle with, and what was the decision you took? Also, consider how you have changed since day one at your first real job. What do you know now that you didn't know then? What other key events or forks-in-the-road have caused you to grow professionally?

Stories: Your career and work choices are all little stories in themselves. What was the dilemma, what were the circumstances, what did your loved ones want you to do? Did you do it or not? Then what happened?

Analysis: How have the significant experiences and decisions in your career shaped and changed you into who you are today? Where you have had hard choices to make, what made you choose the route you chose and would you do the same thing again? How has the experience changed and "grown" you professionally? How do you feel about the professional field you are in? What has reinforced your certainty that this field is ideally suited for you and prompted you to pursue it further via an MBA? Or, what has led you to want to change career emphasis via an MBA?

10. Difference and diversity in the workplace

Points: What is it about you and the mix of forces and circumstances in your work background that is unique? What is it about your set of professional skills or experiences that distinguishes you? Which valuable proficiency or experiences can you contribute to business school? If you were to get a letter from Adcom saying they had admitted you because you bring one, single, hard-to-find special professional skill or experience to the class, what might that be?

Stories: What are the stories and events associated with your special professional attributes? How did you come to develop your unique mix of skills? Is there a case where you have added a unique differentiating attribute to enhance a group's success on a project?

Analysis: How does your difference or special proficiency influence who you are at work and who you might become? How might it enrich those working around you?

11. Values and philosophy

Points: Have the work lessons you have learned so far come together in a set of principles that influence who you "are" at work or the way you interact? What are these? Have you developed insight into yourself in relation to the world of work—how you want to work, what you want to do, and who you want to work with? Do you have a professional philosophy or workplace code of honor and is it different from your personal philosophy? What do you currently do in the workplace that concretely speaks of your values?

Stories: What anecdotes can you tell about events that have shaped and developed your value set? Has anything happened to you along the way that has tested or reaffirmed those values, and how did you respond?

Analysis: How does your professional code and outlook affect the way you manage yourself and other people? How do you get your professional values into your everyday reality? How do they affect what you do and how you do it? What does that say about the kind of career choices you are likely to make?

12. Goals

Points: What important things do you want to do in your career? What are your dreams in the long term and what short-term goals will take you there? When you look back on your life in 50 years time, what would it take for you to consider your professional life a success? What will it look like, if it all works out?

Stories: What events have happened, or what anecdotes can you share, which show when and how you began to see your goals more clearly and so came to develop the career aspirations you now hold?

Analysis: Why do your goals fit who you are? What does this say about your priorities? What does that tell you about what you need from a career? How and why does the MBA fit into these professional aspirations? Going beyond the general benefit of the MBA, and beyond monetary rewards, how will your degree promote and accelerate your career and lead you to higher, more fulfilling professional achievement?

If you don't know your own mind exactly at this point, congratulations, you're human. Note the discussion in the goals essay section in Chapter 10 on the pros and cons of specificity, and how you are expected to be receptive to the career and life growth the program will provide you. As mentioned there, better applications are those that present career goals that show evidence of purposeful thinking. They expect you to change your mind as you grow through your MBA, so you don't need to have a watertight career blueprint. You just need to demonstrate well-thought through plans that evidence your motivation and a sense of purpose.

Extracting the value

If you've done this brainstorming honestly and thoroughly, you should have a lot of notes across three columns, over various pages. Lots of stuff should have come to the surface for you to chew over. The next steps are:

- to select what you need to build a clear profile, with a definitive message and clear themes based on a solid application platform;
- to map your message onto the questions;
- to plan, write, and edit your essays and prepare to take the same message forward into the interview process.

The first of these steps will be dealt with in Chapter 9. The following two are the topics of Parts Three and Four.

9 Positioning, messaging, and mapping

We are now at the point where you have surfaced key parts of you unique story, and the stories and experience that go with them. The next step is to sift and select from your brainstorming, choosing and arranging the material you want. You are moving from "profile exploration" to "profile definition," moving towards defining a clear position for yourself and a clear valuable message to convey. After that, the next step is to figure out how you will convey it across the essays and in your interview, which is the "mapping" phase.

Avoid "achievement soup"

The first thing to understand in moving to the profile-definition stage of your application is that you cannot and should not try to say everything important about yourself, not even all the positive things. You will just overwhelm and confuse your reader, and demonstrate your lack of judgment about what is central and what is peripheral. You don't need your reader to know everything about you; you just need her to know the key things of value about you. Yes, you have loads of leadership examples, extra-curricular activities, accomplishments, etc., but you don't want to dilute or cloud these main points with a jostling mass of competing information. Simplicity and focus are your best weapons. You want to isolate what are the most important things about you that Adcom simply *must* know, and build a compelling, detailed, persuasive admissions argument around this.

If you are able to extract your key points and focus on them, you will avoid one of the standard mistakes in business school applications. Applicants routinely jam their essays with every positive point they have, for fear that whichever one they omit will be some secret key that turns the lock in the gates of admission. There is no such key. Don't go down a track that sounds like:

> After college in Madison Wisconsin I worked for CNN in Atlanta, and then for the Georgia State Legislature, while taking evening classes in economics at City College, and followed this with a year in Taiwan, before coming back to work on my school applications, which I postponed for a year because my father had bypass surgery . . .

Not only does a listing of activities and accomplishments dampen the reader's interest, but all you are really saying is that you have no idea what is important in your profile, or you can't be bothered to extract it, focus it, and package it.

Such "essay stuffing" hurts you because it does not allow you to develop a clear portrait of yourself, or a memorable message, or to make a cogent argument for your admission, or to demonstrate any real self-understanding. It does not allow you to differentiate yourself from the next applicant—whose record will also be full of good points. So the real skill is prioritizing, and then having the stomach to let go of the rest of the also-good stuff (or relegate it to a brief mention somewhere in your resume, data sheet, or short questions).

Serve the reader

It's helpful to think of creating the kind of experience for your reader that you would if you were having her to dinner in your home. You would consider all the possible food you could buy, and all the things you could cook, and *exclude* most of it. You would settle on one starter, one soup, one main course, and one dessert. Your menu might have a few common elements or spices running through it (an Indonesian theme, for example). You would then shop, chop, cook, and present the meal in three or four elegant courses. You wouldn't take everything out of the refrigerator, empty the larder and take down from the shelves all your condiments, and put everything onto the dinner table and ask *her* to figure out what goes with what and how it all comes together.

It takes guts to leave out parts of your story. But to nourish your reader properly you have to pick a meal plan and stick with it. You have to be ruthless in leaving out some interesting tidbits because it is *your* job—not the reader's job—to select, prepare, and present a coherent informational "meal." You must make the call as to the one best meal you can create with your available ingredients, and you must prepare it to be attractive to consume and easy to digest. Each essay in your set then becomes like a course in a fine dinner, expanding one, or at most two, of the ideas that contributes to and is thematically integrated into the whole.

Applying marketing principles

If you recognize the construction of a clear, themed, goal-oriented message targeted to the needs and interests of a particular audience as classic marketing—you are right. You are positioning yourself as attractively as possible in the eyes of your consumer, fitting with their needs while differentiating yourself from your competition; and finding the clearest and most compelling way to express this differentiated value.

Note that *excluding* extraneous data is also a basic marketing technique. When General Motors launches a car, they could tell you a hundred things about it, but they don't. They may create a marketing message for "Car A" using the interweaving themes of safety, comfort, and style. "Car B" might be positioned as a youthful, active, performance car. "Car C" may be framed with the themes of enviro-friendliness, hybrid-based low fuel consumption, and advanced engineering. In each case, marketing professionals are choosing and expressing themes to organize the transfer of a clear, swift, compelling message that will resonate with a chosen target segment. Everything else is excluded.

In the case of MBA admissions, your target segment is known and fixed. With small exceptions, admissions officers need and want to see the same things in candidates (as defined in the attributes section in Chapter 2). Knowing who they are and what they are looking for, your job is to find the parts of your profile that correlate with these requirements and preferences. You then need to construct a themed message that expresses your differentiated and superior value in these desirable areas—just like marketing anywhere. You will repeat your message in various different and subtle ways throughout your essays and interviews, and indeed throughout the whole application "campaign."

The alternative communications metaphor, as mentioned earlier, is thinking of yourself as the politician campaigning for election: you simplify your candidacy by creating themes (causes) that interweave to become an overall message (a election platform). You research the needs of your "electorate," devising a position closer to those needs than your competing campaigners do, and therein become electable because of differentiated and superior value. You repeat your message on every podium, at every speaking engagement, judiciously adapting it to different circumstances. When answering questions, you credibly tackle the question—but you always look for ways to insert your campaign platform message.

Profile definition

Selecting and grouping

To focus your message wisely, you first have to sort and group your profiling output. Look over your profiling notes, over all the things you've done and all the things you are, and all the ways you do things; at your memories, your stories, your preferences, your aspirations. Look for patterns and themes—words, ideas, or situations that show up repeatedly. Look for organizing categories or themes that summarize various pieces of who you are or what you've done, or where your interests and skills lie. Note down anything that links different pieces of you together, or which suggests itself as a grouping mechanism in defining who you are.

For example, you may have achieved your Padi "Dive Master" certification, led a student outreach trip in Kosovo, and helped immigrants learn how to apply for social services, which could all be grouped under a "practical leadership" theme. Or you may have won a math Olympiad, worked in tax consulting for PWC, and developed your own method for beating the House in Vegas, which could all be grouped under a "superior quant" label. As you group your profiling results in this way, your notes may point to, for example, a "people person," "foreign experience," "biomedical competencies," "creative problem solver," "language buff," and so on.

Each category you come up with organizes the events and stories in your life into bigger, more easily understandable and communicable units. They help you and therefore your reader make overarching sense of your story and synthesize your apparently diverse personal characteristics and experiences into a coherent whole. There are no right or wrong categories. Almost any non-trivial theme can work, as long as you can connect it to your key value proposition (your application platform) and your proposed future.

Every individual point you make now has—via the theme it links to—a way to become part of the larger pattern and argument you are presenting. When your themes are in place, any time you tell a story or invoke a memory, or an aspiration, it will no longer just be a loose data piece—you will be able to lead the reader to see how it fits consistently within the group of points going in the same direction. This allows you to create a message that is richly detailed, yet easily followed.

The groups you settle on are, in rough form, the key value points or themes of your application and the building blocks of your message to Adcom. Suitably vetted, they will become the key points about you that you want the admissions officer to get, if he gets nothing else. You will structure your essay set around them, repeating them judiciously in different ways to drive home the point to your busy reader.

Developing themes

Sometimes, your theme may be the obvious link between different activities you are involved in; at other times, it may take a bit of mental "massaging" to get from the activities and interests to the underlying theme. For example, it is likely that one theme will derive from your professional specialty, but you may have to define it more broadly than it first appears. So, if your background is in software development, for example, you might take it beyond merely IT and link it with other things you do to create a theme around being "a designer of complex solutions." Similarly, if you are a NASA engineer, your theme could simply be "aeronautics expert," but it could also be linked with other activities and elaborated to "engineer of new-frontier-technologies." If you are a lawyer, you could create a theme around legal skills, but depending what else you've done, a more telling theme might be something like "dispute and negotiations expert."

To demonstrate how themes may be used, consider the following example. Say you are a Mexican with an undergraduate degree in politics and economics and your main work experience has been with the Mexican embassy in Ottawa. Assume also that you have a passion for software, and a long track record of working with children, particularly those from underprivileged backgrounds. The themes you arrive at might be: (1) "political animal with diplomatic savvy"; (2) "software and Web expert"; and (3) "child mentor."

In your essays you would make points and tell stories that reinforce these themes as often as practicable. If asked for your best achievement—although you have many—you might choose the time you helped a child in an orphanage to be interested in the world by leaving a Web-interactive pocket computer game at his bedside. That is, you would be promoting your child mentor theme *and* your software expert theme. Or, if you are answering a question about your teamwork abilities, you could talk about the time you used your diplomatic skills to save an embassy task force from breaking down, promoting your diplomatic theme along the way.

Positioning: Which themes to choose

The themes you arrive at will categorize you and therefore define your application and position it with regard to the competition. There are broadly two types of themes: those of core value and those of differentiation.

Themes of core value

These themes are, simply enough, themes around candidate attributes that are valuable in admissions. A full list and various cross-cutting principles are provided in Chapter 2, and this can be used as a way to jog your thinking, but should not be considered a blueprint. First, you can't have all of these themes, and second, you may have others that are not on this list. Also note that if a value theme is obvious via your file data (e.g. themes such as academic ability or international work experience), you can use the essays or interview to develop less obvious themes about yourself.

Every applicant is different. But the core of applications value is quite consistent. No matter where you apply and what you seek to do, the four themes—leadership, teamwork, community values, and innovation—are pretty much essential to have going for you. You may not be able to make a big play in all four, but consider how you can at least check the box in each of these categories, using evidence from your present and past activities.

Try to avoid themes around the MBA core courses—you don't want to be "marketing expert" or "financial genius." Not only is it uncreative, but too much of this could also suggest you may be sufficiently skilled to achieve your goals without the MBA, and your place could go to someone with apparently more to gain from being in the classroom. As a rule, don't apply based on your prior knowledge of business fundamentals. There is great admission benefit in business experience, but no great benefit in knowing business fundamentals, which is what the MBA program is there for.

Themes of differentiation

As mentioned in Part One, people with the same personal or professional backgrounds, or the same aspirations, compete with each other in a mini-race for admissions. (For the purposes of class balance, a school will only let in so many McKinsey consultants, or so many private equity aspirants, or so many Indian applicants, etc.) Because your positioning of yourself very significantly determines the school's positioning of you for admissions purposes (depending on how well you communicate, they may not be identical), you should expect to be competing directly against the people who position themselves in more or less the same way as you do.

Therefore you should choose less common themes as far as possible. Beyond your themes of core value, look for themes that speak about you and you alone, that really do encapsulate your singular identity, achievements, and passions. You cannot separate yourself from the crowd if your profile never escapes the default categories. There may be obvious themes in your background such as "quant" or "international," and you should use them if they are strong. But even if you are a very mainstream applicant, with mainstream employment goals, you can still find different and memorable defining themes.

For example, you may not be able to do anything about being an Indian computer science major working at Cisco, but with judicious grouping and a creative approach you can marginally differentiate your positioning. By playing up your Pakistani relatives and your volunteer experience in Kashmir, for example, you could use a "bi-nationalist" or "peacemaker" theme. By playing up your intellectual curiosity and experimentation you may be able to position yourself as a "creative intellect" rather than just "smart." In these ways you move between and across categories, and so position yourself outside of oversubscribed applicant sub-categories. There is a balance to hit here and one can definitely "over-reach" for uniqueness. You do want to offer the school a value proposition that nobody else does, but you don't want to end up in the "weird" box.

Be aware also that things that you think make you unique will be statistically quite common in an applicant pool of 8,000 or more. You were in a bad car accident. So were lots of people. You lost a parent. So did lots of people. And so on. In fact, the only thing that is reliably unique is your take on things: what you thought, what you did, what you think now and would do now, that includes the details of your situations and the anecdotes only you can tell. If you do this, not only does it give you a uniqueness that nobody can duplicate, but it one that is natural. If you try too hard to be unusual, you may end up sounding weird (and also making the mistake of writing what you think Adcom wants to hear).

Extracting and refining your themes into a profile position is a crucial task. Don't skimp on it. Positioning focuses the major thrust of your message, isolating the value points you most want to highlight. Once you arrive at the right, powerful, persuasive value-based themes that put you both inside and to some extent outside the most common categories, your application message will more or less write itself. This means your task in your essays and interview will be greatly simplified.

In general, somewhere between three and five themes is fine (in addition to the necessary "leadership," "team player," and "innovator"). Fewer will suffice if they are especially multifaceted, or if the school only requires very short essays. With more you lose the benefit of clarity that themes give to your communications with Adcom. A good spread will make sure that you have a balance between variety and focus throughout your application. Too few and you will be banging on about the same things all the time.

Say hello to "the elephant in the room"

If you have a major issue in your application that needs addressing, the chances are it will need to be factored into your positioning. If you took six years to graduate college because you decided to take time off to protest destruction of the Amazon Basin, at minimum you need to talk about it obviously and clearly. And you may be able to turn it into an (environmentalist or social activist) theme. Adcom misses nothing in your background, certainly nothing major, so if there is an issue there, it needs airtime in your application. There is nothing more self-condemnatory (and junior) than an applicant who rambles on about this and that while avoiding the burning question.

The application message

When you add the key positioning themes of your application, and add the interesting things you want to do with your future, and add why you need an MBA to do it, and why you and your educational needs fit with a particular school, you'll get your application message. Your message is that sentence or three that sums up who you are, why you are valuable and unique, what you want to do, and why you need to go to the particular business school to do it. It is your application "take-away": the absolute core of what you want the admissions officer to know; what you want to be impressed on her brain after she has closed your file; what you want her to remember about you a month later when all the minor details of your story are long forgotten; and what will come to mind when she sees you in the school's hallway on your way to class a year later.

In the Mexican example above, your message might be: "Business school will build on my diplomatic background, giving me the training and contacts to build a large-scale Web-based education initiative involving children from the US, Mexico, and Canada. It will give me the credibility and skills to fundraise, develop, and lead this dream project." The following section offers techniques to sharpen your message development and delivery.

Message techniques

The elevator speech
One way to focus and simplify your message is via the "elevator speech" exercise. Imagine you get into an elevator at the ground floor with the head of admissions from your dream school. You recognize her from the glossy brochure in the lobby. She's already pressed the button for the 18th floor. You now have about 45 seconds to introduce yourself and to say the most important things about you, including why you are applying, and to leave a memorable, lasting impression, so that as she leaves she says: "That's very interesting—what's your name again? I'll certainly look out for your application."

These few seconds are your elevator speech. It will be about four or five sentences long. It will serve you to have written it out and learned it by heart so that every time you need to explain briefly and clearly who you are and why you are applying, and what's uniquely interesting and valuable about you, you will be able to do it faultlessly. Write it down, print it out, have it pinned to the noticeboard above your desk. Say it to yourself before you begin work on your essays or before you head to an interview.

Labeling
When people are dealing with message statements all the time, even a short message can be unwieldy. It will commonly be contracted to no more than a label. The

label may not even be particularly appropriate or accurate, but will nevertheless be the quick handle that everyone refers to. For example, if members of Adcom were referring among themselves to the Mexican applicant described above, they might refer loosely to "the Mexican diplomat" or "the Mexican child project guy." These labels are not carefully thought out. They just express, in a busy admissions office, what appears at a casual glance to be the most distinctive profile markers that define a candidate. The next file that comes up could be "the ABN-Amro fixed-equity guy", "the Bridge-player," or "Hans, the Swedish dog-breeder."

Your label is important because it makes a difference if you become labeled with something interesting and valuable-sounding that can have a positive influence on undecided members of the committee, or something generic or flippant-sounding that could harm your chances. You can't pick your label, but you can influence what it is, and make it more likely that it works in your favor. That is, you can work to make sure that your label is in fact an accurate contraction of your differentiated, valuable position. The more you define it yourself, the safer you are.

You positively affect your labeling by being crystal clear above what your themes are, and what your message is, and how it all fits together—so that it is less likely that Adcom will light on a mistaken or contingent label. The accuracy and differentiating quality of the label you acquire in the admissions office are a reflection of how successful you have been in communicating your message. Another, bolder technique is to develop a label for yourself—and slip it into one or more of your essays. You could refer to yourself as "the Texan Quant" or "the Melody Maker," and so on. You want something that adds value and is highly sticky—in other words, memorable to the point of being unforgettable.

Staying on message

Among both sales staff and politicians on the campaign trail, you will often hear handlers repeat the communications mantra: "Stay on message!" This means, don't stray from the topic you want the target audience to know about, and how you have decided to tell them about it. Avoid blurring your message with extraneous information. Don't develop other, potentially confusing points that might be challengeable or at odds with your basic position or the position of your product.

In the same way, in the essays and in your file as a whole, your task is to define your message and then stick to it. You can delve widely into your past and your future, your successes, interests, values, and beliefs, but all the things you say have finally to be woven tightly into one clear message, and that message is the only thing you should really concern yourself with. If it is not "on message," don't say it.

Not selling

Nobody likes being "sold." People are rightly prone to become quickly irritated by pitches and high-pressure sales tactics, and soon learn to get through life by discounting if not ignoring them. If you give Adcom a sales pitch, it will be you who will be pitched (into the bin). Of course you are selling yourself, but you won't get anywhere by talking to Adcom like a cheesy infomercial. Treat them like a discretionary *audience* whose attention you are lucky enough to have for a few short minutes. Engage, enlighten, and entertain them, and leave them clearly under-standing your value proposition. If you are genuinely valuable, and obviously interesting and likeable, that's all the selling you need to do. They will be bending over backwards to see you as impressive and full of potential.

Mapping your message to the essay questions

You are finished with the profile part of your preparation when you have done your personal and professional brainstorming, have grouped your results, can clearly enunciate the main themes or value points of your profile, and can express them together with the essential elements of your future goals and "why an MBA" in a short application platform message.

Note that throughout this profiling phase of your application, you have *not* looked at the essay questions. In fact, you have pointedly created your message completely independently of the questions. Now is the moment to examine the question set in your first application. As you do it, realize that your task is *not* primarily to answer the questions, it is to communicate your message via the questions. In fact, with your message ready and honed, you are—with a small amount of adaptation—prepared for any questions you may face. You task is not to decide "what do I say?" It is to decide "which parts of my message do I place here?" You map your message onto the questions.

In this way you will be guided in what you write by the message you want to communicate, not by the questions you are asked. You must, of course, make sure that the questions do get specifically and closely answered too—that's the game. Adcom will be severe with you if you avoid the question or write off the point. They will either assume you can't think or can't write, or you have boiler-plated your answer from your applications to other schools—or worse, from someone else's application.

Think of each question as an opportunity to showcase part of your profile. So, for each application you make, you will now face one simple task: Finding the best fit between a piece of your pre-existing message to Adcom and the questions in front of you—without compromising either your message or the questions. Each new school, with its slightly different essay set, will present a new strategic jigsaw puzzle as you decide where to place each piece of your profile, and how to get all the pieces shoehorned in and knitted together. You will have to do this "mapping" of message to question set quite differently for each set, but always with the same goal—to communicate your pre-existing message via the questions.

Towards question archetypes

The key to high-quality mapping is knowing what each question seeks—what Adcom expects from your response in each case and what bonus information can legitimately be added. But schools all ask different questions. Or do they? They appear different, but if you look closely, almost every essay question is a variation of the classic questions that business schools typically ask. There are, in fact, only about ten classic question "archetypes," and practically all questions are an adaptation of one of these archetypes, or part of an archetype, or a combination of two or more archetypes.

If you recognize and understand the archetype, you will see the basic MBA essay question which lies behind the obscure one you are posed, and you will more easily be able to determine what is the relevant answer information, what is additional, and what is superfluous. This will provide a solid basis for deciding which parts of your themed message go with which question, and this will greatly empower you to use the questions as a vehicle for your message. The ten archetypes, and suggested responses to them, are detailed in Part Three.

PART THREE
Essay and Interview Management

10 The MBA essay question archetypes (part 1)

In the previous sections, you developed your profile, investigated your strengths and weaknesses, understood your interests, found your stories, and developed your value points and themes. Then you turned these elements into an application positioning and created a clear message to communicate it. You did this completely independently of the essay questions, making sure that your answers would be driven primarily by the message you set out to communicate, *not* by the questions. You are now ready to talk to the admissions committee.

Almost every question you will get is an archetypal MBA admissions question, or an adaptation of the archetype, or a combination of two archetypes. Familiarity with the archetypes allows you to turn whatever question you are faced with and shape it to archetypal form. This enables you to best sort and place your profile across the questions and transmit your message through them. Recognizing the archetype tells you what kind of answer is demanded, the kind of topics you can raise, and what is extraneous. It helps you map your message to the questions more closely and more effectively. However, first, a few key items on the unique role and purpose of the essays.

The role of the essays

To write good essays, it is first necessary to understand why Adcom puts them there. As we have noted, each different input in the application process—the GMAT, recommendations, interview, resume, etc., all have their unique purpose, all test the applicant in a different way, as do the essays. So what is specific to the essays? What is their particular purpose in the application package?

Part of the apparent oddness of the essays in an MBA application is the fact that a business school is mostly a logical, quantitative, rational kind of place. Much of it is concerned with making numbers work out and you're never far from your Excel spreadsheet. So you'd think that MBA admissions would be a logical, quantitative, rational kind of process: taking an applicant's GMAT and under-graduate scores, applying a weighted average for credentials and achievements, feeding it all into a computer, and admitting the top 10 or 20 percent would surely be the most equitable solution. Not only would this be quick and fair, but it would make operational sense too, given the thousands of applicants MBA admissions officers have to process each year.

But, by contrast, schools typically ask applicants to write between three and seven relatively long, open-ended, reflective personal essays on their life, achieve-ments, goals, motivations, failures. These essays absorb an inordinate amount of admissions staff time in assessment and deliberations and introduce a large dose of subjectivity into the applications process. Why? What makes them ask the open-ended kind of questions they do? Why do they make the application process longer, more subjective and more resource-intensive than it apparently needs to be? Figuring this out is key to knowing what you need to do to write a successful essay set.

Fine-tuning selection

To understand what's going on, once again put yourself in the shoes of the admissions committee whose holy grail is: (1) to select the best applicants; and (2) to balance the skills, aptitudes, backgrounds, and experience of the incoming class. Any decent school can take half of the applications it receives and throw them in the bin: "not enough experience," "lukewarm recommendations," "poor GMAT," "too old," and so on. That's the easy part. The challenge is what to do with the top half—that is, how to distinguish between the excellent candidates that remain.

In other words, the truly difficult part of Adcom's job is to distinguish between excellent candidates and super-excellent candidates, and achieve a balanced class, while operating with the rather serious handicap that they know actually not that much about the people they are dealing with. Truth is, if they were to take the academic and file data from all competitive candidates with "good numbers" and proven attributes, and compare them all with each other, they would all be remarkably similar. Generally, the college grades would be in a similar band, as would the GMATs, the quantity and quality of work experience, the source and merit of the recommendations, and so on. Any other aptitude or psychometric test they could run would also not significantly separate the candidates either. So, when they are faced with a GMAT 720/GPA 4.0 banker from Chicago, a GMAT 720/ Oxbridge graduated systems analyst from Glasgow, and a GMAT 710/Chinese Fulbright scholar, and they can only take one, how are they going to choose?

Schools set hard, open-ended, searching personal questions precisely to allow them to choose between excellent applicants. (The interview, and recommenda-tions help further in this.) Asking what really motivates her, why he needs an MBA, which of her achievements matters most, how he copes with failure, how she envisions her future, and reading the results over four or five pages, provides Adcom with subtle distinctions between those with an apparently equivalent good claim to admission. Through the essays, the truly compelling candidates make themselves known.

Therefore, the essays are the testing instrument that give admissions officers enough "deep information" about every candidate to be able to fulfill the function of separating the great from the merely good. They are the tie-breaker between excellent candidates. So, unless you are an Olympic champion or are Prince Harry, you should assume that your essays will be the key difference between you and the other great applicants in the admissions pool. You are not going to get yourself ahead of your serious competitors without doing well here.

Sensemaking

The second key reason the essays are there is they give Adcom a filter through which the rest of your file can be read and understood. The things you choose to highlight, and the way you connect the dots in your life story, will provide (and significantly influence) the way the reader makes sense of your data record, resume, and will promote an integrated understanding of your choices, including the choice to do an MBA at this point in your life. All the pieces of your application are, just that, pieces. The essays are what draws them all together and allows them to be understood (that is, you to be understood) as a whole.

Rewarding communication skills

The other key reason the essays are sought by the Adcom is that they test the candidate's ability to communicate ideas and, in particular, to communicate them in English. No matter what kind of statistical and quantitative Excel-jock you are, or what kind of numerical paradise you may be expecting your career to be about, make no mistake that the ability to communicate—to pitch, to persuade, to negotiate, and otherwise get ideas across to colleagues, customers, investors, and stakeholders—is *the* key to business and leadership success, and becomes more so the more senior you get in an organization. This is true all over the world.

The committee doesn't need or want you to be Shakespeare, but they are looking for people who can succinctly organize information and eloquently brief a reader or a listener, as they will have to do many thousands of times in their careers. The essays test this skill and separate those who can do it from those who can't.

Meeting the essay requirements

The essays are therefore a fundamental, deciding part of your application. If you plan to "just get them over with," don't even waste your time and money applying. Given their specific role, it follows that your task in writing them is to communicate well, provide profile sensemaking, and showcase enough differentiating, high-quality material about yourself that Adcom is motivated to make subtle distinctions in your favor. The test of a good essay is the extent to which it adds value to your file, providing stories, insights, and perspectives that turn you from a data set into a fully three-dimensional human being with interesting and valuable qualities. Your personal statement should "open a window" into your single and unique life, and through it Adcom should feel they have met you and come to know you and identify with you as a person, so that they can distinguish you from the crowd.

You achieve this by selecting and sharing personal events and stories, and analyzing and reflecting on them in an honest way, so the readers get to understand what you stand for, are interested in or are motivated to do, and what you aspire to in your life, and why. You have to go beyond your resume and work progression and tell Adcom things they can't find in your application and even some things your colleagues and possibly even your family members don't know about you. Differentiating, high-quality material is not hard to recognize:

it is anything that turns you from a database entry into a unique, memorable person on an interesting path. That is, someone they want to meet and to get behind and offer a place to.

Exercise

If you are having trouble knowing what it means to add value to your file in this way, imagine yourself at a cocktail party with 10 other competing MBA applicants and one admissions officer. You all work for the same company and you all have the identical GMAT score, but only one can be selected. You each get about five minutes to talk to her—what do you say about yourself that is interesting, insightful, provoking and memorable? *That is your essay material.* You've succeeded when she no longer thinks, "MIT undergrad, science major, 3.8/710, ex-PWC," but instead, "The guy who majored in botanical studies, left consulting to create a successful small business in exotic East Asian seedlings and now needs an MBA to develop a community-friendly agribusiness worldwide. By the way, he also has big-6 consulting experience and great numbers."

There are many tools and techniques that will improve your essay development and provide a reliably good recipe for winning personal statements. Part four is devoted to these topics. As the first step to this, we consider essay questions recognition and management via the ten essay archetypes in the rest of this chapter, and the following two chapters.

The MBA question archetypes

Understanding what the relevance of the essays is, we can now look at the key types of questions that come up, and how to best approach each type. The following ten archetypes are the classic questions in all business school applications (Figure 10.1).

The archetypes may come at you in any order in a question set. We deal with the first three question archetypes (why an MBA, Successes, and Failures) in this chapter. The following four (leadership, diversity contribution, ethics, teamwork) are covered in Chapter 11, and the final three (key influences, personal inquiry, innovation) are dealt with in Chapter 12, along with advice on how to tackle other common essay types including the "optional" essay. Bear in mind in the discussion that follows that many question run together two or more archetypes. How to recognize and manage "multiple-archetype" questions is dealt with at the end of Chapter 12.

ARCHETYPE 1: "WHY AN MBA?" / GOALS

1. Examples[1]

Briefly assess your career progress to date. Elaborate on your future career plans and your motivation for pursuing a graduate degree at Kellogg. (Kellogg-Northwestern)

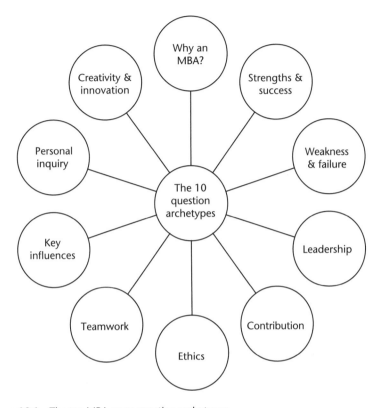

Figure 10.1   The ten MBA essay question archetypes

Think about the decisions you have made in your life. Describe the following (a) What choices have you made that led you to your current position? (b) Why pursue an MBA at this point in your life? (c) What is your career goal upon graduation from the NYU-Stern? What is your long-term career goal? (NYU-Stern)

As a leader in global business, Wharton is committed to sustaining "a truly global presence through its engagement in the world." What goals are you committed to and why? How do you envision the Wharton MBA contributing to the attainment of those goals? (Wharton)

Discuss your career goals. What skills do you expect to gain from studying at INSEAD and how will they contribute to your professional career. (INSEAD)

2. Recognition keywords

Past, present, future, career, goal, progress, plan, aspiration, choices, ambition, decision, position, objective, intention, aim, purpose, life, short term, long term.

3. The underlying issue

Stripped of its verbiage, this question always asks you: Why do you need an MBA, why now and why from us? The question will often be the backbone of the essay set. Note that there are five parts to the question, covering three time periods:

- Past—What experiences have led you to this point and this ambition?
- Present—Why an MBA now, at this point in your career?
- Future—What do you want to do with your degree, in the short and long term?
- Why an MBA at all? (Why not another kind of Master's, or a PhD?)
- Why an MBA from this school particularly?

You should touch on all five topics somewhere in your complete essay set, but be careful to answer this and all questions exactly as posed. If the question is broadly asked, as with Kellogg above, all topics can be addressed in full. Note, however, that other forms of the question ask for some but not other parts of it. You need to shape your "why an MBA" answer carefully to whether the question asks more about your past ("What has led you to want an MBA?") or about your future ("What will you do when you graduate? How will an MBA help you?"). Before getting to the "how to tackle it" part of the discussion, some general observations about managing MBA goals are necessary. As with all the essay archetypes observations, the principles discussed are broadly applicable to the interview process too, as elaborated in Chapter 14.

Managing goals and communicating future aspirations

A very common dilemma is applicants don't exactly know what they want to do with their life. Most people don't really know what they are going to do when they have finished their MBA, and many change direction various times while at school. It's more common than not for a student's career aspirations on graduation to have changed dramatically from what they were on matriculation. So the burning question is: How specific do you need to be about your goals?

Adcoms know full well that most if not all students reevaluate their career goals as their eyes are opened to new opportunities. Adcoms expect this and indeed support it, and this correlates with accepting younger students, as discussed earlier. Harvard Business School Adcom, for example, has said they are looking for students who are receptive to the "transformational experience" of the (HBS) MBA,[2] and has specifically made the career goals essay (What is your career vision and why is this choice meaningful to you?) an *optional* essay. They are saying you do not need to have your life mapped out.

Bear in mind that providing a career framework rather than exactitude does not give you license to hedge on your aspirations. Applicants sometimes say something like: "I want to go to Silicon Valley and create a startup using my knowledge of XPF-Bio data mining. If that doesn't work out, I may go back to my old job at Bear Stearns, or join the family business." That's not a framework. That's drifting. Adcom prefers to bet on candidates who have key part of they story worked out and who will do anything (legal) to realize their dream. If you don't back yourself 100 percent, the committee won't either.

So, at the same time as they want to imprint and transform you, your clarity of purpose and motivation on application are deeply attractive to Adcoms too. They want people who have that kind of mindset and who set themselves goals and achieve them, and they are wary of applicants who appear to be "just drifting along." They are looking for an organized career strategy that rests on solid self-understanding. They want to know why you have made the decisions you made, how they have brought you to this point in your life and where you are going from here. For this reason many schools ask for your short- and long-term goals and see this as a cornerstone of the application.

Bear in mind that a clear goal differentiates you, provided it is well thought through. If you don't know what you want to do yet, you are in a group with many people. If you are an engineer wanting to become a entrepreneur, you are in a group of many. But if you want to be a medical "systems manager" seeking to privatize hospitals in Peru, or a "director of satellite operations" looking for equity partners to roll up independent multimedia service providers, you become singular.

All things considered, the best way to deal with this to consider your own situation. If you do have specific and clear plans, talk about them. If you don't, take heart that you don't need to at this stage, but it is in your favor if you can show evidence of careful and purposeful thinking about your future. You want to appear clear and focused, and to have a framework for making the career decisions that will face you on graduation and beyond, but to be open to the intellectual and professional growth that business school offers and how this will help you refine your choices. It is the motivation and sense of purpose that they are looking for, not a career blueprint.

Mission goals versus functional goals

Most candidates make the mistake of leaving their goals at the level of function—what they seek to do on a daily basis, rather than what they seek to achieve. They will say, for example, "I want to be a commercial real-estate analyst, or an equities trader, or a fund manager." Or, they may say, "I want to run my own firm" or "I want to manage a multinational company." This is okay for a start, but you should seek to move rapidly past function and onto purpose or mission. A mission is something you seek to achieve via the successful exercise of various functions, for example, commercializing your biomass energy company and taking it public, or turning Reykjavik into a free port. Your function is what you do every day. A mission is what it is going to add up to—what you are trying to make or build or achieve.

It is true that many rich and successful MBAs are primarily well-paid function-aries: bankers or consultants or various kinds of day-to-day managers their whole lives. You may well become that too. But this is not the way to get the attention of Adcom. Go past the position you aspire to be in and its functions. The point is, what you will do with the power and budget and connections you will have in that position. What's your purpose?

If you can get from function to purpose in your career aspirations, you solve various other problems in your goal statement, first, explaining why your career goals are interesting and important, and will give you professional satisfaction, that is *why* your goals are your goals. If you are talking in terms of function, you will struggle with this. If you talk in terms of purpose and mission, your deeper motivation will be obvious and persuasive. Second, function is general. Whatever your intended function is, it is likely to be shared by many applicants. But purpose is specific and concrete and therefore differentiates you. It will tell the committee unique and resonant things about you.

Your mission goal is a second admissions ticket

Creating a career mission that is interesting, viable, and worthwhile is like buying another lottery ticket in the admissions sweepstakes. If you are borderline and may not be accepted on your merits as a candidate, you might sneak in on the merits of your interesting and worthwhile goal. Adcom is not in the business of discriminating between different candidate missions. But given a choice between two equal candidates, one of whom has a clear and supportable mission and the other who has merely determined his career function, Adcom will support the mission. It is very hard to turn down a candidate who is hoping to do something interesting and valuable in the world. It is easier to reject the candidate who will be just one more consultant or private equity analyst.

The obvious corollary here is to have a worthwhile career purpose. But all this requires is some thinking about. Your past is behind you and so whatever you have achieved or not, and how important, worthwhile, and interesting it was, is all verifiable by Adcom. But your aspirations are safely ahead of you where no committee can verify them. It's a free hit! So don't hesitate to project yourself into valuable, distinctive roles.

You have to walk a fine line here. On the one hand, you must think big. Whether you want to manage a billion dollars, or create new brain technology industries, or fix Africa—whatever it is, you should communicate high aspirations and a potential career worthy of an MBA graduate from the particular school in 20 years from now. On the other hand, you must demonstrate career-path realism. First, the future must in some way fit with the past or you risk them thinking "dream on." Second, your aspiration will in all likelihood take a lifetime to mature, and even then may not. You should sound like you understand how careers evolve in your field and the ways you might have to "do your time" (even if highly paid) before you become a true titan of your industry and are able to change it.

A place for idealism

There's an old adage: "If you're not a communist at 20, you're a rogue; if you're a communist at 50 you're a fool." The sell-by-date on that adage or on communism itself may have passed, but the idea is everlasting. It is expected of the youth that they are idealistic, that they want to shake things up, improve the world, do things a better way. If you are not thinking like this in your 20s then you never will. Adcom wants your idealism—they want you to want to fix the world. The Adcom staffer can't fix the world, but possibly you, with a shiny new Harvard or Stanford MBA and your whole career ahead of you . . . maybe you actually can. They don't expect you to want to feed the starving or save the orphans. Just building new industries or rebuilding old ones would be nice. Once again, the committee is not in the business of choosing between idealistic aspirants. But when faced with a choice between someone with a possibly naïve but breathtaking vision and someone who want to join a bank and work his way up the ladder, they will lean toward the visionary.

Acknowledge the career arc

Your post-MBA career, if it all works out as planned, will look something like a rocket launched into sub-orbit. You will shoot very quickly upwards, then you will progress more slowly and perhaps in less of a straight line to your highest point, after which you will begin your descent into quasi- and eventually full retirement. There are broadly three phases: the climb, the peak, and the dénouement. Very often in the last phase, successful career-minded MBAs go in a new (but related) direction and turn more attention to community and philanthropy. They start consulting firms with direct community benefits, or turn their lifelong hobbies into businesses. Women, but increasingly men as well, may take time out for parenthood along the way, but the shape of this broad life and career arc will still apply.

In your career essay you should be able to say how this inevitable arc applies to you, how the sections will fit together and what broad themes will go with you all the way through your personal and professional life.

The "why an MBA" for career-changes

The MBA is very commonly about career change. It has always been, and remains, the degree that prepares functional experts for a career in management. That is, by definition, most people on graduation will be going from a role as some kind of specialist, analyst, or technician to a role as manager, broadly defined, which may include entrepreneurship. This is a path Adcom is most familiar with and doesn't need particular motivation. However, there are also many applicants who are looking to change sector (e.g. go from print media into environmental management), or to go from one functional specialty to another (e.g. from the IT side of an investment bank to the trading desk). When this is going on, the applicant has slightly more to do in the goals essay, that is to show good personal research on the new industry or new role—enough so Adcom is satisfied that the move is well motivated and the applicant can make the jump both practically (will be hired) and culturally (will fit in).

Bearing in mind the grass is always greener on the other side of the fence, it is not enough to express a profound interest and motivation in this grass. You have to show you have in some sense "been there," that you understand what is required, what the day-to-day realities are, how you would fit in and get on. You need to show evidence of your proactive and practical due diligence in this matter, which will make the move credible and supportable. If possible, show how your current skill-set and knowledge base fit with and will be beneficial in the new role, and may allow you advantages over your peers in managing the requirements.

It is helpful if your appraisal of a move such as this has matured over a decent period of time—a few years perhaps of developing interest. It is fine to record an eye-opening event that consolidated your thinking in the new direction, but you don't want it to look like you are potentially vulnerable to multiple "Road to Damascus" career-change moments.

4. How to tackle the "why an MBA" essay

This essay should be done in a clear and straightforward way. You can be creative in your answers to many other questions but here it is too risky. Here the committee is looking above all for unequivocal evidence of your professional maturity and motivation, as shown by how much you've thought through your future, and how much clarity of purpose about why you need a business education.

Connect past to future

The committee is asking how your past connects to your future via business school. You need to show that the MBA is the bridge between your yesterday and your tomorrow. Paint a picture of a future that rests naturally on your past, assuming the MBA from the school in question. Past, present, and future can be presented in any order. What works will depend on the details of your situation. A generally versatile template is:

- Start with your direct (short-term) goal on graduation.
- Then give a sense of your long-term (major) goals.
- Say why an MBA is relevant to these goals, and why now.
- Bolster this with what in your past has led you to this point.
- Finish with the particular aspects of the target school that are relevant and attractive, given your stated goals.

Show due diligence on "why here"

The "why an MBA" question is one of the best places to prove you have done your homework on the business school and the MBA program, and to argue that there is a specific match between your agenda and what's on offer. Mention by name the school's features, courses, clubs, extramural or internship opportunities or recruiting "treks," and other key learning opportunities, saying which will boost you toward your life and career prospects, and why. The more specific the goal you have set out, the better you will able to motivate that the program in its particularities is the bridge you specifically need to cross to best move towards it.

Know why now

Adcoms generally believe there is a "right time" in one's career for an MBA and that students who do it at the right time will benefit more both on campus and in terms of direct career boost. Age is a factor in what that right time is, as discussed in Chapter 3, but it is not the only factor. The right time for a full-time MBA generally comes when the applicant has mastered some key skills in their industry, and had formative experiences, but still needs foundational education and experiences, particularly if transitioning into a management role. In answering the "why now" question, you will need to frame it in these general terms, but, as always, making it specific to your story and your educational and professional needs which is part of "the fit" described above.

Show first steps

The best don't wait for acceptance of their business school application before getting on with their dreams. You raise your stock immeasurably if you can show you have already taken steps towards the goal you aspire to. Have you done the certifications you need for your career move? Do you have a plan for attracting investors to the business you hope to set up? Convince the committee that you will make it happen no matter what, even if you don't get into their school, or any school. This is all the more true if you are a career-changer.

5. How to flunk the "why an MBA" question

You will mess up this essay if:

- You don't answer parts of the question asked, or you answer parts not asked.
- Your style for this essay is flippant or frivolous.
- You fail to talk about the specific attributes of the program you are applying to, and why they are relevant to your education and your future.
- You have aspirations that are too low or too dull, or you have not worked to get some clarity on your career path, even if it is, understandably, not set in stone.
- Your aspirations are bogged down in job function and low on purpose.
- Your career goals don't require an MBA, or the role of an MBA is not clear.
- You have goals that are unrealistic or appear a serious stretch from what you have done to this point, or you fail to explain a realistic path to them.
- Your goals are illogical or an extreme stretch given your past, suggesting career flakiness. (You're a Kurdish linguist: you want to be a Wall Street analyst.) The committee will ask: "Is this aspiration logical? Will [he or she] be recruited?"

ARCHETYPE 2: STRENGTHS, SUCCESS, AND ACHIEVEMENT

1. Examples

What are your three most substantial accomplishments and why do you view them as such? (HBS)

Write a brief explanation of your most important professional and personal achievements to date. What do you consider your most powerful strength or asset? Describe a situation where you demonstrated this strength or asset. (ESADE)

What are the two or three strengths or characteristics that have driven your career success thus far? Do you have other strengths that you would like to leverage in the future? (Kenan-Flagler)

Describe your most significant professional accomplishment. Elaborate on the leadership skills you displayed, the actions you took and the impact you had on your organization. (Ross-Michigan)

2. Recognition keywords

Overcome, success, achievement, attainment, feat, triumph, milestone, prevail, accomplishment, strength.

3. The underlying issue

Part of this question is straightforward—it asks for your main personal and professional achievements, to see if you are a success-driven, achievement-oriented candidate, and which concrete things you have done in a competitive company that prove this. In every MBA application pool there will be real outstanding success stories—Olympic athletes, Grammy winners—and these candidates definitely get credit for high-profile achievement. It doesn't hurt the image of the school at all either.

But take heart. Three things work in favor of more ordinary mortals. First, applicants are not assessed primarily on past successes. They are ranked on likelihood of future success. Second, not all accomplishments must belong out there in the hurly-burly of life. Sometimes the biggest and most meaningful accomplishments can be small hurdles that, for one good reason or another, were big for you alone, or show a big heart. Any achievement counts, as long as it is genuinely impressive in some way and real difficulties were overcome. Third, and most important, whether the achievement is big or small, what it amounted to is less important to the committee than why you value it and *what it says about you.*

In other words, whatever the achievement was or wasn't in objective terms, the real test of the essay is that you can extract the personal and growth implications from it and use it as a vehicle for telling your personal story. It's not only about what you've done. It's about who you are. Therefore, almost any achievement will work, provided you can say: why it was meaningful (beyond the fact that it's nice to win and prove yourself); why you set the achievement as a goal in your life in the first place; why you still savor the achievement now; why it makes you proud; how it served to build you; why you choose to talk about it in your essay now, over and above any other achievement; and how this suggests the kind of successes you are likely to pursue in the future.

4. How to tackle it

There are, therefore, two parts to this essay. Part 1 is the narrative story of the success, including the circumstances and build-up that surrounded it. Part 2 is the analysis of the success. You should think in terms of using no more that 60 percent of your allotted word length to tell the story. Remember, the success itself does not count for everything, so give weight to your analysis: why the achievement is significant to you and what this suggests about who you are and the kind of things you intend to focus your talent on once you have, additionally, MBA skills and credentials.

Choosing achievements

Accomplishments imply attributes and strengths—the skills that allowed you to beat the competition or overcome a significant difficulty. Ideally, the accomplishment you choose should be one that implies your command of the strengths valued by MBA programs, including maturity, leadership, teamwork, strong personality, creativity, and perseverance (see Chapter 2 for the 22 attributes that admissions committees are looking for).

Remember, you don't necessarily have to pick the most overtly, externally, impressive thing you ever did. Instead, you can consider your past more broadly, and choose an achievement that is intrinsic to your themes that allows you to reinforce your key message and clarify the basic premises of your argument. As a general rule, if asked for more than one success, give one from your professional life and one from your personal life.

In talking of the attributes that underpin the success you mention, this essay is a good place to show you are a "finisher"—someone who will overcome no matter what the obstacles. Generally, all worthwhile achievements imply a large amount of tenacity. Make sure you extract the presence of such strengths from your story.

Writing about your successes raises the questions: How modest should you be? Should you be understated or trumpet yourself? Careful attention to tone and to cultural norms is required here. It's commonly understood that Americans are more receptive to forthright self-promotion than Europeans. But, in general, in applying to competitive programs, you should be prepared to showcase yourself. Being modest won't get you anywhere, and certainly less so in the US than anywhere else. The best rule to follow is: Be very forthright in claiming personal merit where you have a concrete award, promotion, or other independent proof of your achievement. Go easy on unproven, subjective, positive self-regard.

5. How to flunk this essay

You will mess up this essay if:

- You choose a weak or boring accomplishment.
- You spend too long on the accomplishment story and not enough on the analysis.
- You duck or flub the analysis: You can't say why the achievement means something to you, or what it means.
- You don't give clear insight into the attributes and qualities that underpin the achievement.
- Your story is short on detail.
- You are over-modest about your achievement, or you are insufferably arrogant (both suggest immaturity).

Compete on the analysis

This suggested essay solution introduces the valuable, classic two-part MBA essay answer format—one where you provide factual data (input) in the early part of the essay and an interpretive analysis (output) in the later part. The essay goes from grabbing, captivating, and informing, to synthesizing, interpreting, and convincing. The descriptive part takes the reader into the details of your experiences; the analytical part to your learning and insight. This format will be required in almost all the essays you write.

Stories from different candidates are, believe it or not, more or less equal. It might be hard to swallow, but the reality is that the story data from most applicants is of equal type and merit. Your great wins and unique experiences—travel to Tibet, loss of a grandparent, managing a bad boss, winning a race—might feel very unique to you, but they will be very similar in form and substance to everyone else's. Also your numbers will be similar, and work experience and life path will be similar or of roughly equal value. In other words, it is unlikely that your experiences are better than anyone else's. They have had a full life just like you have.

However, candidates' expertise at, and commitment to, interpretive self-analysis vary hugely, as does their communications ability. Here is where you can differentiate yourself. The obvious implication is that you should compete on the analysis, where there is leverage and where most candidates are weak. Start by getting clarity on what analysis you want to extract, and work backwards from there. Decide which points you want to make about yourself and pick a story that will best facilitate those points, and get the story told quickly enough so you have sufficient space to turn the story into an argument for your admission. Essay structures that emphasize this two-part form are presented in Chapter 16.

ARCHETYPE 3: WEAKNESSES AND FAILURE

1. Examples

Describe a situation taken from school, business, civil or military life, where you did not meet your personal objectives, and discuss briefly the effect. (INSEAD)

Discuss the most difficult constructive criticism or feedback you have received. How did you address it? What have you learned from it? (Tuck-Dartmouth)

Describe a failure that you have experienced. What role did you play, and what did you learn about yourself? (Wharton)

What have you learned from a mistake? (HBS)

Describe a time when you wish you could have retracted something you said or did. When did you realize your mistake and how did you handle the situation? (Chicago-Booth)

2. Recognition keywords

Failure, weakness, learning, unsuccessful, fall short, fault, flaw, limitation, inadequate, criticism, shortcoming, adversity, go wrong, efforts come to nothing, weak spot, imperfection, deficiency.

3. The underlying issue

The weakness-failure-criticism essay is your greatest opportunity to separate yourself from the crowd because it is the one most candidates find the hardest, and it is often the one done most poorly. Applicants to business school very often struggle with these essays because they feel that admitting a weaknesses or sharing a time when they failed erodes their candidacy. In fact, it does just the opposite.

First, understand that the committee does not set the failure essay to see if you have weaknesses or have failed. Everyone has weaknesses and has failed. Second, they are uninterested in your mistake *per se*. What they are testing, above all, is if you have the honesty and self-insight to locate and understand the sources of your mess-ups, and the maturity to address them. The committee wants to know if you can face your own flaws and discuss them candidly and work on them, or if you will try to hide them and/or blame circumstances or other people. They want to know not how you avoided failure, but how you managed it, what you learned, what insight into yourself you gained and how you grew from there.

No-one is comfortable talking about their weak spots and failures. But nobody —not me, not you, not the admissions officer—is perfect or has not failed. The greatest managers and leaders have all made significant mistakes in business and their lives. If it helps you to be candid, remember also that failure is okay (particularly in the American business ethos). Nothing else teaches you as effectively or as quickly as failing does, and a life of failure-avoidance is often a life of experience-avoidance. In fact, odd as it may seem, a failure is often a result of the qualities Adcom is looking for—bold plans, ambition, initiative, creativity, and a willingness to take risks. The committee (and your future bosses, partners, and employees) will generally forgive the mistakes you make, if you are big enough to take responsibility and if you learn rapidly from them.

Take a tip from George Soros, self-made billionaire, philosopher, philanthropist, social reformer, and fund manager extraordinaire—famous for "breaking the Bank (of England)" by shorting the pound sterling in 1992—who shares this candid account of his weaknesses:

> I'm a very bad judge of character. I'm a good judge of stocks, and I have a reasonably good perspective on history. But I am, really, quite awful in judging character, and so I've made many mistakes. It took me five years and a lot of painful experiences to find the right management team. I am pleased that finally I found it, but I cannot claim to be as successful in picking a team as I have been in actually managing money. I think that I'm very good as a senior partner, or boss, because I have a lot of sympathy for the difficulties that fund managers face. When they are in trouble I can give them a lot of support, and that, I think, has contributed

toward creating a good atmosphere in the firm. But I'm not so good at choosing them.[3]

See, the greatest business leaders all have weaknesses and all have made significant mistakes in their careers and their lives. Real leaders know their weaknesses, and can admit them to themselves and others—in order to work on them, or work around them. It shows self-insight and points to seniority. It is, in other words, a primary indicator of your real leadership ability and potential, and a significant test of your readiness for senior leadership.

Crucially, admitting weakness and failure allows you to showcase how hard you work on improving yourself, which is a key characteristic of a good leader. So go ahead and own up to the mess-up. Own up to the underlying weakness, if applicable. Talk about how you propose to correct the weakness, then be positive and move on. Show your growth and your continued, undiminished, can-do spirit. Show Adcom that you have the insight into yourself and the personal resources to come back from failure when it occurs, and that you are not the kind of person who makes the same mistake twice.

Adversity is your friend in MBA admissions

The weakness-failure essay archetype usually brings up life, business, or career adversity and how you faced it. Adversity is a valuable topic because it pretty much begs you to talk about character, resourcefulness, and ingenuity. As many dot-com hotshots and banking bravuras have found out, it's easy to be a good businessman in good times, but when the weather turns, that's when your mettle and your creativity are tested. True leaders show their stuff when the odds are against them. If you can demonstrate to the committee that you have proved mettle in adversity, either for your business or yourself, your application will get a significant boost.

Choosing failure topics

The first thing to be clear on is what "a failure" is. A failure is a situation where there were operational objectives and/or responsibilities and/or aspirations on your shoulders, which for reasons to do with *your own actions or omissions* turned out poorly. A failure must point to weaknesses of your approach, understanding, judgment, aptitude, execution, or character. A failure could be missing a deadline, breaking someone's trust, underperforming when others are counting on you, misjudging a situation or a person, and so on.

In addition, the best kinds of failures for MBA admissions purposes are:

- a failure where you were faced with more or less the same set of circumstances a second time. In this you can show how the lesson was learned, not just claim that it has been.
- a failure with an implied weakness for which the MBA curriculum, learning, experience or socialization is part of the proposed solution. Then admission becomes the first step on the road to overcoming your weakness or lack of experience.
- a failure that allows you to develop one or all of your themes and reinforce

your message. (Your scrambled recovery from failure, or your learning and working on a weakness, can lead into a discussion of one of the themes of your application message.)

Failure topics to avoid

As explained above, it is *not* admitting a weakness that will get you dinged, because it's like waving a red beacon that betrays inexperience and a junior mindset. If you "have no weaknesses" that just tells Adcom that you don't know what they are yet or that you're too immature to face them. It says you don't know yourself, therefore you don't yet know where you will mess up. You are a liability to yourself and your company. These are failure essay strategies and topics to avoid:

- *Non-failures:* The fact that you have some culpability for a mess-up does not mean it is a personal failure. A failure must be the result of a weakness. Therefore, getting caught doing a prank or any other high-spirited loss of control is hardly ever a failure—the time you got drunk with your buddies and the cops stopped you and someone had to bail you out of jail at three in the morning is not a failure. It is just youthful exuberance.

  Similarly, anything that is mostly bad luck or mostly an accident is hardly ever a failure—crashing your car, getting your girlfriend pregnant, or any other event that goes wrong, even if you have some culpability for it, is not a failure (or is only failure to plan or take precautions). If you pick an accidental failure, you will not be able to talk about a weakness underlying it or a personal fix you have put in place.

- *Fake failures:* Don't be so naïve as to think you can slip a fake failure or phony weakness past the admissions committee. Don't say you failed to do something but in the end nobody found out so no harm was done. Your failure must be an episode where there was egg on your face, either at the time or some time afterwards, because part of the story is how you fixed the situation and dealt with the egg. And don't ever, ever, ever say "my weakness is that I have no weaknesses." If you choose a trite failure or non-failure, you will indeed fail this essay on maturity grounds.

- *Childhood failures:* Don't present a childhood failure—it's an obvious cop-out. Unless there is a very good reason to go back further, your failure should be something that happened to you after the age of 21—that is, when you were a full adult and cannot hide behind natural age immaturity.

- *Inappropriate failures:* Don't pick an ethical or moral failure. The reader should get a sense of a mess-up, but she should not be scandalized. If you stole, lied, or cheated, or worse, the admissions officer will think you might do it again. Moral failings are too hard to shake. If you want to confess, go to confession. Also, don't suggest any failure related to mental health. At some more ideal future time, mental illness will be better understood, but we are not there yet. Any mental illness—even something as apparently innocuous as attention deficit disorder—will hang like a wet cloud over your application. Anxiety, depression, anorexia, bi-polar disorder or anything else like this will finish you off, no matter how much you claim to have beaten it.

Don't pick a failure that takes you into territory that normally stays behind closed doors. If you conquered impotence, for example, MBA admissions is not the place to talk about it. Stay clear of topics where the very fact of broaching them may suggest social or professional ineptness on your part.

4. How to tackle it

This essay is similar in form to the achievement essay, discussed above, in that you have an event story followed by analysis. However, in this case the story typically has two parts—your failure event and your scramble to put things right. The analysis will also have two parts: The first analyzing the reason for failure and the weakness present that caused it; and the second extracting the lesson and considering how you would manage the situation differently if you were faced with it again (or better still, how you actually did manage a similar situation more successfully the following time).

The standard template for this essay is thus:

1a. Story—failure
1b. Story—damage control
2a. Analysis—understanding of your mistakes and shortcomings
2b. Analysis—learning, growth, fix, situation revisit.

Start with the story. Don't dress it up or make it pretty—tell it like it was—how you were responsible for a big red-faced mess-up. Talk about it honestly and don't duck it. Stand up, in the way a mature person would. Remember to pay attention to the gritty painful details—they make your story immediate and interesting: don't say you caused the company to lose "a lot of money," say you cost them $1.2 million. Don't say you were "underdressed for the client meeting," take us to the moment on the Saturday when you showed up in a T-shirt because you misread the memo, and your boss froze you out. Make the admissions officer wriggle in her seat with embarrassment for you. (For more on using details in your writing, see Part Four.)

Again, your story—parts 1a and 1b—should not be longer than two-thirds of your essay. If there is something significant to say about 1b—that is, if your damage control was bold, ingenious, or somehow shows management talent in itself—you can allow yourself a little more length.

The fix moves the reader from your mess-up to what you have learned and how this has improved and strengthened you. Show how you have addressed the deficiency, providing evidence of real self-work, or how you have learned to manage the shortcomings implied. Go beyond the generalities of how you have become a "better and wiser person," and get to specific situation-management skills you have learned, and people-management techniques you have adopted. Your analysis should deal with such issues as why you present this failure rather than others, why it was a meaningful and valuable lesson, and why it sheds light on you as a person and on your growth path. You should show your insight into the reasons behind the failure, what you've learned, and how you've grown and got smarter.

From failure to success

Ultimately, your analysis should recast your failure event as a "learning experience" that has strengthened you personally and professionally and is fundamental to building you into the mature leader you are in the process of becoming. That is, you reframe the liability of a failure as the asset of experience. Tell a solution story not a hard luck story. Being pathetic might get you sympathy, but it won't get you admitted to b-school. As explained in Chapter 2, you will get in for one reason only: because you add more short- and long-term value to the school than the next person. What matters is how potentially bright your future is, and this includes being able to manage setbacks.

It is therefore also important to be fully "over" the failure experience when you tell Adcom about it, so you can look back and extract the lessons from a position of relative comfort, with all the learning fully understood and digested. You don't want to talk about a present, lingering failure that you haven't sorted out yet. That would hardly show you in a good light.

On the other hand, a common problem applicants have is they insinuate that the failure and weaknesses behind it are absolutely thoroughly beaten. "I messed up—I understand why—I learned from it—that won't happen again." The truth is that some of your weak spots will probably stay with you throughout your life in one form or another. If they are genuine, there is—by definition—no easy way to beat them, and you will fail again because of them, and it's juvenile to think otherwise.

The only thing that improves is your management of your weaknesses. Take heart from Soros' story above—many very important people are managing a chronic imperfection or two. It is fine to tell Adcom that you recognize a long-term weakness in yourself, and explain how you compensate for it, and how you watch vigilantly for where it might still lead you to make wrong moves.

Tone for weakness-failure essays

When you are writing about failure, take care to keep a straightforward, candid, objective tone. Note how Soros, above, is candid, straightforward, and objective in his self-analysis. He doesn't try to slip in softening or deflecting phrases, or hide behind humor; nor is he self-excusing or whining or looking to blame others. If you do this, it will mark you as too-junior. (If you're really struggling with a candid tone for this essay, get your spouse or significant other to write an first draft of this essay—they will give a forthright account of your weaknesses in the kind of tone you are looking for!)

5. How to flunk this essay

You will mess up this essay if:

- You cannot candidly admit failure and weakness.
- Your failure event is weak, or it is a non-failure, or you do not demonstrate that you understand what constitutes a failure.
- Your story is short on detail and interest.
- You don't connect failure to weaknesses, or you imply that your weaknesses are trivial.
- Your tone is inappropriate or juvenile.
- There is too much description and not enough analysis.
- You fail to develop or share insight into yourself.
- You underestimate the transformation required to ensure not failing next time, given the same circumstances. You think that your weak spots are solved rather than managed.

11 The MBA essay question archetypes (part 2)

This chapter continues the discovery and discussion of MBA question types by looking at the Leadership, Contribution, Ethics, and Teamwork archetypes. The final three types (Key influences, Personal inquiry, Innovation) and common additional and auxiliary questions are dealt with in the next chapter.

ARCHETYPE 4: LEADERSHIP

1. Examples

A) What does leadership mean to you? What are the personal characteristics and skills required to be an effective leader? B) Provide a specific example of when you demonstrated leadership skills. Describe a challenge that you faced and the results that you achieved. C) What areas do you wish to develop in order to become a more effective leader? (McDonough-Georgetown)

Describe an accomplishment that exhibits your leadership style. The description should include evidence of your leadership skills, the actions you took, and the impact you had on your organization. (Yale)

Tell us about a time when you motivated others to support your vision or initiative. (Stanford)

2. Recognition keywords

Lead, motivate, initiative, impact, leadership, guide, direct, direction, responsibility, decision, inspire, encourage, power, influence, run, organize.

3. The underlying issue

Leadership will be a guiding theme in every application you do. Adcom asks this question to find out not only what kind of leader you are now and what kind of a leader you might become—whether you've got "the right stuff"—but also to determine your understanding of and attitude to leadership. Part of having the right stuff is knowing what the right stuff looks like. Just having leadership experience doesn't necessarily mean you were any good at it. You have to show them you know what good is. You must also demonstrate an explicit understanding of your particular personal leadership style—how you influence, how you motivate, how you sanction, and so on—and the preferences and assumptions behind your leadership style.

Note that, for MBA admissions purposes, you won't get far with the idea that being associated with an organization is "leadership." If you weren't present and active, directing or co-directing events, it doesn't count. One active leadership experience is worth a dozen organization affiliations.

In some cases, there may be an overlap between this essay and the achievement essay—a leadership event may also overlap with one of your great achievements. But there are crucial differences. First, a leadership event need not be a success. You may present a leadership event where you didn't succeed, if you at least learned a lot about yourself and about leading. Second, while achievement is often the product of personal goals and private struggles, leadership is *always* in the public domain. If nobody other than you is involved, it is not a leadership event. This "public domain" criterion of leadership requires you to pick an event where you created, directed, and influenced an outcome that was achievable by two or more people, of which you were a part, and where your abilities made a difference to others' ability to achieve a goal.

The ability to make a difference by motivating, harnessing, and coordinating the efforts of others is the very essence of leadership for MBA admissions purposes. Therefore, what's also important here is your relationship with other people and your understanding of their motivations and the team dynamics. This interpersonal dimension suggests that your leadership essay will potentially overlap with the team essay too. As a team leader, you need to show a sophisticated understanding of the leadership problems inherent in managing multiple egos and orchestrating group priorities. In all leadership analysis, you should show respect for the difficulties of leadership—if you underestimate how hard it is, you have never really led.

The elements of leadership

Part of finding leadership experience, attributes, and potential in yourself comes in understanding the breadth of what it means to be a leader. It is not all about supervising people and managing budgets. Here are some parts of leadership that are often underplayed in MBA essays:

- Providing inspiration and motivation—a leader gets more out of people, beyond what they think they can do or are supposed to do.
- Providing and communicating vision—a leader sees what is possible, and is able to communicate what this is and how it can be achieved.
- Providing integrity and courage—a leader embodies principles that followers respect and can endorse. They communicate a courage of conviction and respect this in others.
- Providing confidence and humility—a leader has ready plans, but realizes they don't always have all the answers, and so has the confidence to turn to others for solutions, and therefore allows team members to do this too.

Leadership versus ethical dilemmas

Some people think that taking a moral stand—for example, reporting your boss for inflating monthly sales figures—is a leadership event. It is not. It is just an ethical event. Very occasionally, a leadership essay overlaps with the "ethical dilemma" essay (see archetype 6, on p. 124) in that resolving the dilemma requires leadership. For example, there may have been broader organizational dynamics involved in resolving the issues of the inflated monthly sales figures, and you may have challenged and motivated people to see things your way and follow you in taking action. In other words, the ethical event becomes a leadership event only to the extent that you influence a group's action.

4. How to tackle it

The question usually requires the description-analysis format, as discussed above. Once again, you should not overspend your allotted word length on telling the story. Remember, unless you have led in some spectacular capacity (you are already Eritrea's deputy Minister of Foreign Affairs, say), the wow-factor of your leadership story is going to resemble everyone else's, so focus on your analysis, where you can differentiate yourself. Again, for the same reason, it is less important to pick the most impressive leadership event of your life than one that allows you to develop one or all of your themes.

In your analysis, you must explain why the leadership event you chose was, and continues to be, valuable as a leadership experience, what this suggests about how you view leadership and what that says about you as a future leader. Show how your leadership and other experiences to date are defining your emerging leadership style. You should, space permitting, share some of your "theory" of leadership so far—what leadership requires, and how best to do it.

Often candidates feel stymied in their MBA application by the fact that they "have not led anything of note." Remember that if you are MBA-entry age, you are at the stage of life where, no matter how good your leadership skills are, they are still being formed. Most of your leading experience is still in front of you. This makes it appropriate for you to present your leadership skills as a work in progress (and in need of MBA training). Many who are accepted to top programs will not have managed scores of people or taken responsibility for large-scale projects. In your attempt to outgun the competition, try not to fall into the trap of claiming you are a seasoned leader with rafts of senior experience. You will just destroy your credibility unless you can back up what you say. Good solid evidence of leadership *potential* is all they expect.

5. How to flunk this essay

You will mess up this essay if:

- Your leadership event is weak, suggesting you don't have any significant leadership experience.

- You mix up leadership events with achievement events or ethical dilemmas.
- Your story is short on detail, interest, and relevance.
- You hype the amount and extent of your leadership experience.
- Your analysis is vacuous and does not provide insight into you or your leadership attributes.
- You do not show understanding of your own leadership style.
- You fail to develop or share your insights into the nature of leadership.

ARCHETYPE 5: DIVERSITY-CONTRIBUTION-UNIQUENESS

1. Examples

One of the Rotman School's underlying principles is the value of one; this reflects the belief that each member of the Rotman community has unique needs and talents. What are your greatest talents and/or abilities and how would each enhance the experience of your classmates? (Rotman-Toronto)

Assume you are evaluating your application from the perspective of a student member of the Kellogg Admissions Committee. Why would your peers select you to become a member of the Kellogg community? (Kellogg-Northwestern)

Tuck seeks candidates of various backgrounds who can bring new perspectives to our community. How will your unique personal history, values, and/or life experiences contribute to the culture at Tuck? (Tuck-Dartmouth)

How do you anticipate making your mark on the Stern community? Be specific about the roles you will take on and the impact you hope to achieve. (NYU-Stern)

2. Recognition keywords

Contribution, cross-cultural, diversity, experience, knowledge, range, skill, enrich, talent, expertise, impact, proficiency, background, distinctive, attributes, variety, augment, enhance, develop, unique.

3. The underlying issue

Like the "why an MBA" question, this is a question that is asked every time in one form or another—and if it isn't, you should fit the answer into one of your other essays anyway. The committee wants to know what in your background, ability, experience, or training sets you apart and will be uniquely valuable to your cohort and the program in general. Remember, it is a big part of the admissions committee's job to make sure the incoming class is stuffed (and balanced) with diverse, interesting, uniquely talented people. Schools seek diversity because much of MBA learning is peer-to-peer, and candidates with diverse and extraordinary experience have more to give to their peers and can even potentially leave the school better than it was before they arrived.

Various other essays are designed to see if you fit the MBA mold. The test of this essay is whether you can separate yourself from the crowd and get away from being the typical candidate. This one is the talent show. You don't have to be better than anyone else in the show, but you do have to enter with a special skill, talent, or base of experience that is exclusive. You have to find something in your profile that sets you apart. Put it this way: in various other essays and via file data applicants provide reasons for Adcom *not to reject them*; covering all the bases, saying the right things. But doing this is still falling short of giving Adcom a compelling, positive reason to say "yes." In this essay they look for this reason. Among the kinds of things that people talk about in the context of their diversity-contribution are:

- international experience: growing up abroad, or significant travel or foreign work experience and languages;
- unique work experience, or experience in unique industries, including benefiting from unusual training;
- being a member of a minority group: being black, American Indian, or being disabled, gay, or otherwise non-mainstream;
- special abilities and talents: being an occasional baritone with the Austrian National Opera, for example;
- having benefited from a special or unique vantage point on the world—having been on Tony Blair's staff, for example, or having worked in promotions for the Brazilian national soccer team.

These are just example categories. There are almost no rules for what you can bring to the talent contest—only you can know what you have to offer that nobody else does. Often your extramural activities will point the way to your unique attributes.

It's nice to underscore your uniqueness with a certain level of achievement, but achievement is not the primary consideration here. If you merely trained to swim the English Channel, or were a teen counselor in a Japanese orphanage, or grew up on the Columbia movie lot, or spent a month in silent meditation in an ashram, this could be enough. It doesn't always matter that you completed the swim. There are plenty of times in an MBA application where competitive achievement counts, but here the bias is towards the *experience* itself—as long as you can show why the experience adds value to the complex tapestry of interdependent learning at business school.

Even though the experience is more important here than the success, the burden of proof remains important. If you claim you danced in the Hong Kong Youth Ballet, for example, the committee would expect (and be interested in) some details. If you have been to the Amundsen–Scott South Pole Research Station, some first-hand experience would be called for in your account.

Managing an apparent lack of distinctiveness

Similar to an apparent lack of leadership experience, applicants often feel cornered by a lack of stand-out distinctiveness in their profile. "I haven't done anything that special," they will lament. "I have not published a book; never hot-air ballooned over the Atlantic; not pulled anyone from a burning car . . ." The following is a thought exercise for discovering your unique contribution: Imagine you are accepted to your dream school. On your first day there you bump into the head of the admissions who knows exactly who you are, and she says: "From the moment we realized that you would bring _____ (background, experience, talent, other addition) to the school this year, wow, you were in!" Fill in the blank.

If nothing jumps out at you, consider that your unique attribute may be in the *combination* of elements that are otherwise unremarkable. Perhaps you are a Palestinian partner in an Israeli-funded IT start-up. Maybe you are a Major in Cognitive Psychology who has successfully taken these principles into currency trading. In other words, is there some unlikely combination of factors that will make you unique and memorable?

It is of course great if you embody a difference, or have had a unique experience, or done something memorable that few, if anybody else, in the applicant cohort will have done. But there are two types of specialness. Specialness of what you have experienced AND specialness of *who you are*. Not everyone has the first type in their bag, but everyone can have the second. Here are examples of the second type:

- Distinctiveness of who you are and what exactly you do (or have done.) This may sound obvious but you would be amazed how much distinctiveness is to be had by drilling down to specifics of your life. If you say "I'm a researcher in a lab," you have no differentiation at all, but if you say "I'm a materials science researcher with four years lab experience working on next-generation materials at the Adidas lab in Christchurch New Zealand," you are suddenly unique.

- Distinctiveness of your insight, self-reflection, and self-understanding. Unfortunately (but fortunately for you, dear reader), it appears these days that it takes a special person to be willing to reflect on their path, their roles, their identity, their motivations. But this is exactly what Adcom wants of you. That's why they ask complex, motivational questions. The quality of genuine self-reflection is so unique among 20-something-year-olds (and so highly correlated with real leadership ability) that if you can do it right, you'll be special *just for this*. Note: doing it right means being open and honest, but also circumspect, professional, to-the-point, and focused on the essay question using practical examples and stories. It does not mean wallowing self-indulgently as if your essays were for the Agony Aunt magazine column or your personal diary.

- Specialness of communication. Writing and (in the interview) speaking are the basis of your interaction with Adcom. Words are your tools. You do not need to be a fancy creative writing major to write a wonderful MBA admissions essay, but there are basic tools of storytelling and essay building that make a piece of text stand out. Be aware how much turgid, timid, repetitive prose your Adcom reader has to wade through. Getting your point across in a bright, clear, and organized way will make you stand out.

- Specialness of direction and goals. You can't change your past. You should present it in the best light, but for better or worse, it's set. Your future is ahead of you. It can be anything—you can make any claim, within reason. It is a "free hit" in the sense that you are pretty much invited to distinguish yourself from the crowd through the extent of your ambition, and the relevance, interest, and worthiness of your career path.

On standing out and fitting in

Applicants are often so desperate to make the "right" impression that they fear doing anything that would make themselves stand out, and scrub anything from their file that smacks of difference. Don't be scared to be different and be yourself and to make the admissions officer think: "Huh!! I've got to meet this one." Unusual people with interesting pasts get in because they make the class more fun and enriching for all.

On the other hand, business school is a serious place and there are limits to how eccentrically you can play your hand. Certainly the recruitment office won't like it. These limits largely depend on what the rest of your file looks like and where you are applying to. If you are a banking lifer at 28, you have to do something—anything—to make a colorful splash in your essays. But if you're the guy on Venice Beach who made an untaxed fortune renting kite-boards and selling joints, you should run an altogether more conservative application.

4. How to tackle it

This essay is one where candidates are highly susceptible to the tendency to throw everything at the committee in the hope that something sticks. Try not to do this. It's fine to sketch out the spread of your interests—then pick one or one cluster. A standard template for this essay is:

  a. Claiming an interesting and unique aspect, or combination of aspects.
  b. Proving that you have it/them.
  c. Showing why it is relevant and beneficial to the group and the school.
  d. Showing what else it says about you and making links to your themes.

This essay doesn't always call directly for a story, but you should write one if you can, to bring your unique element to life. In fact, one of the tests of whether your uniqueness is valuable and enriching to others is whether you can immediately think of some interesting or enlightening stories to tell about it. As you move from story to analysis, you should show why the unique attribute you offer the school sheds light on you as a person and your potential to succeed at school and in life.

The relevance and benefit of your exclusive contribution to the class must be spelled out clearly. It may be evident to you that being physically disabled, or French-speaking, or the stepdaughter of Robert de Niro makes you different and valuable—but the test is whether you can convince the committee this is valuable to the learning experience of your classmates and/or to the faculty. Also, be as specific as you can. You can limply say that your Communist Romanian childhood gives you insight into "economic, social, and cultural differences," or you can more specifically point out how your many summers at socialist teenage camps will allow you to offer some genuine insight into European labor politics in your human resources classes.

5. How to flunk this essay

You will mess up this essay if:

- You fail to differentiate yourself—your exclusive offering is something others offer too.
- Your diversity attributes and experiences are trivial or not apparently relevant to the business school environment.
- You do not focus your contribution. You give Adcom too much disparate information and make them guess.
- You play it too safe. You profile doesn't have a memorable angle.
- Your proposed contribution is not valuable to your peers or the school, or you fail to explain how it is valuable or to whom.
- You fail to connect your unique attribute(s) and the circumstances of their acquisition to the rest of your file. You don't use them to enlighten the reader about you.

ARCHETYPE 6: ETHICS AND VALUES

1. Examples

Describe a time in which your ethics were challenged. How did you deal with the situation and what did you learn from it? (Carnegie Mellon)

Tell us about a time you made a difficult decision. (HBS)

Kenan-Flagler has five core values: excellence, leadership, integrity, community, and teamwork. If you could add one value what would it be and why? Be sure to explain how you have lived this value. (Kenan-Flagler)

2. Recognition keywords

Morals, ethics, values, principles, standards, ideals, code of conduct, credo, beliefs, philosophy, personal guidelines, integrity, dilemma, decision.

3. The underlying issue

Famously, values are back. Suddenly, after Enron, Anderson Consulting, the "credit crunch," and various other serious breaches of public faith, public attention is squarely on business ethics and long-term sustainability of decisions, and business is clamoring to show its good side. Therefore, MBA programs and MBA Admissions follow suit, and therefore so should you. Be sure that business schools will be looking harder than ever for people who will stand up to ethical tests through their careers. Rightly or wrongly MBA programs have take heavy criticism for turning out dubiously self-enriching managers, and MBA Adcoms have taken plenty of stick too for filling classes with greedy self-profiteers, and so are under more pressure than ever to pick a better kind of person.

The tricky thing about the ethics essay is that everyone knows what good values are and everyone claims ownership of them. And yet the world is full of scheming, self-serving scoundrels in both large and small enterprises. The public scandals are the top snowflakes on the tip of the iceberg. So, writing a nice essay that shakes its head at known elements of business and personal immorality— stealing, cheating, falsifications, payoffs, etc.—while professing allegiance to fair play, good governance, honest dealings, and hard-working self-reliance, is . . . perfectly worthless. Talk is cheap. And it certainly won't separate you from the crowd in this essay. One or all of four things will impress, however:

- Demonstrating some thinking towards your own, unique set of values. Which bits of the values galaxy are your guiding lights and why, and how did you come to this position?
- Showing evidence of how your commitment to your values—however you define them—has been unwavering in the face of temptation, persuasion, or overwhelming self-interest.
- Showing an advanced sensitivity to ethical concerns in areas where others might not see them; for example, how you pushed for the cleaning ladies to be allowed to put their kids in the swanky new daycare center created as a perk for the professional parents at your workplace.
- Providing evidence as to what you have done that serves people other than yourself: evidence that you have volunteered, mentored, or contributed to worthy causes.

The MBA Oath

In the wake of the credit crunch there is even now an "MBA Oath," the brainchild of HBS students in 2009, which has been "pledged" by current and graduating MBAs from most major institutions.[1] It's unclear how long this will last, but it is high on everyone's agenda at the time of writing. At a minimum it is important for MBA applicants to endorse this framework, or not seem to run foul of it.

Some of the Oath is just the usual good-citizen catechism: serving the greater good, demonstrating integrity, pursuing work in an ethical manner, balancing interests of shareholders, co-workers, customers and the society (triple or quad-ruple bottom line), not advancing one's own narrow ambitions, upholding the law, reporting accurately, and being accountable. Broadly, the Oath also sets these ethical goals:

- bringing people and resources together to create value no single individual can create alone;
- creating value for society (not just self or company);
- developing other managers under your supervision;
- appreciating the far-reaching and long-term consequences of decisions, and acting accordingly;
- pursuing sustainable economic, social, and environmental prosperity (not just fast or big prosperity);
- distributing benefits of prosperity worldwide.

This is a good starter list of ethical attributes that many applicants will miss, but which provide subtlety and differentiation for applicants who understand them, and who can find evidence of them in their personal and professional history.

Ethical challenges vs. ethical dilemmas vs. non-ethical dilemmas

The definition of ethics—for the purpose of MBA applications—is less complicated than it seems: it's about doing the right thing even when nobody is looking. But bear in mind the difference between a challenge and a dilemma. An ethical *challenge* is something like the time colleagues asked you to withhold information from a partner or client; or the time when you discovered the production manager double-invoicing; or when you found out that your boss was spending company money on call girls. These are ethical challenges not *dilemmas* because the lack of ethics is clear and all that remains is the challenge of how best to act on your ethics (most often, how to manage the potential career fall-out that might come if you blow the whistle).

Equivalently, the ethical part of an ethical dilemma implies that the dilemma is more than just a difficult decision: if you have an agonizing choice between staying at work late to finish a project and going on a hot date, it is just an ordinary, non-ethical dilemma. An ethical dilemma, therefore, is where there are ethical issues at stake and *no clear right or wrong answer exists*. As with the euthanasia dilemma or the abortion dilemma, an ethical dilemma will be one where there will be strong arguments on both sides and both choices are bitter-sweet.

Ethical dilemmas in the workplace may, for example, take the form of having to fire someone who is underperforming but who is also a sole breadwinner. Or having to decide whether to use knowledge gained in confidence in a salary negotiation. Or having to decide how much of your work to share with colleagues—benefiting the client but diluting your claim to promotion. The decisions you make in these gray areas speak volumes about your character, morality, and values. Draw out the implications for the admissions committee. There's a chance that Adcom is not going to enforce the distinction between challenge and dilemma, but it's better that you are aware of it.

The personal basis of your ethics

As you do this you should, depending on the question, outline the formal basis of your ethical framework. What are the principles you live by? What would you stand up for, no matter what the consequences? What is the core of your personal code that influences the way you see your choices at work and in life? What might this mean for you as a future manager? For example, you may be an out-and-out meritocrat: you believe in everyone getting a fair start in life, and then each to his own. Or you may be a hard-core environmentalist, and you put the planet first no matter what (and this is why you reported your ex-company's fouling of virgin forest in Argentina to the authorities).

Not being the snitch

Many ethical dilemma essays are of the following type: "Something happened at work that raised my ethical concerns, and I resolved the situation by blowing the whistle." That can work. But if the dilemma was not significant and you still made a royal fuss, you could come across as whining, narrow-minded, or stubborn, and put a question mark against your team spirit and loyalty. Don't assume that your personal moral scale is or should be the workplace standard. Be ready for and respectful of cultural and personal differences. You will routinely be faced with differences of opinion and different adherence to ethics among the diverse set of people you work with. In almost all circumstances your maturity will be shown in your flexibility, humor, and good public relations in the face of such differences.

It's okay to be young and idealistic in this question: the committee expects it. But while taking the hardest line on moral failings may sound good, it can also sound like you haven't lived in the real world much. Business is not a Sunday school picnic. Don't be facile. Don't underestimate the difficulty of being ethical, particularly under competitive conditions where big promotions, adoration, fame and fortune come to those who win. Rather than claim to be a saint, say that you are human but you have an unwavering commitment to certain key beliefs.

4. How to tackle it

This essay also calls for a story followed by analysis. As before, the admissions committee is sure to be less interested in the dilemma itself than in the way you handled it, and the inferences you draw out about yourself. The essential pieces of the essay are:

   a.   Telling the story.
   b.   Processing the dilemma and decision.
   c.   Developing the learning and insight.
   d.   Thoughts on your ethical framework.

Move quickly through the story while providing enough detail for the event to be sharp and interesting. Don't forget to say something about the history or the organizational pressures and responsibilities that led up to the event and made the dilemma juicy. Then process your understanding of the dilemma, the choices you had, and the merits of going one way or the other. Say why you did what you did and whether it worked out, and if it didn't, how you might tackle the same situation now.

As always, the question is not ultimately about ethics, it is about you. Provide some evidence that the situation has led you to self-examination: why this dilemma was important to you, what in your make-up caused you to take a stand on this particular issue, what experiences in your personal or professional past might have created the basis for your stand, and what experiences bear out your holding firm on this issue. Why was the dilemma valuable as a growth experience? Why is your response instructive in shedding light on you as a person and how you might act in the future?

5. How to flunk this essay

You will mess up this essay if:

- Your challenge or dilemma event is weak.
- You mix up ethical dilemmas with other types of dilemmas.
- You claim to be ethical, but provide no evidence of your values in action.
- Your self-analysis is insufficient or not self-illuminating. You fail to develop or share insight into yourself or your guiding moral principles.
- You don't demonstrate growth towards the development of your own set of values.
- You appear as the company gossip.
- You underestimate the difficulties of being ethical.

ARCHETYPE 7: TEAMWORK-GROUPWORK

1. Examples

Please describe your experience of working in and leading teams, either in your professional or personal life. Include any specific challenges you have faced. Given this experience, what role do you think you will play in your first year study group? (LBS)

Please describe a time when you coached, trained, or mentored a person or group. (MIT-Sloan)

Please provide an example of a team failure of which you've been a part. If given a second chance, what would you do differently? (Columbia)

2. Recognition keywords

Team, group, relationship, collaborate, work together, member, partnership, cooperate, association, affiliation, mentor.

3. The underlying issue

The teamwork essay is about the way you interact with other people and manage yourself in groups. No matter what you do in your future business career, you will do it largely in groups. Your team skills are therefore highly relevant to your future success. They are also relevant to your ability to function at b-school, as most schools require intensive team projects and even team-based exams. Like your quantitative skills and your English skills, your team skills have to be good *on entry* to business school.

The challenge of the team essay resembles that of the ethics essay, in that everyone claims to be a "good team player," but we all know many who are manifestly the opposite. Therefore, the attention of the committee is once again on the evidence. Do you have solid experience doing serious projects collaboratively? Can you show a sophisticated understanding of group processes? Does your record show your ability to master interpersonal communication? What evidence shows you can promote group goodwill, balance competing priorities, foster multi-stakeholder solutions, and integrate your preferences and skill-sets with those of others in sorting out tasks and timelines? If you can't show some of this, you are just another Joe who has learned to mouth the right touchy-feely phrases.

Exercise

If you are unclear what your team profile is, do some elementary behavioral testing. You may, for example, take the Belbin assessment, which specifically analyses team role profiles, or any one of the more general personality assessments such as the Myers—Briggs, Neo 5-factor, or Omni, among a host of others. You don't need to make any life choices based on these instruments, but they should give you significant material to chew on in this essay. If you can say, "According to my Belbin team profile, I am a 'monitor-evaluator' and this has the following implications for how I work in teams . . .," your team essay will contain specific, unusually well-researched and documented information about you and will therefore be a better essay. Quick non-professional but good enough versions of many of these tests are available for free online.

Team vs. leadership

The team essay also overlaps with the leadership essay in that both involve your relationship with groups. But where the leadership essay stresses your ability to motivate or enhance the contributions of others, the team essay is primarily looking for the complementary set of team skills: respecting differences, fostering goodwill, deflecting conflict, tolerating, accommodating, and compromising. In this essay, it is not a crime to show that you know when to ease off and let someone else lead while you play a support role, particularly in a field where you are a non-expert.

A note about sports

Talking teams brings up the question of sports. And the answer is, yes you can talk about sports in your essays *so long as* you don't talk about season averages, topspin, point spreads, Manchester United's goalkeeper, or any other factual or technical data. But, it is always fine to talk about competition, adversity, personal battles, team struggles, fears, performance pressure, team bonding, teammate reliance, split-second decisions, triumphs, overcoming odds, disappointment—and how these experiences have made you or changed you. So get off the fanzine stuff and onto the topic in MBA admissions, which is once and for always: you. What is your specific and personal experience of the passions, emotions, insights, and personal and communal growth that make team sports great?

4. How to tackle it

Choosing a teamwork experience story seems simple enough, but take care with it. It will work better to have a story where team synergies applied—where the team worked to be more than the sum of its parts—and you can elaborate on the processes that created this happy outcome. As ever, pick stories that reinforce your themes. If you are positioning yourself as a future Asian private equity dealmaker, don't pick a team story from your Rutgers college dorm. Pick one from your Ernst & Young days in Taiwan. Then show how teamwork leads to self-insight: why the team experience you mention is indicative of you, why it demonstrates your skills, how it illuminates you as a person, and what it suggests about you as a team member in future situations. If your story was a watershed event in your approach to teamwork, say why.

Show also that you appreciate how tough a taskmaster real teamwork actually is—how extraordinarily difficult it is to get teams to be functional and productive, and how much you still have to learn about doing this. If you think teams are easy to be in, you're not ready for a management position.

Your analysis should also include an understanding of your own role in teams. Teams need a balance of different types—evaluators, drivers, facilitators, conflict managers, detail freaks, etc.,—so there are no rights and wrongs to being any one. But you should be able to say which role you normally play in groups and what your style of intra-team interaction is. A detailed appreciation of your team-player profile will take you beyond the banality that applicants come up with all the time in this essay: "I'm a good team player."

5. How to flunk this essay

You will mess up this essay if:

- You don't show significant team experience.
- You appear to lack genuine teamwork instincts or you don't understand what they are.
- Your teamwork story lacks detail and interest, or is not followed by meaningful analysis.
- You fail to develop or share insight into your specific role in teams and the strengths and weaknesses of this role. You can't identify anything you do in a team other than "strongly lead."
- You don't provide detail or evidence of the good teamwork skills you claim.
- You don't show a sophisticated approach to team dynamics.
- You underestimate the difficulties and commitment team interactions involve.

12 The MBA essay question archetypes (part 3)

This chapter closes the section on MBA essay archetypes by looking at the final three types (Key influences, Personal inquiry, Innovation) and common auxiliary questions.

ARCHETYPE 8: KEY INFLUENCES AND FORMATIVE EXPERIENCES

1. Examples

Please tell us about yourself and your background. Include information about your family, where you grew up, your interests, and any other people or experiences that have influenced you. (Haas-Berkeley)

Which recent development, world event or book has most influenced your thinking and why? (Oxford)

Suppose you had to choose two people—people alive now or people from another era—to travel with you on a cross-country automobile trip. Who would you choose and why? What would you hope to learn from them? (NUS-Singapore)

2. Recognition keywords

Influence, background, memory, advisor, mentor, role model, counselor, guide, inspiration, impact, impression, effect, shape, pastime, development, activity, formative.

3. The underlying issue

If you have read any biography or autobiography, you will know that one of the key ways to get insight into a person is to find out who among parents, mentors, and advisors were the defining influences, or what defining formative experiences or activities have been. In this question archetype, Adcom employs the same technique. They want to learn more about you by understanding the forces that have shaped you and continue to shape you. What you know is interesting to Adcom, but how you learned it and who you learned it from consolidates their understanding. They are asking, "Where are you coming from?"

There are two types of mentoring influence: those where you had no say in the matter, for example, your parents, and those later in life which you chose. Early influences are significant because of their enormous formative power. Later influences are significant because, among other things, they show your choices at work. Who you choose to mentor you says a lot about the kind of person you are, and are aiming to become. In addition to wanting to understand your influences, Adcom wants to see your ability to form and sustain mentor relationships. If you can form lasting relationships with senior advisors and protectors, you are a much better bet for big career success. Mentors will groom you for big things, promote you when you are ready, and help watch your back when the blame-pack goes hunting.

Strong influence can come in inanimate forms as well. If you have a fundamental shaping experience or sources of inspiration and guidance—if you are a performing pianist, or did your Peace Corps service on a remote Pacific island, or have rebuilt your life in the army—these are all strong life influences. The committee wants to know about them, particularly if you can say how they will positively affect you in your chosen management career.

4. How to tackle it

Remember, the essay is not about the mentor, or a shaping experience *per se*, it is about you, so you have to be able to say how and why this relationship or experience is important to you and how it advances your candidacy. The familiar questions of self-analysis apply: Why is he a role model for you? Which of her qualities resonate with you? How has the experience changed or improved you as a candidate? How has a formative activity promoted your self-examination and self-learning, or led to an outcome you would not otherwise have achieved? Why is the activity or experience meaningful? How does it nourish you? What would not be there in you if you hadn't "been there and done that"? How has it changed your worldview? In other words, explain yourself through explaining why you chose your major life influences and what it has done for you. And why this is relevant to your claim on a place at business school.

The essential elements of this essay are:

a. an anecdote which points to the nature of the mentor (or other influence) and the nature of the relationship (or experience);
b. analysis, including key qualities of the mentor (or influence);
c. you in action, embodying the principles that you have been influenced towards;
d. why this adds value to your candidacy.

The question may not directly ask for it, but as usual it is better to go with a story: find an anecdote that epitomizes your mentor or your relationship with the mentor. Pick a moment. Where were you, what were the circumstances, what did you say, what did she say? Or perhaps you were not directly involved in the anecdote—maybe you just saw your mentor in action and soaked up the lessons. What happened? Don't say he was incredible, wise and motivating. Say why. Similarly, if you go with an activity type of formative influence, if you can put the activity or experience into a story, you will bring it to life.

The essay should then return the focus to you, using the learning and influence you have gained from the world as you make your way in the world. Give specific examples of you-in-action, demonstrating how you have integrated the mentoring wisdom into your game. Perhaps you have even gone further and adjusted and tweaked your formative teaching to suit you? How?

Choosing the mentor or formative experience

As always, your choices should be led by your value message and what you want to tell Adcom. There is little point in choosing your software-coding mentor at work, or the University of Cambridge Young Scientists club, or the books of C.K. Prahalad as formative in your life if this doesn't allow you to take your application message forward. Choose formative people or experiences that allow you to develop your themes and value points. As we have seen before in choosing stories and events, the choice of mentor or influence is less important than the reasons for the choice. Adcom is less concerned with who or what you pick than why you pick it. Having said that, when thinking of mentors specifically, there are still clear choices to avoid:

- Don't choose someone from professional sports, the movies, or celebrity culture—even if they really have had a great influence on your life. There's no real relationship, so it doesn't count. And it looks like you spend your life on the sofa, or reading gossip magazines, and that is not the image you want to present.
- Don't just choose the most senior person you know. You will trigger the questions: How well do you know this person? How well do they know you? How much mentoring really goes on? If you cannot show evidence of a real ongoing relationship, it will look like you are desperate to impress. (But sometimes it is justified. On my own GMAT prep course, there was a woman who was on Hillary Clinton's staff in Washington, DC—it was absolutely appropriate for her to cite Hillary as a mentor.)
- Generally, you should avoid picking academic mentors, for the same reason you avoid using them as recommenders. Business schools would much rather you are mentored by your VP at Hewlett Packard than by your bearded, tweedy, college professor. Don't ring their alarm bells.

Avoiding junior mindset

You are the junior in your relationship with your mentor and that is normal. But don't juniorize yourself more than necessary. You learned good stuff from someone ahead of you in life or in your field, that's all. Try to keep it factual and objective, and incorporate a level head and balanced criticisms. If you come across as dizzy and star-struck, you might get into cheerleading school but you won't get into business school.

5. How to flunk this essay

You will mess up this essay if:

- You don't show mentorship experience or an understanding of the dynamics of such a relationship.
- You choose your influence badly: someone you don't know well, or who doesn't fit with the thrust of your application message.
- You don't have an insightful anecdote about your mentor or formative experience, or yourself in relationship with such. You don't give examples and details.
- You develop the analysis of your key influence but not of yourself. You fail to show how your influence has changed you and facilitated your development.
- You don't show why what you have learned is relevant to your application or the cohort you want to be a part of.
- You appear star-struck and lack critical judgment of your influence or mentor.

ARCHETYPE 9: DIRECT PERSONAL INQUIRY (WHO ARE YOU?)

1. Examples

What matters most to you, and why? (Stanford)

What is something people will find surprising about you? (UCLA-Anderson)

Tell us something about yourself that we would not find on your resume. (Queens)

How would you like to be remembered? (Cambridge-Judge)

If you had the opportunity, what would you ask the president or leader of your country, and why? (Instituto de Empresa)

2. Recognition

This essay can come in many forms and is recognizable by its direct examination of your character, biography, preferences, passions, and non-work activities; that is, its blunt intrusion into your personal space—often under the guise of asking you to say what other people would say about you. It sometimes asks for a creative format, such as writing the first page of your autobiography, or a letter to the incoming class, and so on. Visual format essays such as PowerPoint shows or multimedia, or other alternative submissions are part of this archetype, although they often also are twinned with the Creativity–Innovation archetype (see archetype 10 on p. 136).

3. The underlying issue

All essays are made better by making them more personal, but in this one the admissions committee is telling you that personal revelation is compulsory. This essay archetype exists due to the general frustration of admissions committees that, no matter how much they ask, in so many ways, for the real person behind the application mask to come forward, they often still don't get it. They get guarded, impersonal, generic, diplomatic statements. So they resort to bald personal inquisition.

The trick, of course, is to take the committee on a real journey of personal exploration and revelation, while staying within your themes and on message, and not losing a strategic focus as to what Adcom will infer from what you choose to talk about. No matter how personal you get, the direction you go in should reinforce the thrust of your application message.

The essay question often targets your hobbies and extracurricular activities, and also sometimes comes close to your "contribution" essay—allowing you to show additional forms of personal interest, diversity, and potential contribution to the class. If you don't get a "contribution" essay in the set, you should use this essay as your primary statement of uniqueness and value-add diversity.

Part of what is at stake in this question is your ability and commitment to your non-professional life. The school is not interested in workaholics. They want balanced people with plenty of attributes and interests that make them more interesting. They won't mind what your non-work passion is, but they will care that you have at least one serious one. (Your non-professional project cannot be a love interest—that's assumed—but it can be children.)

4. How to tackle it

Personal questions are intrinsically uncomfortable. Either you can deal with the discomfort by hoping it will go away and no-one will notice if you offer safe statements with some window-dressing, or you can bite the bullet and provide a real window into you. Guess which strategy works best? Trust the fact that your application is confidential to all outside the admissions office and get on with it. Generally, if you think your answer to this essay is *too* revealing, it is probably about right. On the other hand, it should not be so personal as to leave the reader squirming and uncomfortable.

Of course, personal does not necessarily mean "heavy." Revealing who you are just means sharing something genuine. Drop the mask. Be real. Be engaging. Share your feelings and don't be stiff. Show your humor, and that you're interesting to be around. Your response to this essay must, above all, be unique to you and be filled with details and observations that are intrinsically yours, showing special insight into you and the personal history that has made you "you."

This essay is one where applicants often give the committee too much information and leave them to sift through it. It's fine to start by laying out the spread of your non-professional life and interests, but the key task is to find an angle to your personal life that best represents you, and to focus on it. If you focus your personal statement around an activity, you must take the reader to your passion for it. Even if the admissions officer would never, himself, consider joining an amateur electronics club, for example, your presentation should make it clear how obviously addictively great it is, and why it is an outlet for you and what that implies about you.

The committee will not care which extramural passion you present. As with all your essays, the "why" questions are the important ones: Why is it important to you? How has it influenced your perspective or your choices? How has it changed you or grown you? How does it relate to your wish to go to business school? Why should Adcom consider it important to your application?

Integrating the personal and professional

The most effective essays in the personal category are the ones that show an integrated, cohesive whole across professional and personal life—how the one feeds the other. If your themes stretch from work into leisure, and integrate the two, then you really start to come across clearly and strongly. For example, if in other essays you are proposing a career in media management, you could use this essay to share your passion for 1940–1950s radio-theater nostalgia, saying how you have a vast collection of tapes, how you formed (leadership) a West Coast radio theater society and allied website, how and why all this is personally meaningful to you. You therefore deepen your media theme, show how it is a passion as well as a profession, and thereby show a multifaceted but integrated life.

5. How to flunk this essay

You will mess up this essay if:

- You don't respond personally to a personal challenge. Your response is too generic and safe.
- You don't say enough to differentiate yourself or raise interest about you.
- You don't demonstrate a real passion for the non-professional interests you have.
- You don't appear to understand yourself at a personal level. You fail to develop insights about yourself or share them with the reader.
- You don't make the connection between your personal attributes and the attributes demanded by business school or business life.
- You present a jumble of personal facts and interests, without focus.
- There is little or no link between your personal interests and the rest of your application message.

ARCHETYPE 10: CREATIVITY AND INNOVATION

1. Examples

At Haas, we value innovation and creativity. Describe a time when you created positive change in a group or an organization. (Haas-Berkeley)

Comment on why innovation is critical to success. (Schulich-York)

Please describe a time when you went beyond what was defined, expected, established, or popular. (MIT-Sloan)

2. Recognition keywords

Transform, adapt, change, innovate, new situation, original, imagination, inspiration, ingenuity, inventive, creative, resourceful, vision, advance, improve, pioneer, expected.

Additionally, this essay archetype is also recognizable by an alternative or multi-media format request.

3. The underlying issue

The business world is now so geared to rapid transformation in response to new technologies, shifting markets, demographic change, globalization, and changing social values that probably the clearest test of leaders and managers today is their ability to deal with change. The spoils of corporate war go to those who most clearly see the shifting sands and are the savviest in adapting and renewing their enterprises. Creativity, once banished to the "ladies in marketing," is now front and center as a management skill.

At the same time, careers are not what they were and job security is not what it was. Among the tests that you as a business professional will face in the future is career change: moving to a new part of an organization, or a different organization, or a new industry, or all of the above on the other side of the world! Your ability to adapt, learn, and creatively manage your career under inconstant conditions will be rigorously tested. Schools want to know that you have the ability to survive and thrive in an atmosphere of change. They want to see evidence of your innovation and creativity. By the way, using the term "out-of-the-box" is now a marker of dullness of mind, not innovativeness or creativity.

Career innovation and renovation

Show, also, that you are part of the breed of "new" managers who expect situational and career change, and who know how to function in contingent, project-based work situations. If you appear to cast yourself in a professional future where you work your whole life at Acme Inc., steadily inching your way towards the corner office, you will appear mentally unprepared for the twenty-first century. On the other hand, the committee is also looking for your management maturity and stability, so take care not to fall head first into "new paradigm-itis." There are good things about change, but lots of mistakes are made. Successful management in times of change often requires a reasonable degree of conservatism, and sometimes just a stolid maintenance of the status quo. Sounding like a *Wired* groupie won't advance your cause much.

Talking about technology

Many students come to business school knowing a vast amount about their techno-logical field. Often they do an MBA to generalize their technical specialty, learn something about leadership, and prepare themselves for senior management. A question on change and innovation may open up a window to their technical specialty and, in the bid to impress with their knowledge, they may suddenly begin talking shop to the admissions officer. The reader is vastly more interested in personal insight than in any technical background. It is fine to give the impression that you are on top of your field and that you will lead, or at least manage, the future in your field. But keep the focus on you and the jargon to a minimum.

4. How to tackle it

This essay usually calls for the now-familiar format—the anecdote followed by implications. Once again you should pick an anecdote that reinforces your overall positioning. As this essay often conveniently takes you close to questions of leadership (it's a leader's job to innovate and adapt), try to pick a story that also casts you in the role of leader.

In analyzing the implications of your story, place special emphasis on your ability to learn: it is the key to adapting to new situations. Also explain the professional or personal growth an innovation has pushed you towards. What self-examination or self-learning has it provoked? How has it helped you gain experience, or become a better manager or leader, or how else has it changed you? What does this say about your abilities or your preferences in situations of change?

The audio or visual project

It has become quite fashionable for schools to ask for "non-verbal" essays, or to give a audio or visual presentation option on essays. This included the Chicago-Booth PowerPoint essay, the UCLA-Anderson audio essay option, and NYU-Stern's "Personal Expression" essay. The trend to this type of essay will grow for many reasons: first, admissions staff love them—they are more fun to review. Second, they give a greater sense of personality—who Adcom is really dealing with. Third, essays are a test of communications skills, and alternative essays test non-writing communications abilities. Further, they showcase talent and demonstrate the key skills of creativity and innovation. All to say that as school get better at managing files (sharing them around all those who need to see them), this aspect of essays is set to grow.

If given the option of audio or video—take it! Ducking it is a red flag as to you having no creative talent, no personality, or no sense of humor. In one sense the essay gives you a free rein as you are allowed to do (almost) anything. But remember that in these essays the basic principle of value delivery as described in previous sections remains valid: you still work off your profiling. You decide what it is you want to say about yourself, what your overall application platform is. Then get your "creative project" essay to say the parts of this that are most suitable to it, working in harmony with the rest of your more conventional essay set.

Managing images—static or moving—calls for particular skills. If this is not something you do on a daily basis, take a bit of time to consider a presentation that you find impactful from a visual point of view. Advertising is a good source for this. Gray out the text or turn down the audio if you have to, to focus just on the visual technique. Consider the placement or sequence of images. Consider the amount of, size of, and placement of text if there is any. Design is its own universe and poor layout will ruin any message. Just as you are not expected to be a Shakespeare in your essays, you are not expected to be a Renoir in your management of space and color, or a professional sound engineer in your word–music mixing. You just have to show adequate skill and attention to core principles of impactful layout and presentation in the medium you are in. If you present a visual or audio handin that is truly baby work, it will suggest little visual literacy and low capacity for development of your creative and innovative side in business in general.

5. How to flunk this essay

You will mess up this essay if:

- You don't appear to be innovative in mindset.
- You don't demonstrate a willingness to deal with change in organizations and in your life, and the lifelong learning this implies.
- Your analysis does not further the reader's understanding of you. You fail to develop or share insight into your style of dealing with change.
- You appear young and naïve in response to change. You don't balance a pro-change orientation with a nod to the classic lessons and practices of management.
- You talk about the changing world, new technologies, and innovative opportunities without integrating this into who you are and why this is relevant to you and your career.
- You fail a basic test of visual or audio literacy and communication skills, when dealing with an alternative-format essay.

Other common essay types

These ten essay question archetypes above will allow you to recognize most of the essays you are likely to be presented with. You should also be ready for four other common essay question types: community service, self-review, how have you learned about us, and the optional essay. Community service doesn't often come up directly but is heavily implied under the surface in many questions. The others are easily recognizable, and always come up in more or less the same way.

THE COMMUNITY INVOLVEMENT/SERVICE ESSAY

It is debatable whether a community service profile will make you better at business school or better in your career, but it is nevertheless very common for schools to want to know about your contribution to social causes or involvement with public issues. There is an undisguised moralistic framework being applied: you are a better person if you contribute to society in some altruistic way. Often this essay dovetails with the ethics essay (archetype 6).

The committee's approach is that, if they are going to boost you to the top tier of business influence at the expense of the next eight or nine applicants, they like to think that somehow, somewhere, you'll be the one who helps others along too. Their best guess about this is based on your history of social contribution in the past. This principle is so important that if you are not directly asked about public or community service, you should still find a way to put a paragraph about it into every application.

You have some latitude here, in that schools usually interpret service very broadly. You do not have to have worked in a soup kitchen or taught inner-city kids. Community involvement may be a better catch-all: anything that is not your job—and not a family, friends, or an obvious leisure activity—and involves social issues and is done for free, is presentable. You can go for a less orthodox interpretation, such as being a web-radio DJ, or doing equipment set-up at your local summer salsa festival.

Community service is a "golden key"

Community involvement can incorporate almost any of the elements that come up in the other essay archetypes, or any of the attributes Adcom seeks. Your community involvement can be a teamwork activity, it can be a success story, it can support your diversity claim, it can demonstrate your values in action, it can be the basis of a mentorship relationship, or it can say something about how you use your personal time. Therefore, the community essay will let you develop one or more of these topics if there is no question that lets you do it directly. Reciprocally, you can talk about community service in any of these essays if there is nowhere else to put community service. This is a great help in plugging holes as you map your message to the questions.

The multifaceted nature of community involvement tasks also means that you can usually find a way for your volunteering to reinforce at least one of the central themes of your application. It should also reinforce the leadership theme if you pick a community involvement where you launched a project, developed an organization or organized a program. Similarly, for choice, talk about a community activity that differentiates you: if you developed a line in free-range eggs on behalf of the local co-op, or you were an assistant on a cycle team for the Tour de France, that's intrinsically more interesting and valuable (to your application) than if you went on a river clean-up. Also, try to keep to recent activities. If you go back to high school to find a volunteer engagement, you flag the fact that you've done nothing since. (But if your high school community service was the beginning of an ongoing and future involvement in a cause you still support, then it signals long-term community involvement.)

As community service has become something of a checklist item for MBA applicants, it pays to be subtle in promoting this part of yourself. Do it as if it were a natural part of who you are and what you do with your time. If you visit an elderly persons home once a week, don't start an essay with, "My community service involvement is visiting an elderly persons home," as if the fact that it is community service is more important that what it actually involves. Just say what you do and let Adcom check community service off their list. As usual in your analysis, be sure to say why you chose the activity you did, and how it sheds light on you and dovetails with the other parts of your candidacy.

What if I have none?

What do you do about the community service experience requirement if you don't have any? Certainly, avoid making lame excuses such as you are too busy, or you travel a lot for work, and so on. First, excuses of any kind on any topic look bad in your application. It is always better to acknowledge a fault, say how you fixed or are fixing it, and move on (see advice on dealing with weak points in the optional essay section, below). Second, chances are there will be many in the applicant pool who volunteer despite heavy workloads, and that only makes you look doubly bad. Face the inevitable: the only way to satisfy the community service requirement is to do some service work. More is better, but even a day's worth will allow you to present a "recent" example of the kind of things you do.

THE SELF-REVIEW ESSAY

This essay asks you to evaluate yourself as an outsider might. You may be "appointed" as a member of the school's admissions committee and have to write the evaluative assessment for your file, or you may be asked to write your own review for a promotion at work, and so on. Depending how the question is phrased, the essay may just ask for strengths and weaknesses, or it may ask for a full and comprehensive evaluation of your candidacy. The broader the scope of the question, the stiffer the test. On the one hand, the committee is saying, "Tell us what you want to, in the way you want to," which is a great opportunity to get your message across without having to pay lip service to the question. You have a blank slate: you can and should put down the cleanest possible version of your application message to the committee. On the other hand, you have nowhere to hide: if you cannot get your argument for admission clearly and definitively made here, your reader will be most unsympathetic.

Your approach to this question should be driven directly by your profiling results and prepared message. Put down your profile, themes, and message, flavor it with some self-criticism, dress it up in terms of pros and cons, and you should be close to done. There are two main dangers associated with this essay:

- As with the weakness-failure essay, you must show enough maturity to own up to faults and weaknesses, and take responsibility for them. As with the failure essay, this also gives you the opportunity to show how diligently you work on your weaknesses.
- This question invites lists of attributes, and it is fine to use listing techniques. But don't forget to select, group, and focus your attributes so that the main points of your candidacy are easy to grasp. No laundry lists allowed.

THE "WHAT HAVE YOU DONE TO LEARN ABOUT US" QUESTION

It has become fairly common for a school to directly ask what the applicant knows about the program and what they have done to find out about it. There are no tricks here. They just want to see your good due-diligence. They are doing theirs by checking you out thoroughly; but have you done yours? Or are you just applying because it's a top school and you'll figure out what it can do for you once you're there? There are many, many ways of finding out about the program, from students, alumni, the school's media, MBA tours, campus visits, and so on. To all this, burgeoning social media options has added another layer. No one way is better than another, but a good study of a program will need to use various channels. Also, good hard work shows your passion to get admitted, and that never hurts you. Remember when you study a program you must study its community too. You are applying for a place in a community, not just a place in a classroom.

As schools want to be reassured that you have done your homework, the principle of evidence applies strongly here. It is hopeless to say you have "talked to alumni" or "read student blogs assiduously." The only way to get that to count is to be able to name the sources and mention what interesting/valuable things you have learned. If you can present a lot of pertinent knowledge of the school and the program, then you must have done your due-diligence.

Be aware also that good due-diligence is also a way of differentiating yourself (archetype 5). The truth is, a lot of applicants don't bother to get deep into their research of programs they are applying to. Those who do, stand out with their knowledge of the program, and knowledge of how it furthers their educational and professional goals. Paradoxical as it sounds, if you understand why the school is different from its competitors, you differentiate yourself from yours.

THE OPTIONAL ESSAY QUESTION

Often the final question in the set is one that gives you the chance to say anything you feel is important, that you think the admissions committee should know, that you have not been asked about. There are mixed opinions as to whether to do this essay or not, and there is no right or wrong answer. The advantage of doing it is you get more space to make your claim; the disadvantage is that the criterion of relevance and interest is far higher. If you waste the reader's time a bit in the other essays, well, that's time they have committed to you anyway. If you ask them for more time, and you waste that, you're in trouble.

In deciding whether to do the essay or not, don't worry about drawing attention to your bad points. Unless the admissions officer has had too many martinis (not likely), all your bad points will already be unmistakably blinking on a spreadsheet. Ask yourself, is this extra essay definitely going to add a *new dimension* to a potential problem, and more generally to Adcom's understanding of my claim to a place? If the answer is "no," don't do the essay. If it is "yes," then go ahead, particularly if you have genuinely not been able to find a place for an important piece of your profile, and that piece really changes the picture. Make it crystal clear what the relevance of the extra information is and how it relates to the rest of your candidacy. Remember that there is normally a word limit for the optional essay, but there is no call to use all the space you have. Make your additional points and sign off.

Dealing with weak points

Many people use the optional essay to excuse negatives in their profile—bad college grades or GMAT score, or work gaps and unemployment—so much so that there is a default assumption that the extra essay will be about this. The excuses can get pretty lame, so disassociating yourself from this tradition is an excellent reason not to use the optional essay at all if you can do your necessary explaining in one of the other essays.

If you have to use the optional essay to renegotiate your weaknesses, be sure to explain the situation without excusing yourself—let Adcom excuse you or not. Be brisk and forthright. If there is some circumstantial information the committee should know, tell them straight. If you made a mistake, acknowledge the mistake, say how you have worked on yourself not to make it again and move on. If you dwell on it, so will they. Here's how to think about whether to excuse yourself in this essay (or any other):

- Is your problem a finite thing that is definitely in the past? If you can show that it was a one-off, related to a specific mix of circumstances, inexperience, timing, and bad luck, or any factors that are definitely over or you have unequivocally fixed, then you are okay. Say what happened and, if learning is appropriate to the event, what you've learned. Stay optimistic and upbeat and assume future success, given better circumstances.
- Is your problem a factor that continues into the present? If it is not clearly over—if, say, you got a bad GMAT result because you have test-taking stage fright, or you have a stormy relationship with your spouse—obviously the committee will be thinking this problem could recur at any time. Better that you don't say anything.

Don't ever whine, moan, or curse your luck. Don't blame the GMAT system or any other system or committee or person. Don't tell a sob story. There's no sympathy vote to get you into business school. As in the professional world, you are either on top of things or you are not.

Multiple archetypes in one essay

You can now recognize the broad archetypes of the questions the committee will ask you. Be prepared, however, for the fact that there will not usually be a direct match between the archetype and the question posed: it is very common for schools to try to scramble up the picture by asking questions that incorporate two or more archetypes. They do this because they have more topics they want covered than the number of questions they can ask; because they try to stop applicants cutting-and-pasting material between different applications; and because they don't want people hurting their application by buying last year's model essays on the Web. The following are some examples of double- and triple-archetype questions:[1]

> Why are you seeking an MBA or IMBA from the University of Chicago Graduate School of Business? What do you hope to experience and contribute? What are your plans and goals after you receive your degree? (Chicago-Booth)
> *Archetype analysis:* **Why an MBA? + Contribution**

> Leadership is highly valued at the Johnson School. Describe a leadership decision made by a person who you admired and respected. What outstanding leadership skills were demonstrated and what impact did the decision have on you? (Cornell-Johnson)
> *Archetype analysis:* **Leadership + Mentors and influences**

> Recognizing that successful leaders are able to learn from failure, discuss a situation in which you failed and what you learned. (Harvard)
> *Archetype analysis:* **Leadership + Failure**

> What is motivating you to seek an MBA education at IMD? Why do you believe you should be admitted to the IMD MBA program and what will you be able to contribute that is unique and would make you a valuable addition to the class? (IMD)
> *Archetype analysis:* **Why an MBA? + Contribution**

> What makes work fulfilling? Describe a situation where, as a team member or project leader, you have made work more interesting or enjoyable for your group. (Ross-Michigan)
> *Archetype analysis:* **Personal inquiry + Team**

> The Darden School seeks a diverse and unique entering class of future leaders. How will your distinctiveness enrich our learning environment and enhance your prospects for success as a leader? (Darden-Virginia)
> *Archetype analysis:* **Contribution + Leadership**

> Why did you choose your current job? What is your most notable achievement and most notable failure in your current job? How do you hope to see your career progress over the five years following the MBA programme? (LBS)
> *Archetype analysis:* **Achievement + Failure + Why an MBA?**

> On the basis of your experience of working in and leading teams (either in your professional or personal life), please reflect on how you plan to contribute to your study group and the wider school community. (LBS)
> *Archetype analysis:* **Team + Contribution**

> Upon completion of your MBA at the Johnson School, what will classmates say about you or how will they remember you? (Cornell-Johnson)
> *Archetype analysis:* **Personal inquiry + Contribution**

Tackling the double- and triple-archetype question

Here you are facing two or three essays in one and, obviously, you have to cut your cloth to cover them all inside the word limit. Generally, you should give each part equal weight, but if you have a strong story or an obvious way to promote your themes in one part, and for the other you have nothing special, then weight the essay towards the archetype you deal with better. The committee will not take out a slide rule to check that you wrote as much for part A as for part B. First prize in this kind of multifaceted essay is to find the implied synergy between the two or three archetypes that the school has put together. Very often the question specifically asks for it, as with Harvard above. But sometimes it does not.

13 Essay approaches and content mapping

Mapping your message to the essays

In the profiling section (Part 2) we discussed how to find and organize the elements of value in your profile. In the previous parts of this section we looked at the key questions that business schools ask, recognizing them by archetype. You are now at the point where you can recognize each question you actually face by its archetype, and therefore judge what content it demands in its answer. This will greatly assist you in judging which part of your profile goes with which question in the set, where each part of your message is most relevant, and therefore which of your value themes to elaborate in each location and which stories to use to back them up. The process is one of "mapping" your profile value points to the essays and it's easiest to explain via a worked example. Here is how to map an essay set.

Step 1: Archetype analysis

This section, which uses a past Columbia Business School essay question set as a sample, takes you through the process of mapping your application onto the essay questions. First, take each essay in turn and do an archetype analysis:

1. What are your short-term and long-term post-MBA goals? How will Columbia Business School help you achieve these goals? (Limit 1,000 words)
   Archetype analysis: **Why an MBA?**

2. Please cite and explain a specific situation in which you demonstrated initiative. (Limit 500 words)
   Archetype analysis: **Leadership + Creativity and innovation**

3. Describe an experience in which the relationships you developed enhanced the outcome of a team effort. (Limit 500 words)
   Archetype analysis: **Team**

4. Please select and answer one of the following essay questions: (Limit 250 words) A. Please tell us about what you feel most passionate. B. If you were given a free day and could spend it anywhere, in any way you choose, what would you do?
   Archetype analysis: **Personal inquiry**

5. (Optional) Is there any further information that you wish to provide to the Admissions Committee? (Please use this space to provide an explanation of any areas of concern in your academic record or your personal history.)

Step 2: Assess the gaps and openings

Note first that the archetype analysis reveals that you have *not* been asked directly for strengths/achievements; weakness/failure; diversity/contribution; ethics; community; or mentors/influences. However, some of these topics are, of course, too significant to leave out. Depending on how important they are to your particular profile, you must look for subtle ways to include them. You could do the following:

- To talk about your mentor, you could say that you would spend your free day with your mentor.
- To talk about community involvement, you might say you are most passionate about the community of kids you teach inline skating to on a Saturday afternoon.
- You might talk about community or about your profile strengths in the team effort essay, or you could put profile strengths in your demonstrated initiative essay (or both).
- You could use the optional essay to explain that you are an orthodox Jew, and how that gives a certain ethical framework to your business outlook.

In summary, as long as it's plausibly relevant to the question, you can frame your answers in such a way that significant parts of your profile and message get aired, even if they are not directly asked for.

Step 3: Revised mapping

Once you have opened up the possibilities of the questions in this way, and mapped everything in your message onto them, a revised result might look like this:

1. What are your short-term and long-term post-MBA goals? How will Columbia Business School help you achieve these goals? (Limit 1,000 words)
   Archetype analysis: **Why an MBA?**

2. Please cite and explain a specific situation in which you demonstrated initiative. (Limit 500 words)
   Archetype analysis: **Leadership + Creativity and innovation + Profile strengths**

3. Describe an experience in which the relationships you developed enhanced the outcome of a team effort. (Limit 500 words)
   Archetype analysis: **Team + Community + Profile strengths**

4. Please select and answer one of the following essay questions: (Limit 250 words) A. Please tell us about what you feel most passionate. B. If you were given a free day and could spend it anywhere, in any way you choose, what would you do?

Archetype analysis: A. **Personal inquiry + Community; B. Personal inquiry + Mentors and influences**

5. (Optional) Is there any further information that you wish to provide to the Admissions Committee? (Please use this space to provide an explanation of any areas of concern in your academic record or your personal history.)
    Archetype analysis: **Ethics and values**

Themes and echoes

In mapping and creating essay approaches, you need to put as much consideration into the balance and combined impact of your essay set as you do into each of your individual essays. Remember that the reader will probably read them in one sitting, probably within 20 minutes. Although each essay contributes in its own way, the full set must interlock and make a coherent statement, and reflect a consistent positioning, while each essay works to emphasize a particular part of your value.

Note that some value points are made in a number of essays. This is fine. You wouldn't want to be drumming on the same theme in essay after essay, but it is natural and desirable that your key points get played out a number of times, in different ways and at different lengths. Your essay communication usually takes place over four or five essays. Think of a play in five acts or a symphony in three movements: key themes or motifs will be stated upfront, and may be the focus of one movement, but will also be reprised later on, but not in exactly the same way. That is what will happen when a good set of essays is all working together. Each has its own identity, but they all also are clearly interwoven and part of the same overall statement.

The essay approach: a tweet for each essay

Once you have completed a mapping process such as this, and you are therefore clear as to which part of your message each essay will carry, the points you will convey, and which of your stories to use to do it, you will be in a position to create a one- or two-sentence essay "approach" or "essay mission statement" for each essay. This statement summarizes your intention for the essay. The approach should clarify for you which value point you are focusing on; how this advances the argument for your admission; what memorable event or examples or specifics you will use to back up what you say; how you will link this to the question posed; and how this will complement but not overlap the other essays in the set.

For example, for essay two, above, you could guide yourself with the following statement: "In this essay I will show how I demonstrated initiative by discussing the day I stepped in as an emergency producer on a live TV show (media player theme). I'll discuss the leadership qualities and creativity under pressure required, and demonstrate strength of adaptability, mental toughness and maturity."

Better still, a great exercise in this day and age is to get on Twitter and get the core of the essay into a 140-character tweet. That will force you to find the absolute essence of what the essay is about. That essence will be your guide when you write.

Key points that support it should be included. Any points that don't fit with it should be discarded.

Note, this is not the same thing as an outline. An outline is about getting structure of argument and paragraphing correct (discussed in Chapter 16.) The essay mission statement is to guide you as to what, fundamentally, you want to say; what your content purpose in the essay is. It should hold the message fundamentals and keep you "on message" as you write, so that everything that is necessary gets said, but nothing superfluous creeps in.

The "unlucky 13" essay pitfalls to avoid

Before we go leave content behind and proceed to the nuts and bolts of writing, which is the topic of Part 4, some basic content "do's and don'ts" of content are important. The following section warns of approaches and content topics that should be avoided both in essays and interviews.

1. Don't mess with the truth

Don't stretch, twist or otherwise mess with the facts. Don't make claims that sound dodgy, even if true, unless you have thorough corroborating detail. Not only must what you say be true, it must be easily perceived to be true. The admissions officer, who has probably read 5,000 essays, has an ear for a tinny sounding claim and unconvincing use of evidence. This is your first and, hopefully, last time doing MBA applications, so just assume that she is better at essays that you are. Play the smart odds and stick with the truth. Anyway, you don't need to make things up—chances are, your true stories, if told well, are just as useful to you as the ones you might be tempted to make up.

2. Don't suck up

Don't waste your own and everyone else's time telling Adcom about the excellent reputation of the business school, the wisdom of the faculty, the astuteness of the admissions committee itself, the beauty of the grounds, the size of the endowment, the outstanding nature of the student body, the power of the alumni network, or any other form of eye-batting flattery. You are there to talk *about you* and why you will be a unique benefit to the school. Stick to the topic. (It's fine to refer to a school's excellence in highly specific terms, for example, saying how your proposed career in real-estate finance would benefit from being at, say, Wharton, which according to your research has the top faculty in this field.)

3. Don't be a tin soldier

Show your intimacy and vulnerability. If you don't feel a twinge of embarrassment in sharing a certain story, failure, or ethical decision—if it would be no problem if some prankster were to email your completed essays randomly to people in your personal and professional circle—then your essays are not personal enough.

Adcom treats your essays as confidential because they expect them to need to be. Don't disappoint them in this. They don't have a prurient interest in your private life and thoughts, but they are serious about getting privileged "insider insight" about you.

Your essays are, obviously, still a professional task and you must stay on the right side of professional norms. Being personal is one thing, being inappropriate is another. Don't confess to being a shoplifter. Don't discuss bodily functions, etc. In other words, don't say anything you wouldn't say one-to-one to a trusted professional mentor. If you can maintain this personal–professional balance, you will distinguish yourself from most other applicants.

4. Don't try to be someone else

Many candidates try to be what they think the generic business school applicant is: conservative, respectable, quantitative, "businesslike," and so on. It's natural to want to fit in with the business school ethic, but it's a big mistake to second-guess the committee and try to feed them what you think they want to hear. Trying to be "the model applicant" is not to your advantage because, as explained earlier in the book, there is no desired business school type. The real business school ethos endorses a broad mix of backgrounds, experiences, and opinions. If you try to reinvent yourself as something more normative, you will trade your individuality, personality, and interest for anonymity—a poor trade indeed. Trying to be someone you are not practically screams lack of self-confidence and low self-worth. If you're going to be rejected, at least be rejected for who you are. It is truly pathetic to pose as someone else and be rejected.

5. Don't be generic

You will only get in if you differentiate yourself in a valuable way. The committee wants to know who you really are and what is particularly special and different about you. Therefore, you should at all costs avoid feeding them generic information, and by contrast be sure to focus on what you have that is memorable and unique that stands out.

How do you know if something is generic? Easy. If what you say could be on the next applicant's file or the next after that, it's generic. If what you say could only have been said by you, it's specific and unique. Forget what MBA applicants are supposed to be like and supposed to want. Talk about the career you want. Talk about your actual goals and motivations. Share your real hopes, dreams, and fears. Give voice to your own values, your genuine beliefs, and your real ethical or personal struggles.

6. Don't go along with your own stereotype

When dealing with your profile, try to anticipate and then *break* the stereotypes of background, ethnicity, and job definition that may be associated with it. If you are an auditor, don't be a "suit"; if you are a research scientist, don't come across as though you talk to lab mice. That is, rather than letting the reader loll comfortably in the personality types he might associate with you as a scientist, a Christian, an immigrant, an IT professional, a lesbian, an Asian, and so on, surprise him with non-conforming attitudes and attributes. Drill deeply enough into yourself so as to get below your type, so that you can challenge the typecasting with what you have that is interesting and special.

7. Don't try to be over-competent

Of course, the tendency in a competitive application situation is to present yourself in the best light possible, and that is good. But you can go too far. Not only is nobody perfect, but you as an applicant for professional education are by definition incompetent in many respects. You are a work in progress, and that's okay. Often, in the effort to demonstrate achievement and appear successful, applicants portray themselves as so competent that Adcom can only be wondering how much they really need the MBA. Leave space in your application for the school's curriculum, faculty, cohort, and clubs and societies to have plenty to add to you.

8. Don't repeat material presented elsewhere

This shouldn't need explaining. The reader will have your complete file, so any repetition of its contents in the essays is a waste. You can, of course, reframe or cast a new light on facts appearing elsewhere in your file. Just avoid the dullness of repetition. Also, steer clear of what is already obvious. If your GMAT is 750 and your college GPA is 4.0, don't write essays arguing your intellectual competence. It's obvious. Use your essays to show you are not just an egg-head.

9. Don't provide facts that are not integrated into the message

It's always a burden to follow a writer into the details of his argument. The reward for the reader is that the details ultimately make a solid case. Not so if they are irrelevant. Facts that are not interpreted or integrated into the story are just frustrating "noise" the reader has to filter out. Don't make the reader work harder than she has to. Remember, your job is to pick, describe, and analyze the most important things about you: you must work hard so that the reader doesn't have to.

10. Don't lose sight of your key message

Your job is to communicate a message. Where necessary, make choices that narrow your horizons but strengthen your punch. Get as many of the details and facts about you—employment history, awards, positions held, and so on—into the application short questions so you are free to use the essays for chaneling your message. The essays are not there for you to tell the committee, didactically and encyclopedically, what you've done. They are there so you can show them the essence of who you are and what you are aspiring to become.

11. Avoid unsubstantiated "I am -itis"

Don't make positive judgments about yourself, or compliment yourself. It is much more powerful and persuasive if you just give the facts and let them speak for you. Any general assertion of your capabilities—"I am a fast learner, I'm a problem solver, etc."—should be automatically deleted if you cannot corroborate it with evidence (details) of successes that demand this skill, or specific examples or numbers in your favor, or credible merit awards, or a believable story where the qualities you claim are apparent. Don't say, "I am proficient at . . ." Tell the story of what you did and let Adcom think, "Hmm, he is proficient at . . ."

12. Don't blame or point fingers

In MBA admissions, don't ever say anything negative about anyone, or any group, or nationality, or company, or anything at all, no matter who did what to you or how badly it has affected your life. If you must, kick the dog, but don't say anything bad or finger-pointing in your MBA essays or interview. Avoid racist, sexist, and all other forms of unkind speech. If you come across negatively, or as a recriminator, you will not be admitted anywhere. It's better to say nothing.

13. Don't get onto controversial topics

Stay clear of religion, politics, abortion, inner-city poverty, the war on drugs, 9/11, the Middle East, and social or ideological opinions of any kind. Not only could this be an automatic red light if you get the "wrong" reader, but all the time you spend on this you are not adding anything about why you are special and therefore valuable to the MBA program. Your goal is to get in, not to convince anyone of anything. The only relevant topic is you. The reader won't care what your precious position is, and chances are they won't be reading long enough to figure it out either way.

You can make an exception to this rule if an ideological perspective is an obvious part of who you are and what you plan to do in your career. If you are a veterinarian and passionate activist for animal rights, for example, and you plan to launch an international animal medical foundation, you can make the necessary supporting ideological claims.

14 The interview

We have seen how the key elements of your profile may be taken forward into the essays, and in subsequent chapters will look more closely at how essays should be structured. In this chapter we look at how the fruits of profiling can be used in the other key piece of MBA admissions communication: the interview, and broadly consider how to manage the interview part of the application process.

Over time, the interview has become a standard part of the process for all schools of note. Some do offer acceptance without it, but it's becoming rarer, particularly in the top-25. Sometimes, in long-distance situations, interviews are conducted by phone, but the trend is strongly toward face-to-face interviews in every case. The rising importance of the interview in admissions is due to increasing competitiveness in the admissions process and a growing overall emphasis on personality and communication skills in management. While interviews are just one element in the overall assessment, it is now quite unlikely that anyone will get an offer from a top-tier school without a superior interview.

Different b-schools have different policies as to if and when in the admissions cycle they interview, how much prescreening they do beforehand, and how they organize the process. The issues behind a program's decision to interview you or not, and how that fits into their overall progression of your file through the admissions process, were dealt with in Chapter 5.

A test of personality

As noted throughout this book, each piece of the MBA application is there for a specific reason; each tests the applicant in a different way, or asks for something that the other testing mechanisms do not address. So what does the interview do for Adcom? What does it tell them that they can learn no other way? It tells them how you come across in person in a one-to-one situation; how you communicate verbally, and how well you present yourself. It tells them about your personality. Just as an employer is not going to give you a job without meeting you, so a decent school is not going to offer you a place without getting a sense of you in real life via an individual personal meeting. They have a lot of information about you on paper, but numbers and words on a page tell only so much. The interview lets them get a sense of the person behind all this. The corollary, of course, is that to be successful you have to "leap off the page." You need them to feel the force of personality, the motivation, vitality, intelligence, depth of your persona, that *je ne sais quoi* that memorable people carry with them. It's not easy to do.

Note that you will *not* be asked to analyze a case study or demonstrate your mastery of any business subject matter. Their aim is to give you a chance to talk about yourself, your motivations, your experiences and preferences, etc., and see how you come across. The interview tests:

- the interpersonal dynamics and rapport you create
- the skill and maturity of your interaction
- your honesty and openness
- your non-arrogant confidence
- your communication skills and articulacy
- your drive and purpose towards your goals
- your passion for the program.

They will of course ask specific questions that probe whether or not your goal makes sense for you, or if you have the required experience, or have worked well in teams. But remember that all the relevant facts about you are in your file and they could easily look them up. So the interview is all about the deeper and more important layer of questioning that is unspoken: Are you *a fit*? Do you *seem* right? Does it *feel* good that you will carry the school's name through your career? Are you *one of us*? It is the "who" not the "what" that counts.

Other that getting this overall sense of your personality, they have a direct interest in how well you manage yourself in interviews because you will be interviewing for summer internships or a job within a few months of starting your MBA. If you are going into management—which is what the MBA is all about—you are going into a world where communication and self-presentation are not nice-to-haves, they are core skills.

It's not a chat

A personality interview of this sort can be a relatively free-form experience. You sit down, they say "tell me about yourself"—or some such, and you talk a bit and they talk a bit. It's all very friendly, and it is easy to be lulled by this informality. Don't be. The interview is an exam and probably one of the stiffest professional tests you'll ever go through.

The basics should hardly need mentioning. Treat it like a business interview. Arrive early and follow formal protocol. You should be in business attire and be overdressed rather than under. Whether male or female, manage your attire and accessories as if it was a job interview *with an investment bank* and you've got it about right. Once seated, take your cue from the interviewer: if she lowers the formality of the event, follow suit. When you get talking, be ready to back up everything you say with specifics. Know the details about the school and its program. Have prepared examples and stories on possible major question topics: future goals, leadership, teamwork, strengths, and weaknesses. Be particularly ready for questions where profile appears weak or trajectory unclear.

In sum, don't let your guard down. Just because your interviewer is friendly, it does not mean that he likes you or thinks you are doing fine. There are many post-interview reports of situations where it was all-nods-and-smiles and a ding letter ensued (and where applicants got a real mauling, and got accepted). Don't assume a friendly interviewer isn't ultra hard to please. Stay on top of value delivery from the first moment to the last.

The tricky thing is, despite the take-no-prisoners test you are under, you have to appear relaxed and apparently "informal" to play your part in making the event a genial, personable interaction. The point is: can you do this? Can you play the game of situation management so that it looks like there is genuine ease of association in the room, no matter how high the stakes? People with senior management potential can. In this light, feel free to ask for a clarification if you don't understand the parameters of a question as you would in any other meeting. Respond to ice-breakers and be appreciative of the interviewer's humor, if offered. Play your part in creating a dialogue that approaches a normal conversation—don't under any circumstances let it become question, answer, silence; question, answer, silence, because if it does, you may as well get up and leave.

Adcom or alumni? On-campus or off?

The types of MBA admissions interview on offer can be described in a 2×2 matrix (Figure 14.1), just as a management consultant might do it. You will be interviewed either by a member of the admissions committee or by an alumnus (alumna).[1] And you will be interviewed either on-campus or off.[2]

Note that all interviews are equivalent. There is inherent advantage to being in any of the quadrants. Your location will play a great role in determining the choice.

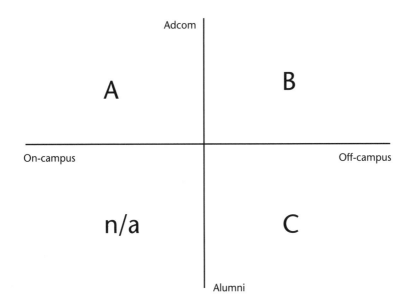

Figure 14.1   Field of MBA interview options

Where it is obviously reasonable that you come to campus they will expect to interview you there. That means you will get an Adcom member (which could be a 2nd year student). If you are coming to campus to interview, it is quite common that this will be packaged with a class visit and a structured opportunity to meet current students. All that is quadrant A.

If you live across the country or across the world, you won't be expected to get to campus (but welcome if you do.) Then your off-campus choices depend on whether you are near an interview "hub" where Adcom staffers are flown to (quadrant B) or not. If not, you will get an alum who lives or works in your city (quadrant C.) If there are no alumni within reasonable range you may be given a phone interview (not diagrammed,) which will be with a member of the Adcom staff.

Using these heuristics and the text of the interview invitation you get from the school, you should be able to know in advance which type of interviewer you are getting, an Adcom member or an alum. It is important to know because it makes a big difference to the type of interview you are likely to get, and therefore the way you should prepare.

Adcom vs Alumni interviews

The admissions staffer and the alum have similar motivation—to find and select the best candidates for the program. However, the difference between them is crucial: one is a professional admissions officer, the other a professional at something else entirely. The officer will have conducted many hundreds or even thousands of interviews, the alum in all likelihood just a few. If you go to campus on an interview day you will feel this strongly. You will sit in a waiting room (looking at your competitors who are also dressed to kill, also there early, also waiting). There will be various interviewers coming and going, taking their "wannabees" off down the corridor, and bringing them back 25–30 minutes later. It's a routine, and that's how they get through the numbers they have to get through. You are batch processed.

This does not mean you will get a poor or uninterested interviewer. On the contrary, they are likely to be of a consistent excellent standard (better than the alumni, in general, because they are professionals at exactly this kind of stuff). But having done eight people before you, and 12 the day before, and countless before that, the process they take you through will be more routine than it may appear. They will have in their head, if not on the writing pad in front of them, a specific set of questions to get through—designed to extract information on particular topics and/or focus on the "core" questions, discussed below. They will have their pet alternative or surprise questions too, but will essentially drill you with the basics to get as quickly and surely as possible to the nub of whether you impress in the interview or not, so they can get the report into your file, and get onto the next interview. (Their impression may be formalized in an interview assessment sheet, where they give you a grade on various items, for easy comparison with other interviewees.) If you interview at a national or global hub, these parameters will apply too.

Alumni interviewing puts you, by contrast, in a much less structured situation. While alumni are often provided with guidelines for how to conduct interviews, and sometimes score sheets, and may even get a "cheat sheet" of questions to ask, the schools are quite light on them in terms of process and tasks. And alumni can hardly be fired, so they can do more or less what they like, and do. Schools are just grateful that alumni give up their valuable time to do it at all.

This is not to imply that your alum will be bad either. The point is, what you get is going to be far less the product of a routine-bound and regulated engagement. With admissions staffer you know what will happen within a small order of uncertainty. With an alumnus, anything can happen. It's more "Wild West," which could play in your favor, or not. It is more likely that an alum will allow you to circumvent an area of weakness, but he may also ask you something "weird" or try to trip you up or put you under a stress test (perhaps acting upon a grandiose sense of how good an applicant needs to be to be allowed into the same hallowed hall as he was). It is more likely that an alum will seek a lively exchange and seek to debate an issue—which you should avoid.

Further, it is quite likely that meeting you is an interest point in a day that is otherwise about fairly dry stuff, and the alumnus will really want to talk about what interests him. He may see a mention of PADI certification on your resume, and the next thing you have spent 15 minutes comparing the virtues of the Maldives vs. the Dutch Antilles. As discussed below, there are ways of moving the conversation back to the matters at hand, but it's a very tricky dance, and often-times it's not at all a bad thing to get off-topic on a matter of interviewer interest. It can be time (a) the interviewer probably enjoyed spending with you, and (b) not spent on answering tricky questions.

If you get (or choose) an alumni interview, you will most likely be asked to come to their place of work. If it is a senior person you could be meeting in their office; if it's a more junior person, you will more likely get the meeting room on their floor. An alum may equally schedule the interview over lunch, in which case they will probably pick up the check, but don't assume so. Also, when going the alumni route, don't make any plans based on your interview starting or ending on time. Some-times they get an important call and keep you waiting. Sometimes they just go on and on talking. Generally a long interview is a better sign than a short one, but not a guarantee. If you had a short interview they might just be having a busy day.

Interviewer research

It is unlikely you will know who you are getting on-campus ahead of time, but if you have an alumni interview, or an off-campus interview with an admissions officer, chances are you will be able to find out who it is and learn a bit about him or her. If you can, then you can check them out via the Web, and get a sense of what their preferences are, or what topics they may be receptive to, or what topic areas they may question you closely about. If, for example, you are positioning yourself as an entrepreneur with a specific business idea, and Adcom, in it's wisdom, matches you with a venture capitalist, expect questions something like *Dragon's Den*.

Preparation

If you read interview advice that is put out by schools you will see that it mostly says they want to "meet you," "have a chat," "no advance preparation is required."

Yeah, right. They definitely want you to feel relaxed and they certainly don't want you to learn your answers off pat. But to "chat" competitively—to outcompete your equally capable applicant competition—you need to prepare. Getting into the room and having a seamless, natural delivery requires extensive preparation and practice. The more you prepare, the more natural you will seem.

Everything said in the first sections of this book is relevant in preparing for your interview. You need a good sense of what schools value, and have worked on eliciting your profile elements, key value points, and application message. When you get the interviewer's questions you will "map" your value onto them in the same way as discussed in the previous chapter, and in such a way that he or she is left absolutely clear as to your distinguishing mix of attributes and qualities and potential contributions, with nothing important left out. The difference is, of course, here you have to do your mapping in real time and make sure it comes out evenly across a series of questions that you can't fully predict. However, you can know a fair amount about the questions that commonly get asked.

Foundation questions

A well-conducted interview will cover most of the core questions, such as:

- What are you doing now professionally, and career history?
- What are your career goals?
- Why do you want/need to do an MBA?
- Why now?
- Why an MBA from this school particularly?
- What will you be able to contribute to the program?

You may be asked them all together as in: "Please explain your career progression and future aspiration," for example. You will also quite likely be asked about leadership experiences, teamwork and mentoring, successes, failures, international or cross-cultural experiences, or ethical challenges—the essay standards. You should go in knowing what stories you will reach for on each of these topics.

As with the essays, these questions can come up with a bit of spin on the ball. You may not get the bald format: "What are the most important attributes of leadership to you?" but rather the disguised: "Who's the best boss you have had?" It is, of course, the same question. But having done your profiling and written essays for a few schools, your recognition of alternative forms of questioning the core topics should be sharp. Understanding the essay question archetypes discussed in Chapters 10–12 is highly relevant here.

If asked why you want to come to their program, or what about their program is going to help you meet your goals, you need specific, concrete reasons that show close understanding of what particularly is on offer. As with the essays, you get no points for parroting what is on the Website or praising the school in generalities—for its "excellent faculty" or many "exciting" clubs and societies. Talk in specifics or not at all, always linking back to your broader motivations. If a particular club is interesting to you, why? If you are drooling to take a particular class, why?

Anything interesting or unusual on your resume is very likely to be a topic of discussion. Be particularly ready for questions where your profile appears weak or your career trajectory meandering. As mentioned in the weakness-failure essay discussion, don't be defensive about weaknesses in your profile. Everyone has them and everyone has failed. Acknowledge yours, state what you've done to mitigate them, and look to move the interview on. Don't excuse yourself or blame anyone else. Don't be flip, cute, or a smart-ass about it.

Finally, within the framework of core questions, the interviewer can also be counted on to ask you at least one thing about your life outside work, often: "Tell me what you do when you're not at work." Or "what do you read for fun?" And so on. Further, you are reasonably likely to be probed on "competitive framing" questions: that is, asking if you are applying elsewhere, and where, and whether the particular program is your first choice. You may also be asked what will you do if not accepted.

"Tumbling" with the other questions

This foundational question area covers the "certainties" to come up one way or another, so before you go in, you should know pretty much exactly what you will say on these topics, and have rehearsed it well enough so it flows. After that, or more likely interspersed with it, the interviewer may ask you pretty much anything that comes into their head to know about. The important thing is you can only prepare for these questions inexactly.

There are many places on the Web where you get samples of MBA interview questions, and a brief scan done by this author suggest there are well over 1,000 reported questions. Trying to prepare for them specifically would be like preparing for a quiz show by reading the encyclopedia. Beyond the core questions, the chances of any particular question coming up are so remote that it's not worth prepping any one of them. You need a different strategy, a strategy of "tumbling" with the question until you can legitimately get back to what you want to talk about. Tumbling means answering the question to start with, but quickly looking to link it to something you do want to talk about. It is tumbling like a circus clown—standing strong for a moment, then falling and rolling and springing back up somewhere else.

Let's say you get a question like "How do you feel about public speaking?" This is a perfectly legitimate question, but also one that is so low-probability that you'd be within your rights not to have actively prepped it. What do you do? You can't stare blankly at the interviewer and listen to the clock tick while you rehearse what to say. You have to tumble. There may be an obvious and good public speaking experience you've had that pops into your head, in which case you would lead off with that, explaining where and when it was, and what happened. But maybe nothing pops into your head at all. Then you would have to go sideways, talking about a good speaker you have seen, or the importance of public speaking in leadership, or maybe (you're scrambling here) how you uncle Jack is a translator at the UN Assembly in New York. The point is, like a robber on the run, if your best transport doesn't show up, you have to get going instantly with whatever vehicle presents itself, and then (assuming the topic in the question posed is not one of your strengths or important themes and you're looking for a way out), as you're talking, you would be scanning for "exits" that allow you to get across to a better track for you. The public speaking event you get talking about may have come when you were working for Marriott, and you could quickly segue to: "that speech was when I was in the hospitality sector, where I picked up a lot of good skills, not only public speaking. There was also . . ." and you're off and running on the track you want to be on.

Behavioral questions

As mentioned in Chapter 6, in explaining why profiling is necessary, the kinds of questions you face in essays and the interview are behavioral rather than factual. A factual question elicits a "what" or "how" or "who" or "when" answer. A behavioral question elicits the "why." A factual question is: "How many times have you been promoted in your job?" A behavioral question would be: "How has moving up the corporate ladder changed your perspective on the workplace? Why is that?" It shines a light on your behavior in situations, probes your choices, looks for your motivations, and examines your preferences. Here is a flavor of the kind of behavioral questions that commonly come up:

- Why did you choose your job after college, or the one after that? Why is it time to move on?
- Tell me about a difficult problem you solved. Is that typical of the way you solve problems?
- What is your preferred role in a group?
- How would you respond if you were faced with . . . [description of an ethical dilemma]?
- Why have you chosen to get involved in [name of extramural activity]?
- What is your favorite part of your job? What would you change? Why?

These are samples, and again there are so many of these questions it makes no sense to prep every one. Obviously, you must also be ready for standard fact questions that hone in on specific examples or detailed descriptions of events, projects or experience as well. For example: What are your interests? Describe your typical workday. What will you do if you are not accepted? And so on. But in an interview like this, to do well, you need to quickly turn fact questions into behavioral questions and address them as such, *even if they are not asked that way*. If asked about your typical workday a "C" answer would say what it is you do; an "A" answer would say that, and then move onto which parts are less or more interesting, and why. If asked "What has been your most important accomplishment?" you would likewise need to push yourself past the "what" to the "why" part of the answer.

On the day: managing the interview

We now assume it is the day of the interview and you are in the final stages of preparation. Give yourself a fighting chance. Get good directions so you don't arrive late and frazzled. In fact, if you do this kind of thing, take a hot bath or meditate or do whatever works for you to put yourself in a positive, confident, clear frame of mind. It helps to remember that by inviting you they already think you are worth spending time on. They are already halfway to accepting you, and if you relax and genuinely enjoy it, you will more likely shine than not. Above all, remember they are not ever looking for cookie-cutter applicants. Be your best self, but be yourself.

On the day, or the day before, make sure to reread the essays you wrote for that particular school. It is more common that the interviewer will interview you "blind" (having seen your resume only) in order to avoid carrying their prejudices into the interview. But at some programs the interviewer will have read your file, and will re-scan it right before he meets you. If he says "in your essay you said 'xyz'," and you give a blank look because you wrote the essay months ago, that's perfectly understandable, but you still come across as a dope. It is fine when going in to ask your interviewer if he has read your file, because it is perfectly professional to adjust your answers in order not to repeat things he already knows. If the interview is blind, then you can tell the same stories as in the essays; if it is not, you can reference what you wrote but you have to go beyond it.

1. Going in, breaking the ice

Sit when invited, and not before. If you haven't already, get rid of any overcoats, etc., but keep your jacket on. Assume formality unless it is directly countermanded. You do not need to provide a copy of your resume—your interviewer will have whatever she needs. But you may want to have your own paper copy in front of you unless you know it cold. Get out a pen and pad of paper, which has the effect of making you look prepared. Don't take notes or even suggest that you might take notes on your laptop or iPhone or otherwise "techno-smart-ass" the situation. Everything electronic you have with you should be turned off.

Your pad of paper is for notes you take in the session. Do *not* have your key points already written on it. Your interviewer will inevitably see them, or see you looking down at them, and you will appear unconfident. Also, no matter how hard you try, having written points to make will tempt you into checking how many points you've got to shoehorn in before the interview closes. This will make a natural conversation really difficult to have. It is better to forget a key point while making the rest well than to make every point in a stilted way. Remember, the content is secondary. What really matters is the rapport you create.

As you come in or as you sit down, take the opportunity to say something about the weather, about the city (if you've traveled to it), about the building, about your ride into town—anything. Don't just come in and sit down, allowing in an awkward silence and sense of discomfort that you are trying to avoid. You want to get talking on a light and genial note—to get the conversation flowing really as soon as possible—even while going down the hallway to the interview room. It will relax you and relax the interviewer. You may find it is a full five or ten minutes before you get talking about "real" stuff. Of course every word and gesture counts, from the minute you say hello. If you can relax the situation in this professional "ice-breaking" way, that probably means you have been in pressure interviews or pressure negotiations before, and this counts in your favor.

If it is possible to slip it in without killing the icebreaking phase (and if you don't already know from the schedule roster) ask: "how long do we have together?" It's a legitimate question because it will help you know how long and in what depth to answer questions. You don't want the interviewer to get up and offer you a handshake after 20 minutes, when you've spent most of it talking about the architecture of Chicago.

As you exit the icebreaker, be prepared for the first question. It is very likely (9 times out of 10 likely) that it will be a general pipe-opener: something that lobs the ball into your court and allows you to get going introducing yourself on your terms. The question will be something like: "So tell me about yourself" or "So why do you want to come to INSEAD?" or some such. The question will not be tricky and will not be narrowly focused. You should have a well-prepared answer to a pipe-opener question, giving a brief overview of your biographical highlights and intended purpose going forward.

First impressions
In Chapter 5 we spoke about "Blink" and how first impressions count at every stage of your application: the first contact with your file, the first view of your essays, and so on, and the start of the interview is one of those times when first-impression antennae will we waving furiously. If you are appropriately dressed, apparently well spoken, able to get seated and break the ice naturally, the first impression index will go in your favor. This puts you ahead of the game. If you fail the first-impression test, you have to come from a long way back.

Body language
An important part of making a first impression, and then an ongoing factor through the interview is "body language," that is, all the things you "say" even when you're not talking. Body language is often talked about as if it is some esoteric phenomenon. Any attempt to correlate exact motions to exact thoughts is spurious, but more generally, making enough eye contact, smiling at appropriate points, sitting upright and an appropriate distance from the interviewer, and so on, all counts in the larger equation. Everyone has their own style, which is fine, but that does not give you permission for bad body language: don't fidget, don't tap your foot, don't spin your pen, don't play with your hair, keep your hands away from your mouth.

2. The ongoing conversation

Five minutes have gone by and you are now warmed up and into the main body of the interview. These are the things to pay attention to:

Take responsibility for a "conversational" style
We have noted above that schools want the interview to feel friendly and informal and conversational. It is most certainly *not* a chat, it just has to be played that way. So, first, steer away from anything that even vaguely sounds pre-rehearsed. You do want to have prepared yourself thoroughly on your key points and stories, but only so that you can deliver them as organically as possible. Don't sound as if you're reading your own autocue. Second, don't let the interview be a "question, answer,

question, answer" session. You have to work the situation so that it feels like a genuine dialogue. Sections below offer tips on how to do this.

Leading the interview

Listen to a genuine conversation and you will notice how its "leadership" changes hands in a fluid way. For a while one person will be leading the discussion; then the other takes over for a bit; then it reverts again. If this didn't happen, it would soon feel one-sided. So, to achieve a conversational effect, you need to take your opportunities to lead as they come up. It is not appropriate to ask questions of your interviewer, her life, her career, her goals, so you can't go that route. But it is okay and very much desirable (1) to segue your answer to a new point and continue with that; or (2) to pose yourself your own follow-up questions to a question, and answer them.

For example, if asked why you want to join their particular program, you would answer it, but when you feel yourself coming to the end of what to say, instead of stopping and waiting for the next question, you could say something like: "which leads me to the point: what unique skills and experiences would I bring in?" Or you could be wrapping up and say "all of which begs the question: why do I need an MBA in the first place?" And you would then be off again and running with the new question. If you do it as if it were the most natural thing to do, it is unlikely that the interviewer will cut you off and say "No, I didn't ask you that." They want to get you talking and seeing how you handle the conversation and what topics *you* choose to raise is all part of the test. Remember, a million times, the content is secondary.

Other than making the conversation more two-sided, the benefit of driving the conversation forward yourself is you get to steer it where you want to go. If you're at the helm of the speedboat you can steer clear of the rapids. You will obviously not pose yourself a question on a topic you don't want to talk about; you will specifically go towards what you do want to address, which best allows you to deliver value.

Stick to value delivery

The approach of this book has been to know what is valued in MBA students, find that value in yourself, and communicate it across your application inputs. So here, in the interview, this is once again the guiding principle. You need to get your value points and application message across no matter what questions you get. It's simpler when you get the basic questions like "What do you bring to your team?" but harder when you get a question like "What is your favorite magazine?" Nevertheless, for every question, as you hear it, what should flash through your mind is: which value point or points can I legitimately address in answering this question?

If asked something random like your favorite magazine, you could trot out that you read *Newsweek*. And that may be the perfect truth, but it is low on differentiation, and hard to establish a value point around. But, say you are looking for a way to talk more about your design background and time in Italy and Switzerland, on hearing the magazine question your whirring brain may think: "Magazines . . . magazines . . . What about *Casabella*? That allows me to get onto my value points." And you will be on your way to delivering them. Of course you have to select from items, events, and experiences you really do know about, otherwise you will make a real mess.

Balance depth and breadth
When you get a question, you should answer it thoughtfully and fully, showing the question due respect. But you don't want to over-answer it (spend 5+ minutes on it) such that your time is cut short for other important value delivery. So you have to manage answer length very carefully. How long you go will depend on how long you have in total (which you should ask if you don't know), and also the style of the interviewer—which you can deduce as you go along. Some like to move along at a real clip. Others are more *laissez-faire*. Look for signs of impatience, and if you see any, tail off your answer promptly. Also, if you feel you're repeating yourself, stop. A point is mostly powerfully made when made once.

While being aware of not going over-long, one of the most hidden perils of interviewing is saying too little. Be more than ready to talk at length about where you are coming from, why you need an MBA now, and what your aspirations are. Then be bristling to talk at length about what you do outside of work. Then be champing at the bit to talk in detail about what you need to learn, or what you will contribute to peer learning, and so on. Your interviewer should feel like there is a lot more you would say, if you had the time. They will worry if it feels like you are short of something to say and by the end of the question you really couldn't squeeze out another word.

Give details and proof
The standards of detail and proof we have highlighted for essay development apply here too. The only way to breathe life into your candidacy and rouse the interviewer's interest is through a generous sharing of detail, stories, personal observations, and insights. The only way to deliver value is to prove it. If you assert your qualities and attributes without proof, you may as well have just opened and closed your mouth like a fish, because you have said nothing. Use examples and stories to illustrate and confirm.

Also, in elaborating your biography or telling stories, don't take background information for granted: your interviewer may not know the first thing about software client-interface systems or the Kansas City Chiefs, or anything you know deeply. So if you are telling a story (quickly) support it with enough context so that your interviewer "gets it."

Keep it on you
Again, as with the essays, it is all about you. Neither your company nor your work team nor your family nor anyone else is being evaluated for a seat at business school. Everything and everyone around you is context—definitely important in framing you and explaining who you are and the choices you have made and why you are valuable—*but* only valuable in framing. It is all about you and only you. Don't allow yourself to get sidetracked to waffling on for half the interview about the World Bank or your famous film director uncle. Sure, digress for a moment, but then come right back to you.

Don't debate

Don't be drawn into a debate about anything. Don't debate the environment, banking regulations, the Middle East, race relations or any matter. Similarly, don't be defensive about your weaknesses such that you are tempted to debate the merits of criticism of you. Any debate you get into has two problems. First, the debate is "the skirmish"; who wins is irrelevant. The only thing you need to win is "the war," of getting in to business school. Second, any time you spend on any debate takes time away from the key topic, which is you.

Go beyond your numbers and file data

Don't get stuck on the facts of your story. They are in your file, remember? The facts are a means to an end, and the end is telling your story—interpreting the data, explaining your choices and motivations, and so building up a 3D picture of you that the facts alone can't. Also, once again, the content is secondary. Creating a rapport with the interviewer is more important than any single thing you say. Concentrate primarily on how you come across, on your tone and poise, and building a real connection with your interlocutor.

Balance "I can" and "I need"

As much as you possibly can, focus on your strengths. You want to give the impression that you are able to meet and exceed the rigors of an MBA education, be they physical, psychological, social, and intellectual. Not only that, but you will contribute in fabulous ways too. However, be sure to stay on the right side of the line between complete self-confidence and cockiness. Be open to acknowledging the skills, experiences, and attributes you don't have and how you need to improve.

Also, where appropriate, generously acknowledge the assistance and support of your mentors, teammates, friends, and family in making you what you are. Remember at all times that you are not just applying to go to a business school, you are applying for the right to be part of its community. Judgments about your role in and potential contribution to the community are being made as you talk.

Manage cohesion

Finally, a live interview situation demands your active attention to cohesion. In your essays you can go back and rework sentences or move paragraphs around. When you're talking in real time you need to closely attend to clarity and cohesion as you go along. Bend over backwards to make sure your overall life story has a beginning (your past to now) a middle (the MBA and what happens next) and an end (longer-term goals) and that the purpose and motivations taking you forward are as clear as daylight. If you bring in a story, make it clear how it relates. If you go on a tangent it's your responsibility to bring the conversation back on track.

3. Wrapping up: your questions

As things start to wrap up in the interview you may be given an open "Is there anything important we have missed?" or "Anything you wished you were asked?" kind of question. This is a structure similar to the optional essay that most schools provide, which is a net to catch anything that might have been missed. However, where the optional essay is associated with mitigation of apparent weaknesses (see Chapter 12), in the interview it is not the case. Here the interviewer just wants to see they have not missed anything important, and obviously this your chance to jump in with anything you have not yet had a chance to say.

You may or may not get this catch-all question, but you will definitely get the formal opportunity at the close of the interview to ask one or two questions of your own. Even if you have asked questions during the interview, you will still get a "Do you have any questions for me before we close?" question. This has two functions. First it is the interviewer's way of signaling time is almost up. Second, it elicits your questions.

On getting the time's nearly up signal—which you may think of as the "two minute warning" (without timeouts)—you cannot and should not ask for more time, by saying something like "Oh, I really wanted to tell you about . . ." If that something was so important, you should have got it in earlier. If you push to say one more thing, your interviewer will probably allow it, but mark you down, and you will have to make your point in the face of a much higher standard of critical appraisal: "So was this extra point really something worth going over time for?" she will be thinking to herself.

But you do get your own question. What you ask says a lot about your judgment, and they are tricky to get right. On the one hand, you want to use them to sum up and refocus your interviewer on your strengths, goals, and resonance with the program. On the other hand, your question has to be a real question, and not only that, must target an area the interviewer can reasonably be expected to know about. If you are talking to an admissions officer, you can ask a question about the program or extramural opportunities (that is not obviously answered on the website) and how it fits your goals. If you are talking to an alumnus from five years ago, a better line of questioning may be how the school's brand holds up in the job market, or how the alumni organization really works.

Using your questions to sum up and refocus your interviewer on your value points, could be done as follows. Assuming you bring strong skills in HR and you want to leave having underlined that fact, you may say something like: "Given my extensive experience in applying the 'balanced scorecard,' will there be scope in the management accounting electives for me to continue to broaden my specialization in employee evaluation?"

Your questions: do's and don'ts

If you are dealing with an alum, you can ask questions based around where you are in the world and what you know of the person. If you are sitting in the Goldman Sachs office in Johannesburg, you can ask about the business school in relation to developing economies, for example. Be particularly careful to ask questions based on information about the alum's situation that is obvious or easily accessible. Don't ask them about something that is deep in their own resume or about something you got off their Facebook page—that will give them that "stalked" feeling and you don't want that.

Generally, keep questions at a high level: ask about the school's approach, emphasis, or future direction rather than seeking perfunctory information about library hours or gym facilities. Don't ask questions the answers to which are available on the Web or in the student guide, or anything you should know already or could easily find out yourself. Further, do not ask your interviewer to judge the school in the marketplace or compare it to others; or to sell the school to you, as in "Can you give me three reasons I should come here?" (Believe it or not, it happens.)

Do not, under any circumstances, ask the interviewer to give an on-the-spot assessment of you and "how you did." In fact you should expect to walk out without any commitment from them as to how it went, or whether you are going to get a good or a bad report, particularly if dealing with an Adcom staffer. Their professionalism demands that they smile, shake your hand, and say something like "Thank you for your time," and that's it. That's all the feedback you're ever going to get until your letter arrives in the mail. Do, however, send a thank you note. Email is fine for this. (It's okay—very touching in fact—to ask them for their card in order to do this.) When you write the note, reference your interview conversation in some direct way, which will make the interviewer remember you specifically, and suggest that your thank-you note writing is not just rote and perfunctory.

PART FOUR
Writing Tools and Methods

15 Managing the reader's experience

Part Three was about how to recognize the questions you face and how to parcel your application message (developed in Part Two) onto them strategically. It was about what content to use and where to use it. Now we move to the writing itself. This section will be about how to write an essay that gives your message the best possible promotion. We will examine the various tools and techniques of managing the reader experience, and getting her to absorb and remember your message.

In this chapter we deal with overview principles of attracting and retaining a reader. In the next chapter we talk about the mechanics of essay organization, idea discipline and argument flow, and then writing a first draft. In the final chapter we deal with how to improve expression and achieve writing polish and professionalism.

The art of persuasive writing

Writing can have many different goals: to inform, to entertain, to direct, to transmit ideas, or to persuade and convince. Whether it succeeds or not as "good writing" depends on the goal the writer has. Scriptwriters write primarily to entertain; journalists write to inform or persuade; poets write to create verbal beauty and transmit ideas; lawyers write to direct or to persuade, and sometimes, to obfuscate.

MBA admissions essays fall into the category of informing and persuading: you are writing to persuade Adcom to admit you, and you do this by providing sufficient, relevant, and compelling information about yourself, particularly your value as a candidate for admission. Your essays don't just describe you; they "argue your case" in front of the admissions "jury." Whatever the surface details of any point you make, underlying this you are always saying one identical thing, which is: "I deserve a place in this business school ahead of the next candidate because (I have this quality) . . . (and here's the proof)."

Arguments rely, above all, on good structure. Structure is what orders the parts of the argument and ensures they fit together to move the reader towards the conclusion you want the reader to draw. Structure knocks out waft, ramble, and clutter, to allow your reader to better follow you, understand you, and therefore—the holy grail—agree with you.

Crossing the river

The structure of a persuasive argument is not merely a string of points following each other. A persuasive argument has a form appropriate to persuasion—a form necessary to take the reader from where he is to the place you would like him to be. Think of a persuasion essay as helping someone across a river: you take him by the arm and you lead him from one bank to the other, hopping from rock to rock. Each rock is a step that connects to the previous one and to the next one in a logical sequence. Just as you would plan your path across the river, you should plan your path to your essay's logical conclusions. Don't go in any direction that doesn't take you to your goal. Just as you wouldn't choose to land on stepping-stones that don't get you further across the river, so your essay should not include information or steps that don't support the goal of getting the reader across the river, that is, to your point of view.

Managing the finite resource of reader patience and interest

The reader's attention is a finite resource. All writing competes for attention with other writing, and with other calls on the reader's time. As you sit down to compose your essays, take a moment to visualize the last moments in the life cycle of your essay: there it sits, buried in the middle of a pile on the reader's desk, making its way to the top as she tries to get a few more done in between meetings, emails, phone calls, fetching Mickey from daycare, and getting to the gym. Remember, on average each application gets about 20 minutes per "read," and each essay about two to three of those minutes. And reading, as we know, is hard work at the best of times.

Now she's reading your Essay 1. Her mind is half on the emails she has to send and the Dean's recent memo. Chances are, as soon as there's a confusing or boring bit, her eyes will lift off the page and land again further down in the essay, like a stone skipping on water, perhaps reading a sentence somewhere in the middle—another obvious bit—skip again, looking a little further down the page, right, yep, read the last sentence and done.

You don't want this. Being important and relevant is a start. But you also have to produce and package the information so that your copy goes down quickly and easily, like ice-cream on a hot summer's day. You want the reader to pick up the essay, be able to tell where it's going in the first sentence or at least the first paragraph, be sucked in through a good story, be clear why each part is there, and why the next part follows the preceding one, and be fully aware of what key points are being made. She is reading you out of obligation. It is her job. But you want to turn that obligation into a joy. You want her to put her nose down at the first word and not to lift it again until the end, along the way "high-fiving" your successes, commiserating your weaknesses, holding her breath in the tense bits, nodding warmly as she gets to see why your story leads you to an MBA and through it to something inspirational, and so on.

Ask yourself, can you read a book twice? Maybe. Ten times? Never. This is because soon your mind craves something it hasn't read. Adcom readers are obliged to read basically the same stuff in application after application after application. What benefit will accrue to you if you give them a break in their routine! If you can write something fresh and interesting that they have not seen 10,000 times before. Here's how to do it.

Stick to what is relevant and important

The art of being read begins with understanding what's important, relevant, and attractive to your specific reader at a specific time. If you write about something a reader needs or wants to know, when he wants to know it, your text becomes intrinsically attractive. A person is only going to read the newspaper's front page if he wants to know what's going on, or the instructions for the DVD player when she wants to connect it up: that is, when there is benefit to reading because an informational (or entertainment) need is served. If your content is outside the reader's current field of interest or need, it will be unattractive no matter how well you write or how "grabbing" your introduction is.

Similarly, your admission essay readers won't be attracted to your text unless it helps fulfill their need. So, what do they need? They need to fulfill their various responsibilities to their stakeholders by succeeding in the two tasks that admissions officers are responsible for: selecting the best candidates and constructing a balanced, diverse class. When they read you, they need to find out how good you are, what you might bring to the school, and what differentiates you from the other applicants, so they can accomplish these two selection tasks.

In considering what is relevant and important, bear in mind, as discussed in Chapter 1, career admissions officers are human resources professionals with the general set of interests and skill-sets that you might expect from this profession: they are trained and experienced in analyzing human motivations, challenges and choices, and people's ability to function in organizations. They are interested in and responsive to insightful, carefully motivated self- and life-path analysis. They are not primarily business or technology people.

Pass the "so what?" test

Expect your reader to constantly be asking the pointed question that all readers (including you) are asking themselves all the time. That question is: "So what?" For Adcom, if you give them a fact, a story, an observation or any other piece of information, they will want to know: Why is this relevant? Why is it important to know this about you? What understanding about you do I get from it? What am I learning about your growth, transition, development, experience, or insight? How and why does this advance your candidacy?

It is your job to answer these "so what?" questions by showing how each piece of your essay connects to you and your argument for an admissions ticket, and framing this, at least in part, in human resources and organizational behavior terms. Just as you skip the dense bits in the magazine story in search of what's interesting, so the admissions officer will skim over anything that doesn't take her to more relevant information and insight about you.

So when you are writing a story on your musical education in Chechnya, or the day you pitched a perfect Little League game, or why pandas shouldn't be kept in the National Zoo—be clear in your mind that the admissions committee fundamentally doesn't care about all that stuff. If they were reading for fun, they would be reading the novel on their bedside table. But they are not reading for fun. They are only following your verbal meanderings through your activities and philosophies as a means to an end, and that end is knowledge of you and whether you are worth a place at their business school. Therefore, it is your responsibility to make it obvious why each detour furthers their insight and helps their assessment of you. Anything in your writing that doesn't take the reader closer to significant insight about you fails the criteria of relevance and importance. It is, therefore, bad writing.

Delete the bits that readers skip

The simplest and most important guide to good writing is this: when you write, leave out the bits readers skip. If you want to know what readers skip, think what you try to avoid reading—that is, the kind of writing you find in legal documents, academic tomes, technical manuals, and the like, including:

- generic, impersonal statements and other forms of "official speak";
- lists of facts, dates, places, and figures;
- all forms of generalization and abstraction.

We've already established that readers will also skip when:

- they have information that is not important or relevant to them, or they can't work out its relevance;
- they are given information they already know.

The other standard causes of reader fatigue are:

- boring, dull, bland, monotonous language and sentence construction, and clumsy phrasing;
- writing where it is hard to piece together the argument or unscramble confusing or apparently irrelevant information.

Throw out "the written word"

For many people, writing means manufacturing an arcane species of language called "the written word." When we "put pen to paper," the way we talk is suddenly not good enough, and we strive for higher, more literary prose with different, bigger words, longer sentences and more complex, indirect constructions. The self-important obfuscation of most academic, legal, scientific, business, and government writing serves to harden these habits. What we get is artificial and impersonal text that fogs up the communication window between writer and reader.

This would not be too much of a problem if all we ever needed writing for was to record a scientific experiment or compose a letter to the electricity company. But it turns out we often have to attract, stimulate, and capture a reader.

Professional writers who do this for a living have all had to unlearn the formal style and, if you want to write good MBA essays, you need to too. Listen to the rhythm, structure, and vocabulary of (educated) everyday speech and write like that.

Write what readers read: human-interest stories

One of the things that professional writers have to learn is not to overestimate readers interest in theory and analysis. Readers have little tolerance for it. Nor do they generally like to read about ideological debates and other high-minded matters. What they do like is interesting facts and, particularly, human-interest stories. People are naturally drawn to stories, particularly stories about people in novel or challenging situations. Stories are what we first heard in the crib and what we had read to us on our grandparents' knee, and basically, as readers we never grow up. If you are in any doubt about this, think about what you read for preference—and what magazines are full of: sharply written stories about people doing stuff that we are curious about.

So all writing professionals know the art of being thoroughly read by satisfied readers rests heavily on telling human-interest stories. If that's what it takes for professional writers to get read, all the more so for you. In an MBA admissions essay, this means talking about a key memory, an important lesson, a transitional experience—giving a sense of the actors, the context, the action, the outcome, and so on. If you don't follow this principle, if your essays are just wordified resumes or theoretical arguments in your favor, your reader will soon be drifting and skimming and turning the page no matter how good your prose technique is, or how organized your analysis. Further, stories lower people's resistance to accept your ideas, make things easier to understand, and tweak emotions like nobody's business. So, tell stories to arouse and retain reader interest.

Bear in mind that if you are a typical MBA applicant, at a typical workplace and product of a typical university, you've spent much more time in your life writing depersonalized, analytical papers and reports than interesting personal stories. You are better at analytical writing and you are more comfortable with it. Bad luck. While you do need to closely back up what you assert, the personal, reflective, human-interest story is what makes an MBA essay.

Worse news yet, simply putting the story out there is not enough. Bad story technique makes the reader plow through a watered-down, reported version of events. A good story immerses the reader in the action and explores the personal drama. All good stories contain conflict and predicaments, and work towards resolution. Rather than simply report what happened, recreate the series of incidents and experiences for the reader. Let him experience what you experienced, and live through the event as you relive it. And tell it as if you were actually telling a story. Say who was there, what happened, what was said and what happened after that, building momentum towards a critical decision point or showdown moment. A story like this will be not only gripping, it will be differentiating, because you can be guaranteed that no matter how large the applicant pool, nobody else will tell this same story in this same way.

Choosing stories and the "carry freight" principle

In your profile analysis, you recorded stories associated with each of the brainstorming prompt questions. If you have lived a reasonably full life and you have done your brainstorming right, you will have many interesting, enlightening, and amusing anecdotes relating to your main profile points. Given the tight word limits of most MBA essays, you will be faced with hard choices about which stories to include. How do you decide between them? What are the criteria that separate a story more useful to your application from one that is less useful?

Apply the "carry freight" principle. In well-written movie scripts, every scene, event and piece of dialogue advances the plot and/or character development, and works to further the main narrative. Nothing is superfluous. Any scene that isn't a vehicle for character and plot gets axed. In the parlance of movie scriptwriters, every scene must "carry freight" for the movie as a whole. In deciding which story elements to include in your essay set, or which essay to put them in, you should be driven by the same principle: every story, and every element of every story, must carry admission freight for you. Ask yourself: Is this story a vehicle for my message? Does this story say what I'm trying to say, or prove what I'm trying to prove? If I'm trying to show the admissions officer that I'm a supportive team member, does this story do the job? Or does another anecdote do it better?

By implication, if you have a favorite anecdote that doesn't clearly advance your profile and message, it is useless to you. (Or, if you want to use it, you will need to change your message.) For example, you may have an "IT specialist" theme that collects together various points from your personal and professional life. In your profiling you may have recorded the story about the time you got a call from a New York client when you were in Bahrain; it was three in the morning and you had to go downstairs to the hotel lobby in your pyjamas to find a computer to get online to sort out a server crash thousands of miles and many time zones away. That story will advance your profile in terms of IT technical expertise, work ethic, international experience, and team spirit. It won't say anything about leadership, your personal preferences, or your career goals.

Obviously, where possible, the story that says various things about you—values, strengths, goals, unique attributes, and so on—is usually better than the story that says only one thing. But sometimes it pays to focus the reader's mind entirely on one attribute.

Be emotive: chicken soup for the Adcom soul

Your essay will be more prominent and penetrating if you "touch" the reader in some way. Don't be afraid to open up where this is where your story takes you and that's what's required. Think *Chicken Soup for the Soul*, the book that turned into a publishing empire. Why? Because people could not stop themselves reading those tearful, feel-good stories. Or think Oprah. Why did her show explode into the television legend it has become? Touching stories is what it is all about.

This does not mean you should burden your Adcom reader with your own slice of Mills & Boon. But you should aim to be emotionally moving and to elicit responses: a sympathetic surge of pride, a moment of happiness or sadness, a flash of anger or despair shared with you. Emotions show that you are human, that you are alive inside and that you can connect with the humanity of your reader. If his eyes water at the sad stuff ("smoke get in your eyes"), and she feels pride with you at your unbelievable success, bingo! You are getting through.

Bear in mind, also, the real-world reality that people (your admissions officer included) very seldom make decisions based only on facts. You don't need to look further than the stock market to see an example of where most people do extensive fact research and data analysis, and then make decisions based on hunches and emotions. You will be well served if you can touch your reader's emotional core, because subjective hunches and feelings will certainly be part of what decides whether you get admitted to a top business school.

How to do it

There is no touching emotional buttons without telling compelling personal stories. And there is unfortunately no short cut to the technique and writing control necessary to manage emotional responses. But even a non-writer who weaves a tight yarn that doesn't back off from personal topics can expect to strike some chords. When you've written your piece, try it out on a friend to see if it works. Word choice counts a lot here: don't disconnect yourself from your subject matter by using a pompous, dry lexicon. Use warm, human, emotive words. For example, don't talk about your "relatives," talk about "mum and dad and Uncle Bob." Don't talk about the "malnutrition" you saw in Mozambique, talk about "hungry people." Don't say you had "acute neuralgia," say you had a "bad headache."

Be visual: show, don't tell

The best writing uses words and actions to paint illuminating, memorable images. Literary critics call this technique "imagery." For example, consider Lady Macbeth, who, cracking under the pressure of guilt at the murder of Duncan, does not walk around saying, "I feel guilty, very, very guilty." That would be a complete yawn. Rather, Shakespeare has her rubbing and wringing her hands endlessly in simulated washing (of the blood off them) saying, "Out, damned spot!"

A picture is, as they say, worth a thousand words. Your application essays are only about 2,000 words in total, so you do the math. For every picture you induce in the mind of the reader, you greatly boost both the extent and the punch of your statement. Images will always be more powerful and easier for the admissions officer to remember than a list of points, qualities, traits, or qualifications—no matter how impressive any of them are.

How to do it

Go past merely presenting a statement; think of a moment in time that encapsulates the state or condition or feeling, and describe the associated picture. For example:

- If it was a wet day at the ballpark, and you say, "It was soaking wet," there is no picture. If you say, "There was mud in my socks as I squelched up the river to first base," you have planted an image in the reader's mind.

- When describing your experiences at an outdoor paramilitary camp in China, if you say, "I was living rough," there is no picture. If you say, "I picked spiders out of my hair at lunchtime," you have an image that tells it all.

Beware the standard clichéd images for certain descriptions and don't use them. For example, if it was hot outside, don't waste your talent by saying, "You could have fried an egg on the hood."

Be specific, detailed, and concrete

Think of the pleasure you get in a good photograph. Part of it is that it is clear and sharp. A fuzzy, smudgy picture is immediately off-putting and unfulfilling. Similarly, if your descriptions are vague and general, you will frustrate the reader. Precise details add life, color, and interest to your story. They make it unique and memorable. The details distinguish it from everybody else's story.

How to do it

Don't generalize or oversimplify your descriptions. When you tell a story, or when you talk about yourself, think of your pen or keyboard as a sharply focused lens that soaks up and reflects even the smallest detail. Talk in specifics and give examples: don't say, "I'm a published scientist," say, "I'm the co-director of the Massachusetts Young Physicists Committee, and I had two published articles in the society journal last year." Be faithful to names, dates, times, what you saw, what you heard, what you felt, what he said, what she said, and all other such details associated with the specific event that will allow your reader to see, hear, and touch the event along with you.

> General: "I'm a 'people person' and I have lots of friends, and I'm always the centre of my social network."
> Specific: "My friends say I have a mobile phone dent on my ear, and it could be true—especially when it seems everyone calls me to find out where we're all meeting on a Friday night."

> General: "I've been good at numbers since I was a child. I was always first in my class at math."
> Specific: "When I was about seven my older brother got a mental arithmetic game. You'd get a problem like 13×29 and you'd have to do it in your head before the egg timer ran out. I always won."

> General: "I've done a lot of sports activities in my life, both indoor and outdoor. This is a big part of who I am."
> Specific: "Open my closet and you will see . . . well, there should be camping gear, but I lent it to Jake. There's my snowboard, my tennis shoes, two pairs of rollerblades (a five-wheeler for speed), my titanium rackets, a battered bike helmet, gloves, baseball bat. You could say I'm an action nut."

Note how the boiled-down, generic versions could belong to any applicant. As soon as you put in details, not only do you get valuable pictures, but immediately the scene is unique to you and therefore you become memorable to the reader. While it is true that the details might take up more words in your essay, these are usually words well spent. Make your deletions somewhere else, where you are making vacuous statements nobody will remember.

The limits of adjectives

While adjectives have their uses, don't expect them to carry you very far. If you say it was a romantic beach, or a thrilling encounter or an interesting book, you are not telling the reader much. Instead, take the reader to the helicopter rescue and let him be thrilled. Or take him to the beach at Marsa Alam and let him think, "How romantic!" In other words, rather than state your judgment—the adjective—let the reader's perception unfold towards the judgment you want them to make due to your good description.

The power of details and numbers

Part of your task in the essays is to convince the committee of the extent, validity, and quality of your experience. The burden of proof is on you. If you were a trial lawyer attempting to prove a case, you would not just say, "There are many indications that the accused is the murderer." You would bring evidence of fingerprints, cell phone numbers dialed, voice recognition, eyewitness accounts, and every other possible detail, down to DNA samples, to make your case. Similarly, details help solidify the claims you make about your past. If you claim to have made a presentation to the Siemens Board at the company's head office in Munich, it doesn't hurt you to mention that from the boardroom you can see half of Bavaria. It's convincing. Let the details talk for you.

Numbers ground your story in the same way. Why say you led "a team of consultants" if you can say you led "a team of 25 auditors and 10 software developers"? Don't say you "implemented a new account management system," say you "fired the HP contractor, took a one-year turnkey solution offered by IBM, and managed the integration of new sales efficiency and reporting systems to increase productivity by 17 percent, while reducing errors by 42 percent and saving the company $1.1 million." (If this sounds like the way you have been coached to do a resume, that's no accident. Resumes require detail for the same reason: to give credibility to your claims of experience and ability.)

Keep your prose, ideas, words, and images fresh

The committee reads a lot of essays, on the same topics, from similar candidates, trying to prove identical attributes. Chances are, if something is a slightly tired phrase to you, it will be a stone dead one for them. Your reader, with at least six years of tertiary education and many more years of professional and life experience, will recognize a cliché for what it is: lazy thinking. Avoid all standard metaphors and known epiphanies. In other words, steer clear of beaches and sunsets and, unless you are a bona fide mountaineer, don't use mountain climbing as a metaphor for your personal or professional ascent. You won't believe how many times admission officers this year will read something like: "Standing on top of that ledge I suddenly knew all my goals were achievable." Yuck! Banalities and platitudes scream that you can't—or can't be bothered to—tell of events or express insights in a way that uniquely reflects you.

For the same reason, don't use jargon, acronyms, or buzzwords, which will make your writing sound like a regurgitation of others' ideas you have read and heard along the way and not got around to passing through your own filter of perspectives or forming your own opinion of. In particular, leave out things used to rev up business and technology magazines. Talk about the companies in your industry, not the "players in your space." Say you want to help your clients succeed rapidly, not to "post early client wins." Say you got people to work well together to develop new ideas, not to "create synergies for thought leadership." As soon as your reader thinks you are mouthing off, or (worse) does not understand you, or (worst of all) is not fully sure that you understand yourself, your application is halfway to the chop shop.

How to do it

Your ideas and prose will be fresh if you think of them yourself and express them in your own way, and it doesn't sound like anything you've heard before. It's that simple.

Be the master of your tone

Every MBA admissions essay you write demands a tricky balance between a personal and a professional tone. It is a frank and friendly chat with one person, where you are trying to create a memorable individual connection, but still requires the business professionalism Adcom expects from an applicant in a formal situation.

Like "body language," mentioned in Chapter 14, your writing tone communicates an enormous amount beyond the actual words. Step back from your prose and try to feel what your tone communicates, and make sure that the "inner" statement is congruent with the image of confidence and capability you are trying to project. Try to spend some of your essay-writing time at this "meta" level—focusing only on how you are coming across. At a minimum, you want your reader to feel you are smart, honest, and likeable. In fact, someone they would like to meet. To get your tone right, it helps to think of yourself as talking to one person, not many. Write as if you are holding one side of a conversation, and the other person is just across the table. Don't write as if you are giving a speech in the Sydney Opera House.

How to do it
The following are the dos and don'ts of MBA essay tone.

- Be animated and optimistic. Project enthusiasm and an interest in yourself and the world. Come across as an upbeat and solution-oriented.
- Be sincere. Your communication should feel open, upfront, direct, and to-the-point. Don't give the feeling you are slyly "giving them what

they want to hear." Adcom can smell a disingenuous statement at forty paces.

- Be humbly confident, neither arrogant nor self-effacing. Go easy on the bluster. Don't hype yourself or any of your experiences or contacts. Don't come across with "attitude." These are days of circumspection in the business world and being mostly successful most of the time is the best you should claim.
- Don't be too guarded. Don't hide behind a professional or academic veneer, using pompous words and a dry "objectivity" to poke gingerly at self-analysis from a safe distance, as though writing about someone else.
- It's okay to show you know what it means to struggle and overcome, but do not allow yourself any self-pity.
- Don't come across as indulged and pampered.
- Be practical and businesslike. Don't be whimsical or dreamy, or appear about to float off in flowery prose. Be emotive but not emotional.
- Don't be preachy or sound like you think you know all the answers.

Making sticky messages

Some messages "stick"—get picked up, noticed, remembered—while most get lost in the information bombardment that we are all subject to. The authors of the book *Made to Stick*,[1] "reverse engineer" sticky messages to figure out why—what makes them so? While it won't tell you what to say, the book draws together cognitive psychology (memory, motivation) and communications, to isolate the principles of "how to say it" so it has lasting impact. In doing this, it offer cross-cutting insights that are exactly consonant with the principles in this chapter and this book as a whole. The six routes to a sticky message are:

1. *Simplicity*: finding the core of the idea to be shared; weeding out ideas that may be important but are not the most important.
2. *Surprise*: getting and holding people's attention via unexpected information or telling that breaks a familiar expected pattern.
3. *Concreteness*: using words and images that are directly approachable via the five senses; avoiding abstraction and intellectualization.
4. *Credibility*: getting belief and agreement through evidence such as authority opinion, supporting data, or convincing details.
5. *Emotion*: getting people to care about the message by stimulating their emotions.
6. *Stories*: telling anecdotes, which provides the best vehicle for enacting the previous five principles.

16 Idea discipline, structure, and outlines

There is no good writing without good thinking. If you have your argument organized in your mind in such a way that your line of thought moves forward in a measured way towards its goal, with all points in clear relationship to each other and to your message, then you are already halfway to good writing. But if your essay is not a reflection of disciplined, lucid thought, no amount of language polish is going to help you. This chapter is your guide to the structure that should underpin your writing, and how you take this forward into a first draft. The next chapter talks about better sentence construction and word choice.

Classic structures

You can and should make your own structure for each essay so that you have one that is best designed to promote your specific argument. However, there are template structures that you can use directly, or adapt to create your own structure. These are the main types.

1. Shadowing the question

Multipart question
The most obvious and often the best structure is to shadow the question, providing answers in the order they are sought by the question. You let the question imprint itself on your essay and shape its outline. This is a natural way to deal with questions that have two or more parts. For example:

> Tell us about the most challenging team experience you've had to date. What role did you play? What factors made it a challenge for you? How did the group address these issues? (Duke-Fuqua)

A shadowing-the-question structure would be as follows:

- Paragraph 1: Introduction—story of my most challenging team experience
- Paragraph 2: Story continued
- Paragraph 3: My role, self-analysis
- Paragraph 4: Factors that made it a challenge
- Paragraph 5: How the group addressed these issues and my role in this
- Paragraph 6: Analysis
- Paragraph 7: Conclusion

Series of examples

Another appropriate time for a shadowing structure is when you are asked for a number of examples, e.g. "Discuss two accomplishments, one professional and one personal." Here again, you can use the question's own structure, providing answers in series and at the appropriate length according to what the question asks for.

A shadowing-the-question structure for this type of question may be as follows:

- Paragraph 1: Introduction—professional accomplishment story
- Paragraph 2: Professional accomplishment story continued
- Paragraph 3: Analysis of professional accomplishment
- Paragraph 4: Personal accomplishment story
- Paragraph 5: Analysis of personal accomplishment
- Paragraph 6: Analysis of skills and temperament common to both accomplishments
- Paragraph 7: Analysis continued and conclusion

When shadowing the question, you are working from a structure the questioner has created, so you can go light on signposting your transitions. Once you start with their structure, it's obvious that when you start with a new section it is going to be the next one in an expected series. You don't need to labor the transition by saying something like: "Turning now to my personal accomplishment . . ."

2. Time as structure

Time structures our days, weeks, months and lives, and it structures the narrative in books and movies. You too can use the chronological sequence of events to give your essay clear form and direction. For example:

> Recognizing that successful leaders are able to learn from failure, discuss a situation in which you failed and what you learned. (Harvard)

A time structure for this essay could go as follows:

- Paragraph 1: Introduction—setting up the preliminary explanatory information, conditions that were in effect before the event and which explain the event
- Paragraph 2: The failure story
- Paragraph 3: The immediate fallout and scramble to fix
- Paragraph 4: Later that day . . . A week later . . .
- Paragraph 5: Analysis (time = now)
- Paragraph 6: Analysis (time = future, what I would do next time) and conclusion

Comparing then and now

Occasionally, you might be asked to compare yourself at a previous age and era to how you are now. For example: "How have you changed since college?" or "By the time you graduate, in what way do you expect to be different to how you are now?"

Or you yourself may simply choose to answer any of the essay questions you face by comparing yourself in two distinct time periods.

In such circumstances, it is natural to use time to structure your essay. You can either spend the first third of the essay in the past and the second third in the present, or vice versa. (The final third should be kept for analysis.) Or you can go backwards and forwards between the past and the present, comparing yourself then and now, item by item, thought by thought, until you reach a wrap-up analysis conclusion. The structure might be as follows:

- Paragraph 1: Introduction—me now, my professional focus, interests and ambitions
- Paragraph 2: Me back then, professional focus, interests and ambitions
- Paragraph 3: Analysis or goals, skills developed and outlook developed
- Paragraph 4: Me back then, personal preferences, interests and outlook
- Paragraph 5: Me now, personal preferences, interests and outlook
- Paragraph 6: Analysis of development in outlook and understanding
- Paragraph 7: Analysis continued and conclusion

Making an essay outline

In previous sections we have described making an argument (for your admission) as like helping your reader across a river. You do better in getting your charge across the river if you plan your route—if you decide in advance which rocks you will land on and what the thread of your journey will be. An outline is a sketch plan of your structure: the point-form design of how your essay will advance the reader toward your point of view. There are two forms of outline planning: visual and linear. Which one you choose is up to you. Assuming the essay topic, "Why I need an MBA," this section describes both approaches.

Visual outline

First, draw a rectangle in the middle of a page. Write the topic of the essay (e.g. "Why I need an MBA") in the rectangle. Next, draw lines out from the central rectangle (keeping the lines orthogonal to help clarity and readability). At the end of each line draw a secondary rectangle. In each one put one major supporting topic, for example:

- short-term goals
- long-term goals
- what experiences have led me to this point
- why an MBA (why not a PhD, etc.)
- why this school in particular
- why now.

From each secondary rectangle (e.g. the one labeled "short-term goals"), draw a line for each of the basic steps in the argument or major categories of information. If there are further facts, details, and examples to support these points, continue the process of topic boxes and lines as necessary.

Once you have the elements of each of your main points in place, you need to decide which points are going to be made first, which next, and so on. You build your case like an architect builds a house: each new piece rests on and fits in with what has been laid down before, and in turn supports what will follow. The simplest way to do this visually is to number-order your points on your diagram (see Figure 16.1).

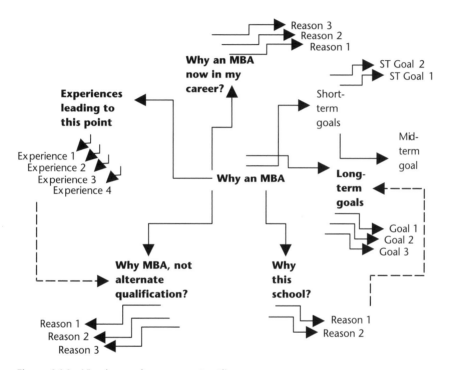

Figure 16.1   Visual map of an argument outline

Linear outline

A linear outline will do the same as above, in list format, using headings and subheadings. Idea-organization software will provide you with a template to do this if you need it. Your essay topic is your main heading, your chief supporting topics are your subheadings, and so on. Under each of the headings you write contributing points, or lists of sub-points as necessary. As you add content around your main and subsidiary points, they should support and reinforce the logical direction of the outline. Arrange and rearrange the sequence of your headings if necessary, as your thinking develops.

Either way, the object of this exercise is to arrive at the point where you have a clear, ordered, point-form skeleton of your argument that you can follow as you write. It should also create content discipline, with all the sub-points under every point grouped together so that they will appear in your written text together. If they do, you will avoid having all points that should go together scattered through the essay, and you will avoid making your reader search the essay for the elements supporting any point you make, or for the implications thereof. All the supporting information or evidence will be right there, attached to the point.

Talk your outline out loud

An outline should make sense on its own. You should be able to speak it out loud. For example: "First I'm going to look at my long-term goal of starting an action leisure company in Montreal; then I'm going to talk about my past experiences in leisure and travel consulting and entrepreneurial orientation that lead me to want to achieve this goal at this stage. Then I'm going to talk about my route to that goal after graduation, focusing on innovations in kite-boarding that will help me successfully launch the business. I will follow this by demonstrating why I need an MBA to fulfill my path. Finally, I'll explain why this specific program is the best one for me and my career plan."

The pros and cons of signposting

There are two advantages in using a clear structure. First, it organizes you and helps you keep the bits together that should be together and marshal them in the direction of your argument. Second, it helps the reader know exactly how you are answering the question and how the points will flow and come together.

You should signal the presence of your structure to the reader by signposting—raising markers in the road that spell out to the reader what is coming up and how it is organized, so that she moves forward with a clear mental picture of the road ahead and can tell at a reassuring glance where each part of your answer is and what order things are coming in. Signaling the reader where you are going is not a "nice-to-have" element. It is an absolute "must-have."

There is a caveat. Longer essays and articles have the luxury of formal signposting, for example: "I intend to deal first with the arguments for and against genetically modified foodstuffs, followed by a consideration of how scientific development in the field is changing the balance between these arguments . . ." But in a 500-or-so word essay you simply don't have the space. You have to imply the signposting, more or less as newspaper columnists do it—suggesting what you will cover and where you are going next, without wasting words saying it.

For example, you may start your success essay by saying: "My most important professional success could not be more different from my greatest personal success, but they are equally significant in explaining who I am." The reader is then ready for a structure where you deal with the professional, then the personal, and then compare and contrast them. In mid-essay you may signal your move from a professional example to the personal one by starting a paragraph: "In the personal realm . . ." which signposts the break without laboring the point or wasting words. Where possible, it is good practice to make the first sentence of every paragraph do its own work *and* also signal what's coming in that paragraph.

Given the tight MBA essay word limits, you will greatly help your cause if you stay within commonly used structures, such as those shown above, which will be what the reader is expecting and which will therefore require a minimum of active signposting.

Thesis statement

The thesis is the core of your argument. It is the reason you write the essay, the fundamental point you want the reader to get. It is the value-carrying content that you want to prove. Previously, we discussed the benefit of writing an approach or mission statement for each essay—a sentence or two that contains the focus of the essay and encapsulates your primary purpose in writing it. This should now be reworded and find its way into your final text as your thesis statement. In other words, your thesis statement rewords your essay mission statement for public consumption.

For example, the essay mission statement from Chapter 13 was: "I will show how I demonstrated initiative by discussing the day I stepped in as an emergency producer on a live TV show. I'll discuss the leadership qualities and creativity under pressure that were required, and state my other main strengths: cool head, adaptability, mental toughness, and maturity." A thesis statement from this could be: "Leaders need to be creative, adaptable and mentally tough, as I learned the day I had to take over as an emergency producer on live TV. I know what's required and I have demonstrated these qualities."

Another example of a thesis statement (for the "Why an MBA?" essay) is: "My success and promotion in the fixed income division of Morgan Stanley have reaffirmed my ambition to be a CFO in a large multinational firm. At this stage, to proceed along that path, I need an MBA from a top financial school such as the Chicago School of Business."

Try to avoid laboring your thesis statement, for example by saying: "The purpose of this essay is to . . ." or "In answering this question, I will attempt to . . ." If you need this kind of scaffolding, use it, but then take it down afterwards.

It is possible to write a good essay without a thesis statement, but unless you are very practiced at focusing and signposting your message, the lack of an identifiable thesis may lead to a meandering essay. Use the thesis statement to focus your essay, and keep strict tabs on your area of focus, and to limit the scope of your stories and analysis. It should guide you by helping you to figure out whether a point ought to be included or deleted. The thesis statement will also help to stop you trying to throw too much information at the reader.

The prominence of your thesis statement for you and for the reader may also be influenced by the kind of essay you are writing. If your line of reasoning is clear (e.g. this is my personal success and my professional success, followed by why they are important to me), then you need a formal thesis statement less. But if you are weaving a tapestry of ideas, moving across topics and across different periods in your life, a prominent thesis statement inserted early in the essay will help you place the pieces still to come, and help the reader to follow your trajectory.

Writing a first draft

By this point, you have isolated your profile elements and understand your key value points. You have worked these into your themes and application message-platform. You've picked your first school and you understand the question archetypes you face in the essay set. You've mapped your message onto the different questions, you've created an essay "approach" and "thesis statement" for each essay, and have created a mini-structure. You understand what's required of the introduction, middle, and conclusion. It's time to start writing.

With all these mechanisms in place, you really can't go too far wrong. The nets you have created will catch you and bring you back to the task at hand. So relax and let the muse do her work. Don't edit as you go along, and don't fuss style or elegance—this is just a first draft after all. There will be lots of time to sharpen and polish later. Just get going, let the words come and record them. Give yourself a chance to get some flow: write as fast as you can in one uninterrupted sitting. It should take you about 60–90 minutes, working quickly, to get a draft down. Write at least one-and-a-half times the stipulated essay length—double is even better—so you will have something to cut.

Where do I start?

The most common problem at the writing stage is getting going. Applicants know what to do, but still say: "I don't know where to start!" Contrary to the advice in *The Sound of Music*, the beginning is not a very good place to start. In fact, leave the beginning for the very end. When you sit down in front of a blank screen, write "Intro" and press the Enter-Return key a few times. Get on with the rest of the essay. The introduction will come to you as you write the body of the text—and even if it doesn't, you will still be in a better position to write it when the rest of the draft is complete.

Work off your essay approach or thesis statement—the point or points you are trying to make in the essay. Jot it down in your text and elaborate it in a couple of lines. This should give you something to focus on and direct your points towards. Then start with the easiest thing to write, which for most people in most essays is the "story" part. Write the story using as much action and direct speech as you like. Once you have the story down, you will be ready to write the analysis and implications, anticipating questions and counter-arguments, and drive towards fulfilling your own essay mission statement. Use the guidance in the essay archetype section above to make sure you are covering the ground adequately. Then recheck your essay mission statement to see which aspects you still need to address. When the body is done, write your conclusion and introduction.

The introduction

Whatever structure you choose, your essay will need an introduction that grabs the reader and introduces the central argument; followed by a body of about four or five paragraphs (for a 500-word piece) that develops the argument;

followed by a conclusion. The following sections provide tips on how to deal with each part.

The introduction is the most important paragraph in your essay for two reasons. First, as mentioned previously, the "Blink" factor is crucial. People make strong judgments, rightly or wrongly, in the first micro-seconds of contact with any situation, and Adcom readers are most certainly people. Their first impressions count. If you start loosely and sound confused or unconvincing, it is almost impossible to come back, no matter how good the rest is. Second, reader attention falls away rapidly. Just about everyone who sets out to read a piece will start at the beginning. Then, depending on their attention span and the value they perceive themselves getting, they go on to paragraph two, or they skip further ahead, or their mind wanders, or they stop reading altogether.

Journalists are well schooled in the following algorithm: if X number of readers read the first paragraph, only $X/2$ will read the second, and so the "half-life" of readership falls away further into the story. The first paragraph is the sole opportunity to entice reader attention for the duration of the piece.

The only way to write an interesting introduction is to start with the first interesting thing. In the movies you don't see the guy getting out his address book, looking up the number, calling it, getting a voicemail, leaving a message, going to get breakfast, eating it, going back to his room, calling, leaving another message, and then getting called back. The scene starts with the conversation. Similarly, when you pick your start point, start when interesting things begin and not a moment before. You don't need to "warm up" the reader with prefaces, histories, and explanations, and you don't need any windup or backswing to get going. Your first interest point doesn't have to be action, but it must be rich in content and relevance. If you have to go back and explain something, do it *afterwards*, in paragraph two or later. There are four basic forms of introduction:

Mirror introduction

This type of introduction directly reflects the question and often reproduces it verbatim. For example, in a leadership essay that asks you for two significant leadership experiences, you might say: "The two leadership experiences I value most are . . ." or "I was a leader among my peers many times while growing up. The following two occasions most clearly point to my leadership potential . . ."

The advantage of the mirror approach is that it is clear and unmistakable. The disadvantage is that it can be pedestrian and the same as everyone else's. The admissions officer will read this introduction many times. This is not in itself a problem, but be sure to get off the launch pad and into the story as rapidly as possible.

Didactic introduction

A didactic introduction is one that seeks to situate the reader in the topic and convey the scope and main points of the message to come. It will contain no surprises and will often be a lead-in to a story. For example: "When thinking about strategies for success, I think primarily of two things: my tough resolve to achieve and my flexibility in decision-making. I learned these lessons in December last year. I was in the boardroom, briefing various vice-presidents and section heads when . . ."

The advantage of the didactic introduction is that it allows you to begin in a clear, balanced way, but without the crutch of parroting the question. It opens up the topic in a way that puts you in charge of it, introduces the main idea and suggests one or more of the threads that will be followed, as well as why this is going to be interesting and valuable. The disadvantage is that, if it is not tightly written, it can be preliminary waffle that the reader loses patience with. It is the hardest type of introduction to write well.

Action-drop introduction

This introduction drops the reader into the middle of the action in a story. In a leadership essay, it might look something like: "We had a compass, but it was broken, and we were down to an inch of water in the jerry-can. There were no flares. The cell phone batteries were dead. Maureen wasn't complaining but after sharing the last packet of M&Ms, I knew it was time to take a few calculated risks . . ."

The advantage of this type of introduction is that you plunge right into the vein of the story. There's no wind-up, no prevarication. You pull the reader into the drama, and the narrative tension and promise of resolution keep him reading. We all read to find out "what happened next," and the admissions officer is no exception. Once immersed, the reader will stay immersed unless you mess it up. The disadvantage of this introduction is that you don't have the scaffolding and inherent signposting of other types of introduction. You have to work harder in the middle parts of the essay to create the sense of argument that your reader needs to understand how and why the action is relevant to your claim on a place in business school.

Cute introduction

This covers any other form of introduction—a quotation, a rhetorical question, a startling statistic, a chunk of poetry, and so on. You might start it something like: "Are leaders born or made? If made, what is this secret alchemy? If intelligence and creativity harden on the anvil of experience in some, but not in others, why not? My life has given me a unique vantage point to answer this question, because . . ."

Using quotations

If you have a quotation or an epithet you live by, and you want to use it to start or finish an essay, that's okay. It will get you noticed. But try not to do it more than once per application. It won't take long before the committee gets nervous about you. Also try to pick something unique to you. You may feel the need to quote Steve Jobs saying "the most important thing is to love what you do" which is very nice, but this is a generic insight. Ask yourself the same questions you would ask yourself for anything else you would put in your essays: does the quotation add to the essay? Does it fit with my essay approach and themes? Does the quotation say something interesting and valuable about me that I have chosen it? If not, drop it.

The body

Amateur writers expect to be read from start to finish. Professionals don't. We mentioned the "half-life" of diminishing reader interest in discussing introduction techniques. One solution the pros have developed is to write the most important things early and then, if the reader loses interest, well, at least the most important things have been communicated. This is called the "inverted pyramid" (the biggest stuff is at the top). This technique also greatly respects the reader's time. You don't make her wait until *you* are ready to tell her the most important information. You just spill it.

Scriptwriters, storytellers, and speechmakers (who often have a captive audience sitting down on chairs in an auditorium) have the luxury of a long buildup employing the techniques of suspense. In a sense your Adcom essay reader is a captive audience because they are paid to read you. But don't rely on it.

Both modes work, and the choice is yours. Just remember it is okay to strike early with the things you absolutely want the reader to know and to let the supporting data and explanations trail behind. At first it might feel unnatural, but you'll soon get used to it. This way you will have made no assumptions that, when you do finally pull your "rabbit out of the hat" after 483 words, your reader will still be in a good mood.

Paragraphing

The body of your essay is all the steps between introduction and conclusion. It includes all the stepping-stones in your argument as you lead your reader across the river to your position. Each paragraph is a step that contains and binds together elements of information that need to be delivered together, at each stage of the argument.

The conventional wisdom is that paragraphs should express one idea only, and as soon as you go onto the next idea you should start a new paragraph. This is appropriate for long-form writing. The MBA essay is too short and dense a beast, with each sentence working too hard, to always follow this rule. However, by convention and reader expectation, paragraphs signal the beginning of a new idea or a new step in the argument. They let the reader know when new stuff is coming, or when you are changing direction. You should be aware of this and try where possible not to have two major ideas in a paragraph, or various paragraphs dealing partially with the same idea. One idea and some supporting observations per paragraph is the expected protocol, the one your reader will be expecting.

Paragraph lengths are a personal choice: there is no right and wrong. It is fine to have short paragraphs—at a push a sentence can even be a paragraph, particularly if it is an important sentence that you want to draw attention. Whether short of long, the goal is to use paragraphing to organize your communication thematically, and to help your reader follow your logic as seamlessly as possible. Organized, one-idea-based paragraphing promotes discipline in thinking and writing, and discipline is what the admissions reader wants from you.

Transitions

As you move from one paragraph to the next, your reader—who is always on the lookout for structure and direction—will be asking: Why does this paragraph follow the one before? How does this link into the chain of the argument? The first part of the first sentence of every paragraph should provide a clear transition from the previous paragraph to the current one. Transition words help you do this by creating relationships between an idea that has ended and one that is about to begin, telling the reader how the new paragraph adds, changes, extends, compares, contrasts, or otherwise relates to the previous one. Control of your transitions will give your essay cohesion and the sense that the information is all going in one direction.

Transition words include "however," "in addition," "furthermore," "nevertheless," "additionally," "notwithstanding," "another," and so on. A transition can also come in the form of a phrase, for example: "Later that day" or "It was to be expected that." Or transitions can come in a sentence, such as: "Nothing would have prepared us for what happened the next morning." The main categories of transitional phrases are:

- *To show time and sequence*: meanwhile, eventually, soon, later, first, second, then, finally, also, besides, furthermore, moreover, in addition.
- *To compare and contrast*: likewise, similarly, in the same way, however, nevertheless, still, on the other hand, on the contrary, even so.
- *To show cause and effect*: therefore, as a result, accordingly, consequently, thus, hence, otherwise.
- *To offer examples and conclusions*: for instance, for example, after all, in fact, of course, in conclusion, in other words, on the whole, in short.
- *To show the result of an argument*: therefore, in summary, consequently, thus, the effect of this was, as a result of this.

If paragraphs flow naturally together, you may not need a transition word, but mostly you do. If you are having serious trouble connecting two paragraphs, and no transition word comes to mind, then the paragraphs probably don't belong together. Rework the outline.

The conclusion

The last sentence or two of your essay are the trickiest. You need to leave the reader with a final positive impression, and take this last chance to reinforce those key things you want him to have extracted from the text. The difficulty in concluding an MBA essay is that standard essay-concluding technique, which involves repeating and drawing together the main points, is *not* appropriate for such a short piece. It's silly to reiterate a point you made only moments ago. Given drastic space limitations, you will mostly have to settle for a one- or two-sentence ending that does not summarize.

These final sentences can state the main point of the essay if you have not done so already, or they can situate the key points of your particular essay within your application message as a whole. It sometimes works to return to the issue or problem posed in the introduction, showing what has been gained in the argument since then—that is, showing the reader that a river has in fact been crossed.

Generally, the temptation is to overwrite the conclusion, winding the essay up towards a grand summarizing flourish by trying to tie up the insights in one perfect phrase. Stop yourself from going for something like: "In conclusion it can be seen that the lessons I learned from my father, and my travel experiences in Indonesia, and my experiences at Accenture all come together at the right time to make me ready to . . ." It's never subtle and it is often excruciating.

On the other hand, you don't want to end abruptly, leaving your reader pressing the scroll-down button, or turning the printed page over, wondering if somewhere along the way the computer system dropped some of the copy. Rely on your structure to help you. If it is strong and follows a natural, obvious pattern, then your arrival at your conclusion will be a clear and expected event. As on a Ferris wheel, what goes out and up is expected to come around and back down.

Be careful to resist the trite "philosophical" insight conclusions that are a favorite of MBA applicants. If you find yourself saying something like, "In conclusion I can say I have learned that my family and friends are the most important thing in my life" or "I really believe that everything happens for a reason" or some such banality, sit on your hands until you can think of something fresh and interesting to say.

Conclusion dos

- *Synthesize, don't summarize.* Move away from the specifics of your argument and towards general perceptions and implications. Frame your discussion within a larger context. Answer the question: "So what?"
- *If appropriate, look to the future.* Leave the reader with your vision and a strong, clear sense of purpose and expectation of success.
- *Reflect the introduction.* This is not always possible, but where it is you can create a powerful sense of integration and cohesion. If, for example, you started your failure essay with an experience that went wrong, you could mention that you have the same experience coming up again soon, but your approach will be vitally different. In alluding to the opening paragraph, it sometimes works to echo its language or phrasing without, obviously, exactly repeating what was said before.
- *Work in your themes and message.* If several of your essays conclude with similar, subtly different but interlocking theme statements, collectively it will all start to add up in the reader's mind.

Conclusion don'ts

- Avoid winding-up phrases such as "in conclusion," "in summary," "to conclude," "in closing," etc. If you are one paragraph from the end of the page, your reader already knows you are concluding.
- Avoid the "ta-dum" finale. Don't try to pack everything into a final flourish phrase.
- Resist the trite, vacuous, insight summary.

- Resist the impulse to highlight your main points again. You don't have the space. If you do still have the space, you should have used it earlier to add something else of value about you.

Summary: the "take-home" message

Successful communication leaves the reader in no doubt as to what the purpose of the communication was, what she should walk away knowing. In the short MBA essay, you don't have the space to underline your message, so you need to be even more careful about being clear the first time. You are working towards a nailed-down argument as to why the reader and her committee should pick you and not the next applicant in the pile, who is probably equally good. You want to emphasize the message, which will ultimately come down to why you are valuable (along the lines of the 22 attributes outlined in Chapter 2), how you will make an impact at the school and beyond, and how you are different to the average applicant.

Whatever it is, don't make the reader guess. Make it patently obvious to any half-conscious reader (even to a drunken orangutan) what your basis for admissions is. Of course you can't just state it like a laundry list. That's a yawn. You have to use the power of interest, examples, and proof to get your message across. But if, when the reader closes your file, your uniqueness, accomplishments, strengths, and potential contribution to the school are not stamped on her forehead, you have not done your job.

The test is to give your draft essay to someone else to read. When they have read it through once, ask them what the main points were. If you get back a clear value-packed and persuasive message, you are doing fine. If you don't, rewrite.

Word limits

A common question is whether and by how much an essay can go over the stated word limit. To answer this, it's essential, as always, to think about any process or task or limit in admissions from Adcom's point of view. Put yourself in their shoes. Why do they ask for it? What are they trying to achieve? How does it help them?

So, what is Adcom trying to do with word limits? First, if there were no limits applicants would ask incessantly: "How long must it be?" Second, some applicants would write the great American novel, which would waste their time and the committee's. Third, limits provide a way of getting essays from different applicants to be more directly comparable, being the same length.

But there is usually some play in the system. The purpose of the essays is to get to know the applicant via their writing, and everyone knows that writing is a creative process and certainly nobody expects you to hit the word count on the nail. Note that in some online systems the computer applies the limit absolutely, and in this case there is no play in the system. But usually you are dealing with a human and this is not engineering or accounting, and anyway, application forms often talk about a word "guide" rather than word "limit." So you can clearly go a bit over, but by how much?

My advice to clients is not to go more than +5 percent in any essay. This kind of margin is a natural "rounding error" in finishing up what you have to say and will not hurt you if your reader is a reasonable person, which we assume he is. More than this will start to look like you are taking advantage and/or asking for an indulgence that your competitors are not getting.

However, if you write a number of essays that are noticeably short, it is fine to have one or two that are commensurately longer, so that the whole comes out more or less right. In fact, Stanford GSB explicitly allows this: its guidance is both per essay and for the essay set as a whole (1,800 words), so you are invited to trade off between essays as you see fit. How well you do this is, by the way, a test of your communications judgment.

What if you are under the limit? Similarly, I advise clients not to go less than −5 percent on any essay. In one sense, like all professional communicators, I believe strongly in "say what you have to say; say it once, strongly and clearly, and then stop talking." This is the royal road to more powerful communications. Certainly there's no merit in padding, waffling, and repeating yourself to fill out the word count. But admissions essays are relatively short pieces of writing, and you—if you merit a place at a top business school—are a multifaceted individual with an valuable track record, and if you can't find things to say to take up the word count, this in itself flags that you have not been able to (or haven't bothered to) properly investigate your own motivations or fully argue your merits, or somehow can't manage the essay process.

A cooling period

You should always—without exception—have a cooling period between writing and editing, and between subsequent edits, and between editing and submitting. The longer you can afford the better, but it must be at least overnight. (Stephen King in *On Writing* claims to leave a newly written novel in the drawer for six weeks before reviewing it.) When you come back to your essay with a fresh eye and cool brain, you will be able to catch errors, improve muddled phrasing, and enhance flow. New ideas will come to you too. If you can stand the embarrassment, it's not a bad idea to read your essays out loud to judge the flow of it and to catch errors that your eye misses.

After cooling, if you have written a draft of the full essay set, read it as a set in the number order—that is, as the admissions reader is likely to. Check that the essays complement each other and add up to a coherent picture, that they do not overly overlap and repeat material, and that each contributes in its own clear way to your message. You should also check for holes in your story. As you read the essays, ask: "What is missing?" Look out for any key piece of yourself or your background that you know so well you just assume it is known by the reader, but which in fact needs to be explained to someone who doesn't know you so they can make sense of your material. It's hard to see this yourself: you may need to prevail on a friend to help you.

Further drafts: revising, rewriting . . . and re-rewriting

Once you have a first draft, you're only half of the way there. It is the nature of writing that it always takes many iterations and many stiff reviews to achieve greatness. All writing starts out rambling and wordy. Concise thought and precise expression come in editing: joining ideas that should go together, smoothing phrases, improving diction, and refining word choice. Each rewrite you do should boil off some of the copy. The first rewrite should lose 25 percent, and subsequent rewrites perhaps 10 percent each. It is like reducing a sauce. Everything that remains will be stronger and sharper. This "sweat equity" principle of writing applies to the world's best writers. The more writing seems fresh and flowing, the more hours of careful revision it contains. Be ready for delays and don't get flustered when they happen. The following is a likely course of events:

- Your first rewrite—your second draft—will probably still be oriented to content issues: what you say, what you omit, what you emphasize, what you put in the introduction and conclusion, and where you add your themes and message. You will also be improving the organization of paragraphs and flow of ideas.
- By the third draft, content elements will mostly be settled and you should focus on the finer points of structure and coherence. You will also be dealing with issues of sentence construction and expression.
- The fourth draft should be mostly fine-tuning—tweaking a sentence here or there. The focus will be on clarity and style.

These are just general guidelines: depending on how quickly you work and the standard of finished product you are happy with, you may take less or more time. You are not finished until you have done a grammar check and proofread.

Why everyone needs an editor

All good writers put their writing through external copy-editing and proofreading. You should too. Not only will another reader find the small mistakes that you don't register because you are too preoccupied thinking about the content, but they will also be able to point out areas that are unclear (but perfectly clear to you because you have the necessary inside knowledge to bridge the gaps in the story). As the author, you cannot ever adequately judge how you are coming across to the fresh reader.

For this reason, if possible use an editor who is not familiar with your story, because, other than picking up errors and inconsistencies, a fresh eye will be able to tell you where you have made assumptions you don't even realize you have made. For example, you may be an energy engineer and you talk about venture capital as a goal, and what you mean—it's so obvious to you that you don't even mention it—is early stage investment in energy-firms, but unless you say that, Adcom won't know. They are not in your head like you are, and an outside eye will help you check for this kind of error.

Reusing essay material for other applications

Work on more than one application at once will put you in a situation where you have many half-essays in play, and every review change you make in one application you'll have to find and change in another, but then it may not work because the essay question is not identical and . . . this *will* drive you to the bottle (or Ben & Jerry's). Spare yourself. Do one application until it is finished. Once it's done, then you have options for reusing your fine text in the next one. The upside of spending many hours getting your essay developed, and value delivery, and phrasing exactly right is that it is there for recycling, where appropriate, in every application you make. The schools themselves recognize that you are likely to apply to multiple locations. They don't mind. It's not reuse that bothers them. It is sloppy and lazy reuse.

In other words, what is important in reusing copy is to make sure you answer each school's questions carefully and specifically. First, this is an indicator of intelligence (and, for foreigners, English competence). If you don't answer the question exactly and in all its parts it could be that you didn't fully understand it, or missed its subtleties. Second, all the schools know each other's questions, and they know that students reuse material, so a lack of exact focus to the question becomes a red flag as to applicant laziness.

For example, Chicago-Booth[1] asks: "Describe a time when you wish you could have retracted something you said or did. When did you realize your mistake and how did you handle the situation?" Wharton asks: "Describe a failure that you have experienced. What role did you play, and what did you learn about yourself?" On the face of it, these two are similar enough to use the same story and make the same points, and they are. But for Booth you have to couch it in terms of something you did that you wished you could undo. For Wharton, you don't, so if you start your essay talking about your wish to retract something you said, expect to get raised eyebrows. Also a failure and a mistake are not the same. A mistake may cause failure, but it may not. If you drum on about a failure in the Booth essay, they will be alert to sloppy essay reuse. What you want to alert them to is your effort and attention-to-detail. Tailoring answers to common questions carefully to their precise question helps them form a positive assessment of your diligence and effort, which is a proxy for how much you really want the place you are applying for. So any paragraph you lift from a previous application must pass these three tests:

- it must relate to the question exactly, and therefore might need serious tweaking;
- it must relate to the paragraphs immediately before and after it;
- it must relate to the argument you are making.

To best set yourself up to reuse material, it is helpful to do the application with the most extensive and demanding essay set first. (You may be tempted to take your easiest and shortest first.) But if you tackle the most comprehensive set first, you will have the maximum reservoir of completed prose to reuse. You will more often have the easier task of shortening and reworking than the harder one of thinking further and adding new stuff.

Proofread to show your hunger (yes, hunger)

Reusing essay material across schools brings us to the topic of proofreading because, if there is one consistent Adcom "pet peeve" across all schools is that the wrong school name often appears in the text. That is, Stanford GSB Adcom gets essays that say: "I would contribute to my peer learning environment at Wharton by . . ." Ouch! Putting the name of another school in the application pretty much screams laziness and sloppiness, an automatic ding. Do check that this does not happen to you. The only way to do this effectively is to wordprocessor search your copy for the names of all the other schools you are applying to.

Proofreading means checking painstakingly for spelling, grammar, punctuation, and typographical correctness. Typographic or other careless errors in your text immediately clues Adcom in as to how (un)careful you were with your text, and this tells them not only how organized and detail-oriented you are—whether you are a "finisher"—but also how much you actually really care about your application to their particular school.

If you could not be bothered to check your work thoroughly, that means you are *not hungry enough* for a place. Ding. Proofread as if your life depended on it because in admissions it does. In this sense, MBA admissions works just like a resume you send out for a job. If there's one error in it, eyebrows will be raised. Two errors and you may as well not have sent it. Famously, the spellchecker will help you a bit, but is not foolproof. It will happily let you say your first mentor was your high school "principle." Nor does it know that Haas is a business school, but Hass is an avocado.

As with editing, the tricky thing is that you, the essay-writing applicant, can't proofread your own work. Obvious errors will go undetected because you will be focused (rightly) on content and value delivery. Proofreading should be done by someone who is seeing the essays for the first time, and who is tasked only with looking for errors.

17 Improving expression: word and sentence strategies

This chapter provides techniques for wielding the knife as you go over your text in the quest for writing that is sharp, fresh, and easy to read.

Be brief

In the spirit of taking out the bits that readers skip, be ruthless in getting every superfluous word or phrase out of your writing. Cut every word that wastes space and blunts your message. Keep going over your text with a red pen looking for shorter ways to say each thing. When you are done, verbal fat should be gone and your text should feel tight and wiry: Homer Simpson will be turned into Lance Armstrong. The following will help you to be brief:

Avoid redundant points

Check that each sentence adds something significant to what has been said before. If not, delete it. If something is obvious, don't say it. Once you've made a point, don't come around and make it again using other words in the following sentence. Make your point definitively the first time and move on. A good structure will help you here. If you have all your sentences that address each particular point grouped together, and the point is addressed once and fully before you move on, it will be easy to see where you are repeating.

A more subtle part of this is knowing when a point is made. Say you want the reader to know that you are good at social media marketing. When you talk about developing, for example, client Twitter campaigns you are adding value, and there is merit in adding your mastery of Technorati and social bookmarking. But by the time you are talking about the fourth or fifth application of which you are an expert practitioner, the point is already made and your benefit returns are rapidly diminishing or becoming negative. Back it up with specific evidence, and move on.

Avoid redundant phrases

Sharpen sloppy, wordy phrases that pass when people talk loosely. For example, cut the phrases [in brackets]:

- The fact [of the matter] is . . .
- The [end] result was . . .

- I returned [each and] every phone call . . .

Sometimes a redundant phrase can be replaced by a shorter, clearer word or phrase:

- "I will finish my application [within a comparatively short period of time]" becomes "I will finish my application soon."
- "I am applying for an MBA [due to the fact that] it will enhance my career mobility" becomes "I am applying for an MBA because it will enhance my career mobility."
- "[There is a chance that] I will take a finance course next year" becomes "I might take a finance course next year."
- "[We came to the conclusion that] the music was distracting" becomes "We concluded that the music was distracting."

Avoid tautology

Tautologies contain redundant repetition of your point. For example: "It was a [false] delusion that caused me to make some early career mistakes."

Don't start sentences that state your point of view by saying: "I think that . . ." /"I believe that . . ." /"In my opinion . . ." If you are writing it, it is obviously what you think, that is, it's a tautology.

Avoid redundant words

Many sentences contain unnecessary words that repeat an idea already expressed. Delete them, and also delete words that readers can infer. For example:

- At first [glance] . . .
- Varda and I bought [exactly] the same marketing book.
- The [basic] fundamentals were . . .
- The printer is [located] near [to] the computer.
- This is done by [means of] inserting the buckle into the catch.

Empty, abstract nouns such as "nature," "position," "factor," "character," "condition," "situation," "aspect," "consideration," "degree," "area," and "case" can cause wordy redundancies:

- His GMAT is [of a] satisfactory [nature].
- Her mentor is not [in a] prominent [position].
- I am now [in the situation where I am] able to begin my essays.

Sometimes a sentence needs to be re-jigged to get rid of the empty noun. For example: "Student demand is rising [in the area of] online services" could be rewritten as "Student demand for online services is rising" or "Students are demanding more online services."

Avoid unnecessary prepositional phrases

Often you can shorten "from," "of" and "by" constructions. For example: "It was necessary to stop people [from] cheating." Sometimes turning the construction into a possessive clause will help simplify it. For example: "The opinion of the working group" or "The opinion put forward by the working group" can be rewritten simply as "The working group's opinion."

Avoid empty qualifiers and modifiers

Don't use "somehow," "somewhat," "rather," "probably," "quite," "considerably," "absolutely," "possibly," "totally," "utterly" or similar empty words to qualify your statements:

- I was so [totally] obsessed with my grades that I became [utterly] self-absorbed.
- He had [considerable] difficulty recognizing the [absolutely] critical nature of the situation.

Besides bulking up your copy and slowing down the reader, overuse of modifiers also makes you appear diffident.

Avoid overuse of constructions using the verb "to be"

Including "be," "am," "are," "is," "was," "were," "will be" and "could be," or "going to be" which slows down the sentence and which also often throws it into the passive voice. For example:

> *Don't say*: In April, when I am going to be presenting at Interop.
> *Say*: In March, when I will present at Interop.

> *Don't say*: It was my low quantitative GMAT result that persuaded me to retake the test.
> *Say*: My low quantitative GMAT result persuaded me to retake the test.

> *Don't say*: There will be indications of how admissions officers are aware which essays are bought on the Internet.
> *Say*: Admissions officers will indicate how they know which essays are bought on the Internet.

> *Don't say*: His results were indicative of a person likely to succeed.
> *Say*: His results indicated a person likely to succeed.

Avoid "that"

There are times when you need "that" in your sentence. But check every time whether you can leave it out, for example: "Read the new book [that] I bought."

Use everyday language

Don't use fancy Latinate, multi-syllabic, abstract words. You are not applying for an M.Litt. The top of your vocabulary register should be no higher than that which you would use in everyday speech in a reasonably formal environment such as the office. For example:

- Say "stop" not "desist from."
- Say "after" not "subsequent to."
- Say "aware" not "sentient of."

If you consult a thesaurus, do not pick a word unless you personally use it often. Do not use a word you have to look up in the dictionary after you find it in the thesaurus. You risk sounding like a phony, even if you use the word correctly, and certainly if you use it wrongly. At the other end of the spectrum, don't use slang or jargon. Say: "she was affected by the decision" not "she was impacted by the decision." Also, avoid technical terms, or be very careful to explain them. The classic test is: if your grandma wouldn't understand it, it's too technical. Don't assume the admissions officers knows anything about technology or business. That's not their job.

Write in the active voice

Use the active voice every time, unless there's a good reason not to. That is, your character should be the subject of the verb, as in: "I arranged the student conference" not "The student conference was arranged by me." The passive voice ("The student conference was arranged by me") has the sentence structure: object–verb–subject. The active voice ("I arranged the student conference") has the structure: subject–verb–object.

The active voice does five things for your essay. First, it reduces words and adds briskness. Second, it is clearer. Third, it is more direct. Fourth, it is more personal: you are obviously present in the story. Fifth, it makes your agency more obvious. For example:

> *Passive*: While I was at business school there was a significant improvement in my work ethic and the growth of my confidence was evident.
> *Active*: While I was at business school my work ethic improved significantly and my confidence grew.

> *Passive*: The bidding system for electives is thought by most students to be fair, but the drain on the IT system has been underestimated by the administration.
> *Active*: Most students think the bidding system for electives is fair, but the administration has underestimated the drain on the IT system.

There are times when the passive voice is appropriate. Use it when:[1]

- You don't know who did or will do the action. Say "Plagiarism will not be tolerated" (to imply this non-tolerance could be effected by any one of various authorities).
- Who does the action is self-evident. "Interview appointments should be made as soon as possible" (by the candidate, of course).
- The agent of the action is less important than the effect (or is unknown).

"Every year, thousands of students are confused by the elective bidding process."

- You want to emphasize the action rather than the agent. "After a frantic search, the interview score sheet was found in the wrong filing cabinet."
- You want to be tactful by not naming the subject. "It appears the role of the recommender has been misunderstood."
- To create an authoritative tone. "No applications will be accepted after 11 January."

Keep subject, verb and object close together

Readers like sentences where the subject quickly connects to a verb and the verb to its object. Be careful about placing subordinate clauses in the way, forcing readers to have to keep a lot of information straight in their heads while they read. Remember, the idea is that *you* work hard to make life easy for the reader. Rework the sentence to make causal links clear. This usually means moving all the complicating and modifying material that interrupts the flow of subject–verb–object to either the beginning or the end of the sentence. For example:

> *Blurred—subordinate clause in the middle*: "My references, because they were written in an impersonal, pompous style, did not make an impression on the admissions committee."
>
> *Sharp—subordinate clause at the end*: "My references did not make an impression on the admissions committee because they were written in an impersonal, pompous style."
>
> *Sharp—subordinate clause at the beginning*: "Because they were written in an impersonal, pompous style, my references did not make an impression on the admissions committee."
>
> *Blurred—subordinate clauses in the middle*: "The faculty's decision to allow laptops in group exams, even if carried out in the next year, or, failing that, phased in over a number of years, will do little to stop people cheating."
>
> *Sharp—subordinate clauses at the end*: "The faculty's decision to allow laptops in group exams will do little to stop people cheating, even if carried out in the next year, or, failing that, phased in over a number of years."

If in doubt whether your subject, verb and object are close enough, apply the following test: Underline the subject, verb, and object. If there is a wide gap between them, rewrite!

Use more and better verbs

Put as many active verbs as possible into your copy. Verbs add action and move the story along. They help you to be direct. It is hard to equivocate when you use verbs, particularly in the active voice. Adjectives and adverbs don't move the narrative in the same way; they don't create the forward momentum that verbs do. In fact, mostly they just slow the reader down.

A common problem in non-professional writing is that the verbs are hidden as nouns or adjectives. For example, "He will make a decision" hides "He will decide." This causes prose that feels long-winded and bureaucratic.

Extract verbs from nouns. For example:

- Say "I conclude that . . ." not "I have come to a conclusion that . . ."
- Say "He specified that . . ." not "He made the specification that . . ."
- Say "The meter measures . . ." not "The meter produces measurements of . . ."
- Say "Tim analysed the situation" not "Tim produced a situational analysis."
- Say "The hiring process must be evaluated" not "An evaluation of the hiring process needs to be done."

Similarly, extract verbs from adjectives:

- Say "influenced" not "was influential."
- Say "glorifies" not "is a glorification."
- Say "prefer" not "have a preference."
- Say "appeared" not "had the appearance."

Other examples include:

Hidden verbs: When the university made a decision to expand its library, it implemented the purchasing of more technical periodicals.
Manifest verbs: When the school decided to expand its library, it purchased more periodicals.

Hidden verbs: Because bottlenecks in the supply chain are damaging to business relationships, the decision of management was to expand the workforce.
Manifest verbs: Because bottlenecks in the supply chain damage business relationships, management decided to expand the workforce.

All verbs are not equal

Try to use verbs that still pack some punch. Basic verbs will do a basic job. Many are washed out or clichéd, and should be avoided. For example, you don't want to say "I slaved at the office all night." Sometimes a little lateral thinking will give you a verb that may wake up the reader: You could say "I remember the day my brother drove up to the driveway in his new Mustang," but you could say something like, "I remember the day my brother slithered up to the driveway in his new Mustang."

Use conjunctions and pronouns

Conjunctions and pronouns help you to write more directly and naturally. They put different parts of a sentence in direct relationship and demand that you clearly commit to what that relationship is. This stops you from writing bureaucratic, impersonal prose. Conjunctions also let you place events in the order that is simpler for the reader—that is, going forward in time. For example:

Blurred: We missed the market despite having bought the consulting reports.
Sharp: We bought the consulting reports *but* we still missed the market.

Blurred: Their increase in revenues came about even though they reduced outlets.
Sharp: They increased revenues *despite* reducing outlets.

Pronouns

You will write better if you refer to people using ordinary personal pronouns, as you would when speaking. If you refer to yourself, say "I" or "me" or "my," not "the author of these essays" or "the writer." When you refer to anyone else, say him or her or they, etc. This will help you avoid the evils of indirect speech, hidden verbs, and other pomposities. For example:

Hidden pronoun: Examination of the evidence is necessary before the judge will be ready to make a decision.
Manifest pronoun: The judge will need to examine the evidence before *he* can decide.

Hidden pronoun: As there was no microphone, it was the speaker's position that the presentation should be canceled.
Manifest pronoun: As there was no microphone, the speaker thought *her* presentation should be cancelled.

Watch parallelism

When you have a series of words, phrases or clauses, make sure their grammatical construction is congruent so that the reader can identify the linking relationship better.

For example:

Not parallel: The candidate's goals include getting into Harvard, Baker scholar recognition, and a Goldman Sachs job.
Parallel: The candidate's goals include getting into Harvard, being a Baker scholar, and getting a job with Goldman Sachs.

Avoid ambiguity

To get clear, unambiguous sentences avoid the following mistakes:

1. *Avoid noun pile-ups*. Too many nouns together are difficult to understand. One way to correct a noun pile-up is to change at least one noun to a verb.
   Don't say: "I drafted a workplace relationship enhancement proposal."
   Say: "I drafted a proposal for enhancing workplace relationships" or, even better, "I proposed enhancing workplace relationships."
   Don't say: "Bain has an interdepartmental gender bias evaluation program."
   Say: "Bain has an interdepartmental program to evaluate gender bias."

2. *Avoid multiple negatives.* Multiple negatives are difficult for readers to unpick. For example:

    Unclear: Less credit is withheld from previous Master's degrees that don't lack quantitative components.

    Clear: The committee gives more credit to previous Master's degrees that contain quantitative components.

3. *Avoid unclear pronoun references.* Be sure that your pronouns ("it," "they," "this," "that," "these," "those" and "which") or personal pronouns ("him," "her," "them," "their," etc.) refer clearly to the noun they stand in for. For example:

    "As the student is better at finance than accountancy, he prefers to take courses in it." (Which one?)

    "Steve told Sean that no-one would take him away." (Take who away?)

4. *Avoid unclear modifiers.* Place modifiers (constructions that modify or add to the information in a sentence) near the words they describe, and punctuate carefully. For example:

    "I booked a hotel on the beach called 'The Robberg' " (is that the name of the hotel or the beach?) should be "I booked a hotel called 'The Robberg' on the beach" or "I booked a hotel on Robberg Beach."

5. *Avoid imprecise use of words.* For example:

    "By predicting a weakness, you can emphasize countering strengths." [Predicting could be what you mean, in which case it is not wrong, but "anticipating" may be closer to the real intention of the sentence.]

6. *Avoid inadequate punctuation and over-punctuation.* Use commas and other punctuation as necessary to indicate relationships among ideas and sentence parts. For example, the following sentence has different meanings, depending whether commas are inserted:

    The applicants who were Canadian received $500.
    The applicants, who were Canadian, received $500.

    On the other hand, too much punctuation makes writing difficult to read. For example:

    "Field trips are offered, in several courses; such as operations management and organizational behavior" is better written as "Field trips are offered in several courses, such as operations management and organizational behavior."

7. Check for unwanted double-entendres. For example:

    Shelly likes scuba diving more than Patrick.
    The mayor ordered the police to stop drinking and driving.

Raise the pace

One way to solve many of the problems highlighted in this chapter is to "raise the pace" of the text. This just means using fewer words and cutting out unnecessary clutter, in order to get the reader quicker to value. For example, you may find yourself saying something like this: "Unconventional ideas often cause doubts to occur in others, and this one I had required my great fortitude and conviction and meeting with many stakeholders to realize its potential. After extended discussion with various team members I was able to convince them to see my point of view more clearly."

This is making various of the mistakes highlighted in this chapter, but, putting it all together, it is guilty of slow value delivery. If you want your smart and busy reader to stay on board you need to raise the pace, for example: "Unconventional ideas are often doubted, and this one required my fortitude and conviction in many meetings, to win over my team members."

But keep a watch on over-brevity

Applying rules such as these should change your prose style from a meandering waffle to a tightly packaged message, which is right for admissions officers who are smart, busy people with little time to waste. Your essay should feel efficient and to-the-point—"businesslike," if you like.

However, brevity does not mean writing short, choppy, simplistic sentences (and never, ever resort to shortened "military-speak"). You must still write plain English, with varied sentence lengths and structure and enough description and elegance to satisfy the reader. It's okay to use words, just don't waste them. The essay should appear tight, not clipped.

One way to keep your copy lean is to list items. There is some debate on whether to use bullet points in MBA essays—that is, whether the test of the essays also strictly includes a test of your ability to express yourself in discursive paragraphs only. This will probably depend on the prejudices of the individual reader. To play it safe, don't overuse bullet points. However, you can still use "first, second, third," etc., to make the points in a multipart argument clear.

Conclusion

This book has outlined a method for creating a competitive business school application involving a series of steps in four phases. Part One develops a picture of what Adcoms at top business school programs are looking for, and their basis for selecting candidates. This gives an idea of the culture of business schools themselves, how they work, what they are committed to providing to the school in the incoming class pool, and therefore the many considerations they have in admitting or rejecting applicants, and how they go about this.

The next phase, covered in Part Two, gives applicants a way to critically understand the value in their own profile, and identify and extract the most important and persuasive parts—their key areas of competitive value—and consolidate them into clear application themes. Adequate, honest, personal diagnostics and profiling is the difference between a generic applicant and an interesting one. The bottom line for the admissions committee is to feel they have "met" and like the candidate, and they can only feel that if the candidate knows him or herself well enough to present candidly at this level. You must do the work to find what's relevant, meaningful, different and memorable in your story, and frame this value within a profile message that is resonant with Adcom's needs, as defined in Part One.

Once you have a differentiated value profile, a clear strategic positioning and a compelling message, the lessons of Part Three are how to communicate this in the essays and interviews. Knowing the best way to advance your value package via the essay questions posed—what to say and which essay to say it in—requires a close understanding of the essay questions and what they are really asking you for. There are, in fact, only a limited set of question "archetypes" and recognizing these is the key to understanding how to divide up a profile between them. The interview involves similar "mapping" of value to the questions you face, but creates higher demands in terms of managing interpersonal dynamics.

The final phase involves the nitty-gritty of actually writing the essays in a way that advances your prospects. The clearer your story is to you, the better you will write it. Many applicants have a well-worked valuable story to tell, but are still not able to tell it in a way that attracts and holds the reader. This requires the techniques of essay structuring, brevity and writing craft, as outlined in Part Four.

The following is a summary of the most important keys to a good application. If you do nothing else, focus on these twelve things:

1. *Show self-knowledge*. The Greek Oracle at Delphi said "know thyself" and this is the golden key to admissions. If you know who you are and where

you're going, and why it requires an MBA, you're more than halfway to getting in. The profiling tool in this book is a quick and effective way to achieve this basic self-knowledge. If you don't clearly understand your strengths, weaknesses, achievements, preferences, goals, and motivations, you'll end up looking and sounding like a generic candidate. Ding.

2. *Show past success.* In an ideal world, business schools would have the time to fully investigate the merits of each candidate who applies. In reality, they can't do this: they have to rely on your past successes and past people who testify to your successes (the referees) as a shorthand indicator of your future success.

3. *Show leadership experience and aptitude.* Leadership is the ability to motivate and coordinate the efforts of others towards a common goal. It is the key management skill and the key to management success. Wherever you have done this successfully so far in your life, the admissions committee should know about it.

4. *Prove it with evidence.* You think you're great, and you surely are. But your opinion is self-serving at best. What counts is the evidence. Any positive opinion of yourself you offer must be immediately backed with evidence. The strongest evidence is concrete: promotions, awards, etc. But stories and anecdotes will do the trick too.

5. *Position yourself away from the competitive categories.* Business schools have oversubscribed and undersubscribed categories. Bankers and management consultants will be common. Tibetan monks and ballet dancers will be under-represented. But even if you're not radically different, look for ways to emphasize the differences in your profile and so exit from the herd.

6. *Have clear, interesting, ambitious future goals.* Nothing turns Adcom off like a candidate who wants to become a consultant or doesn't know what he wants. They don't like to think you will waste their precious education. They want you to make a difference in the world in some unique and relevant (to you) way. Reassure them that you will do so by telling them exactly what this will be. Don't say too little. Seize the opportunity the essays present. If you give more than a muttered safety-first statement, you'll get more back. The reader can only get out what you put in.

7. *Focus on telling your story* and don't try to give them "what they want to hear." Candidates invariably get bent out of shape by trying to second-guess "what Stanford needs" or "what's hot at Kellogg," etc., and often neglect to say who they really are and where their own strengths lie. In fact, all schools are looking for a mix of strong candidates of all types and backgrounds (to achieve class balance). Therefore, their requirements are so similar as to be identical for all practical purposes. If you get your profile right, you can get in anywhere.

8. *Don't praise the school.* They are fully aware of their value and their charms. What they want to know is why *you* are valuable and how you will add value to them. Keep your comments about the school at the level of showing the fit between you and them—how the program will contribute to you and how you will contribute to it.

9. *Don't try to be too competent.* Successful is good. Perfect is highly dubious. Particularly in your twenties, with just a few years of life and work experience behind you, you cannot have fully "arrived" yet in any sense. If you are too good, not only is it suspicious, but you leave them no role to add to your skills and build your profile.

10. *Be personal.* Give Adcom real insight into your character, passion, personality, and self-understanding. Don't think you can escape with the standard platitudes, keeping a cool, distant reserve. You won't fool anyone.

11. *Be unique.* How do you know if your statement of purpose is not unique? Easy: if what you say could be said by the next applicant or the one after that, it's generic. If what you say could only have been said by you, it's unique.

12. *Be likeable.* MBA applicants often walk around with the myth that they have to be industry tycoons-in-training to get into a good business school. Not so. A pleasant attitude and open, fair-minded, reflective values will take you much further. People always choose people they like as colleagues and co-workers, and Adcom is no different.

Notes

1 Marketing to Adcom

1 UCLA-Anderson: Admissions Q&A—*BusinessWeek*. http://www.businessweek.com/bschools/content/may2009/bs20090526_803957.htm, viewed December 8, 2009.
2 Bader, J. "Seven Words to Remember," *SitePro News*, February 4, 2009, viewed December 2009. http://www.sitepronews.com/archives/2009/feb/4prt.html
3 Stanford MBA Admissions, June 2004: http://www.gsb.stanford.edu. Stanford's guide to the applications evaluations process is highly generalizable to all the top programs.
4 Stanford MBA Admissions, January 2010 http://www.gsb.stanford.edu/mba/admission/essays.html

3 Admissions fundamentals

1 There is some indication that the scoring of the GMAT (and/or GRE) will change in the coming years. If so, the numbers will change, but the underlying principles of how these tests are used in admissions will not.
2 www.hbs.edu/mba/admissions/blog.html.

5 What goes on after you hand in your application

1 M. Gladwell, *Blink* (New York: Little, Brown & Co., 2005).
2 M. LeGault, *Think!: Why Crucial Decisions Can't Be Made in the Blink of an Eye* (New York: Threshold, 2006).

6 The profiling project

1 A. Maslow, "Theory of human motivations," *Psychology Review*, 50(1943): 370–96.

10 The MBA essay question archetypes (part 1)

1 Essay examples are selected for demonstration purposes from the real essays schools currently require, or have required in previous years.
2 http://www.hbs.edu/mba/admissions/blog.html, viewed December 2009.
3 G. Soros, *Soros on Soros: Staying Ahead of the Curve* (New York: John Wiley & Sons, 1995), p. 18.

11 The MBA essay question archetypes (part 2)

1   http://mbaoath.org, viewed December 2009.

12 The MBA essay question archetypes (part 3)

1   These questions are from 2004–5. While the literal questions have changed in many cases, the principle of multi-archetype questions remains identical.

14 The interview

1   You will not need any Latin to get into b-school, but this will help you avoid appearing uneducated in your interactions with Adcom. The correct usage of alumnus, alumni is as follows—masculine singular: *alumnus*; feminine singular: *alumna*; masculine or mixed plural: *alumni*; all female plural: alumnae. When using the singular, the gender-neutral "alum" is passable too.

2   Very occasionally faculty are involved. For example, Oxford and Cambridge, UK, have a tradition of "dons" choosing their students, and the business schools have so far maintained this.

15 Managing the reader's experience

1   C. Heath and D. Heath, *Made to Stick: Why Some Ideas Survive and Others Die* (Random House, 2007).

16 Idea discipline, structure, and outlines

1   Questions taken from the mentioned schools' MBA essay requirements, 2009.

17 Improving expression: word and sentence strategies

1   Adapted from The Writing Center, University of Wisconsin-Madison http://www.wisc.edu/writing/Handbook/CCS_activevoice.html (May 2005)

Appendix
Essay revision checklist

There are many things to check for as you revise and improve your essays. The following records just the essential questions you should ask yourself.

Profile

- Does this essay make me memorable? Have I put in enough to be interesting, or am I still a face in the crowd?
- Are the main points about my profile clear? Is it clear why this profile would be unique and valuable to the school?
- Does this essay reflect me specifically, or could anyone else have written it? Does it open a window that gives genuine insight into me personally?
- Have I revealed distinctive, significant things about my values, choices and preferences? Or have I just made the right noises while keeping prying eyes at bay?
- Does this essay provide information about me that the rest of my file data and recommendations do not?
- Do the essays fit with the profile that comes through from the rest of the application?

Argument

- Have I answered the question? Does any piece of my answer not fit with the question?
- Is my message clear? Have I made a precise, logical argument for my candidacy which rests on points that are fully backed up? Have I provided a set of solid reasons as to why I deserve a place?
- Are my themes and highlights absolutely prominent, or did I play cloak-and-dagger with the committee and try to make them guess the most important things about me?
- Do the essays in the set add up to one coherent image, and does each essay contribute in a clear way?
- Have I targeted the school exactly and in detail?
- Is anything (other than my themes) said twice? Are there any obvious or redundant statements?
- Are there contradictions or obvious gaps in the narrative or in my profile?
- Are my conclusions justified by the evidence and examples I present?

Structure and coherence

- Is the introduction engaging? Do I prepare the reader for what's to come?
- Is the conclusion appropriate to the introduction and the argument?
- Is there clear structure and signposting—have I helped the reader to know where I'm going before I get there?
- Are my ideas developed one at a time, each with supporting evidence as necessary?
- Does each paragraph relate to the question, and to the preceding and following paragraphs, and to the thrust of the essay as a whole? Or will I be caught having boiler-plated paragraphs from another application?
- Is my essay one unified argument? Do all parts contribute to the main argument, or are there tangents and digressions?
- Is the transition between paragraphs clear? Are there transitional words and phrases to connect the sentences, or do I lose the reader as I progress through the essay?

Expression

- Have I been brief and to the point?
- Have I used active-voice verbs wherever possible?
- Is my tone consistent?
- Have I varied my sentence structure and length?
- Do I use stories and imagery? Did I just tell the reader what it was like, or did I take him there?
- Have I allowed a tired old cliché or an inappropriate word choice to slip through?
- Have I used details, numbers, facts and other specifics wherever possible?
- Have I deleted every unnecessary word, every unnecessary modifier, every redundant phrase?
- Have I deleted obvious points that can be inferred?
- Are the mechanics of my writing perfect? Have I corrected all spelling and typographical errors?

Index

AACSB, 44
academic ability, 1, 16, 24, 28–31
  assessment of, 53
  see also GMAT; GPA
academic dimension, 22, 24
academics, 10, 13, 33, 133
accomplishments, 72, 73–4, 80
  see also achievements
accreditation bodies, 44
achievements
  achievement and leadership, 118
  archetypal essay question, 101, 107–10,
    144
    choosing achievements, 109
  and diversity contribution, 121
  profile development, 72, 73–4, 80
action-drop introduction, 190
active orientation, 17–18, 24
active voice, 202–3
activities, 72, 73, 80
adjectives, 204
  limits of, 179
adjunct application readers, 10, 52
admissions committees (Adcoms), 1–2, 7
  attributes that satisfy, 15–21
  committee meeting stage, 55
  interviews, 155–7
  perspective of, 9–13
  stakeholder sets, 13–14
admissions officers, 10, 10–11, 49, 53, 173
  engaging, 11–12
  interviews, 156–7
  pressure-reward system, 13–14
admissions process, 2, 51–9, 208
  admissions fundamentals, 28–41
    age, 40–1
    GMAT, 28–31
    international applications, 38–40
    MBA resume, 31–2
    recommendations and recommenders,
      32–8
  all elements of application printed out, 51
  attributes *see* attributes
  class balance, 55–6

  first impressions, 51–2
  first read of the application, 52–5
  marketing oneself *see* marketing oneself
  researching the school *see* research
  timing issues, 56–9
adversity, 112
age, 40–1
agenda, control of, 64–5
all-rounder, 19–20, 24
alternative transcript, 30, 53
alumni, 10, 13, 48
  interviews, 155–7, 166
AMBA, 44
ambiguity, avoiding, 205–6
ambition, 17, 24
American orientation, 46
analysis, 66, 67
  in essay questions, 110
  personal profile, 72–8
  professional profile, 79–84
analytical mindset, 16, 24
analytical writing assessment (AWA), 19, 30
application failure, 1
application message *see* message
application timing issues, 56–9
archetypal essay questions, 3, 93–4, 97,
  100–39
  analysis of, 146–7
  creativity and innovation, 101, 136–9
  direct personal inquiry, 101, 134–6
  diversity/contribution/uniqueness, 101,
    120–4, 135, 144
  ethics and values, 101, 124–8
  goals/why an MBA?, 100–7
  key influences and formative experiences,
    101, 131–4, 144
  leadership, 101, 117–20, 144
  multiple archetypes in one essay, 143–5
  strengths, success and achievement, 101,
    107–10
  teamwork, 101, 128–30, 144
  weaknesses and failure, 101, 110–16, 144
argument, persuasive, 171–2
assistance, acknowledging, 165

attention, reader's, 172–5
attributes, 15–27, 89
  attribute dimensions, 22–4
  cross-cutting principles, 20–1, 89
  forces working in your favor, 25–7
  managing weaknesses and red flags, 24–5
  nobody has them all, 26
  profiling, 72, 73, 79
  proving, 67–8
  that satisfy the admissions committee,
    15–21
  see also points
audio presentation, 138–9

Bader, J., 11
balance, class *see* class balance
basic information, survey of, 53
behavioral questions, 65, 160
Belbin assessment, 129
blame, 152
Blink factor, 51–2
blogs, 9, 49–50
body of the essay, 188, 191–2
body language, 162
brainstorming, 65–7
breadth-depth balance, 164
brevity, 199–201, 207
brochures, 48
bullet points, 207
business scandals, 18, 124–5
business schools
  brand identity, 8–9, 15
  campus visit, 49
  competitiveness for applicants, 14, 40
  due diligence, 26, 48–50, 106, 142
  ensuring correct name in applications, 54,
    198
  foreign applicants and distinguishing
    between, 39
  GMAT score guidelines, 29–30
  the rankings, 21, 44–5
  reputation, 43, 44–5
  researching *see* research
  second-guessing requirements of, 209
  stakeholder in admissions process, 13
  sucking up to, 149, 209
Business Week, 21
buzzwords, 180

call options, 57
campus visit, 49

career
  arc, 105
  changes and the MBA, 105–6
  goals *see* goals
  innovation and renovation, 137
  potential, 17, 24
career services officers, 10
'carry freight' principle, 176
celebrities, 133
change
  archetypal essay question, 101, 136–9
  change and growth experiences, 82–3
chief executive officer (CEO) qualities, 23–4
childhood failures, 113
class balance, 9, 15, 55–6, 57, 209
  works in favor of the smart, 26–7
classic structures, 182–4
cohesion, 165
collaborative team member, 18–19, 24
Columbia recommendation guide form, 34,
    35
combinations of factors, 122
committee meeting, 55
communal dimension, 22–3, 24
communication, 122
  ability, 19, 24
  essays and testing skills of, 99
  priming recommenders, 37
community involvement/service, 18, 24, 89
  essay, 139–41
comparing then and now, 183–4
competitiveness, 1–2
  business schools' competition for
    applicants, 14, 40
  international applications and, 40
  killer instinct, 18, 24
conclusion, essay, 189, 192–4
concreteness, 178–9, 181
confidence, 118
conjunctions, 204–5
contribution, 19, 24
  essay question, 101, 120–4, 135, 144
  profile development, 76–7, 83
controversial topics, 152
conversational style, 154–5, 162–3
cooling period, 195
core questions, 158–9
core value, themes of, 89
courage, 118
creativity, 19, 24
  archetypal essay question, 101, 136–9

credibility, 181
cross-cutting principles, 20–1, 89
cultural influences, 75–6
current students, 10, 13, 48–9, 49–50, 52
current supervisor, 33
curriculum flexibility, 46–7
cute introduction, 190

deadlines, 56–8
debate, 165
decision process, 55
Department of Homeland Security, 58
depth-breadth balance, 164
detail, 164, 178–9
didactic introduction, 189–90
differentiation, 110, 150, 209
    themes of, 89–90
    see also uniqueness
difficulties, 74–5, 81
direct personal enquiry, 101, 134–6, 144
direction, 122–3
distinctiveness see uniqueness
diversity, 1–2, 9, 15, 19, 24, 46
    essay question, 101, 120–4, 135, 144
    profile development, 76–7, 83
double-archetype questions, 143–5
drafts, 188, 195
    letting someone else read a draft, 194
    revising and rewriting, 194, 196
dress, 154
due diligence, 26, 48–50, 106, 142

editing, 195, 196
editor, 196
education, 45
electioneering, 7–8, 87
electives, 45–6
elevator speech, 91
emotions, touching, 176–7, 181
English ability, 39
enthusiasm, 20, 180
EQUIS, 44
essays, 3, 97–100, 139–52, 208
    archetypal questions see archetypal essay
        questions
    assessment, 54
    essay mission statement, 148–9, 187, 188
    mapping your message to the essay
        questions, 93–4, 146–9
    meeting the essay requirements, 99–100
    other common essay types, 139–43

pitfalls to avoid, 149–52
profiling as basis for essay responses, 64–5
profiling and shadowing the essay process,
    67
reading the draft essay set, 195
reflective writing, 12–13
rereading before the interview, 161
role of, 97–9
writing see writing
esteem needs, 70–1
ethics, 18, 24
    essay question, 101, 124–8
    ethical challenges, 126
    ethical dilemmas, 119, 126, 127
    ethical failures, 113
everyday incidents, 68
everyday language, 175, 201–2
evidence, 209
examples, series of, 183
executive MBAs (EMBAs), 47
experience, 40, 41, 121, 122
    inexperience, 81–2
    quality of, 41
external readers, 10, 52
extracurricular options, 45–6
extramurals, 45
extrovert personality, 17, 24

factual questions, 160
faculty, 10, 13
failures
    archetypal essay question, 101, 110–16,
        144
        choosing failure topics, 112–13
        failure topics to avoid, 113–14
    profile development, 74–5, 81
fake failures, 113
Financial Times, 21
fine-tuning selection, 98
finger-pointing, 152
first draft, 188
first impressions, 51–2, 162, 189
first read, 52–5
first steps, showing, 107
fit, 7, 8–9, 15, 43, 48–50, 209
flexibility
    curriculum, 46–7
    deadline, 58
foreign applicants, 38–40, 58
foreign business schools, 40
formality, interview and, 154–5

formative experiences
  archetypal essay question, 101, 131–4
  profile development, 76, 82–3
formative role of the MBA, 41
formative stories, 69
foundation questions, 158–9
freshness, 179–80
functional goals, 103–4
future, 193
  communicating future aspirations, 102–3
  connecting past to, 106
  expectation of achievement in the, 27

gaps, assessing, 147
general requirements, 9
generic, avoiding the, 150
Gladwell, M., 51
GMAT, 16, 19, 22, 28–31
  balance vs superbracket scores, 29
  international applications, 39
  mitigating a low score, 30–1
  target program guidelines, 29–30
  vs the GRE, 31
goals, 209
  career goals, 54, 84, 102–3, 122–3
    archetypal essay question, 100–7, 144
  personal, 77–8
GPA, 16, 22, 28, 53
  international applications, 38–9
  mitigating a low GPA, 30–1
GRE, 31
grouping information, 87–8
groupwork *see* teamwork
growth, professional, 82–3
guest speakers, 45

'half-life' of diminishing reader interest, 189, 191
Harvard Business School, 40, 102
hierarchy of needs, 70–1
honesty, 18
human-interest stories, 175–9
humility, 118, 181

icebreaking, 161–2
ideal MBA applicant, 8, 150
idealism, 104–5
ideological perspective, 152
idols *see* mentors; role models
imagery, 177–8
importance, 173–4

imprecise use of words, 206
impressions, first, 51–2, 162, 189
inappropriate failures, 113–14
inexperience, 81–2
influences
  archetypal essay question, 101, 131–4, 144
  profile development, 75–6, 82
initiative, 17–18
innovation, 19, 89
  archetypal essay question, 101, 136–9
insight, 63–4, 69–71, 122
  see also profiling
inspiration, 118
integration of the personal and professional, 136
integrity, 18, 24, 118
intellectual ability *see* academic ability
intercultural experience and tolerance, 19, 24
interests and passions, 19–20, 135, 135–6
international applications, 38–40
internships, 45
interview, 3, 153–67, 208
  business school policy, 54–5
  managing the interview, 160–7
  preparation, 157–8, 160–1
  questions, 158–60, 162
  research on the interviewer, 157
  test of personality, 153–5
  types of interview, 155–7
introduction, essay, 188–90, 193
inverted pyramid, 191

jargon, 180, 202
joint degrees, 46
judgment, good, 16
junior mindset, 133

Kelleher, H., 29
killer instinct, 18, 24

labeling, 91–2
leadership, 17, 24, 89, 129, 138, 209
  archetypal essay question, 101, 117–20, 144
    elements of leadership, 118
    vs ethical dilemmas, 119
    in the interview, 163
    profile development, 75, 82
learning, 138
  from failures, 114–15
LeGault, M., 51

length of the program, 46–7
life-changing events, 76
life story, 64
likeability, 20, 24, 210
limits, word, 194–5
linear outline, 185–6
listing, 207
location, 45
love/belonging needs, 70–1

major issues, 90–1
making a difference, 20–1
management, and leadership, 17
mapping
    in the interview, 158
    message to essay questions, 93–4, 146–9
marketing oneself, 7–14, 86–7
    Adcom's perspective, 9–13
    communicating your value, 14
    and electioneering, 7–8, 87
    fit with the program, 8–9
Maslow challenge, 70–1
'math camp', 16
maturity, 16, 24
Max-Neef, M., 70
MBA Oath, 125–6
mental health, 113–14
mental toughness, 17
mentors, 75, 82, 131–4, 144
message
    application message, 91–3, 193
        ensuring all facts are integrated into, 151
        keeping sight of the key message, 151
        mapping to the essay questions, 93–4, 146–9
        message techniques, 91–3
        staying on message, 92, 164
        'take-home' message, 194
    sticky messages, 181
mirror introduction, 189
mission goals, 103–4
mission statement, 43
mistakes, 81
MIT-Sloan recommendation guide form, 36
model applicant, 8, 150
modesty, 109
modifiers, 201, 206
morality see ethics
motivation, 17
    analysing your own motivations, 42–3
    leadership and, 118

Maslow's hierarchy of needs, 70–1
multipart questions, 182
multiple-admit strategy, 59
multiple applications, 47, 197
multiple-archetype questions, 143–5
multiple negatives, 206

needs
    analysing your own needs, 42–3
    hierarchy of, 70–1
non-failures, 113
nouns, 204
    pile-ups, 205
number of applications, 47
numbers, 179

object (of sentence), 203
objective reality, 69
off-campus interviews, 155–6, 157
older applicants, 41
on-campus interviews, 155–6
openings, in essay questions, 147
opportunities, seizing, 21
optional essay, 142–3, 165–6
outline of essay, 149, 184–6
over-competence, 151, 210
overlapping information, 32

paragraphing, 191
parallelism, 205
passions and interests, 19–20, 135, 135–6
passive voice, 202–3
past, connecting to the future, 106
perseverance, 17, 24
personal code, 126
personal dimension, 23, 24, 210
personal goals, 77–8
personal inquiry essay question, 101, 134–6, 144
personal life, 149–50
    integration with professional life, 136
personal philosophy, 77, 83–4, 126
personal profile, 65, 72–8
personal qualities, 72, 73
personal values see values
personality
    interview as a test of, 153–5
    strong and extrovert, 17, 24
personality assessments, 129
persuasive writing, 171–2
'philosophical' insight conclusions, 193

philosophy, personal, 77, 83–4, 126
phrases
  redundant, 199–200
  transitional, 192
  unnecessary prepositional phrases, 200–1
physiological needs, 70–1
points, 66, 67
  personal profile, 72–8
  professional profile, 79–84
  proving, 67–8
  redundant, 199
  see also attributes
posing as someone else, 150
positioning, 89–91
preferences, 42–3
preparation for interview, 157–8, 160–1
prepositional phrases, 200–1
presentations, 138–9
prioritizing, 85–6
professional admissions staff *see* admissions
  officers
professional associates/clients, 34
professional dimension, 22, 24
professional goals (career goals) *see* goals
professional life, 150
  integration with personal life, 136
professional profile, 65, 79–84
professional qualities, 79
professionalism, 16, 24, 150
profile development table, 66, 72
profiling, 2–3, 63–94, 208
  application message, 91–3
    mapping to the essay questions, 93–4
  benefits of, 63–5
  brainstorming, 65–7
  finding and developing stories, 67–9
  Maslow challenge, 70–1
  personal profile, 65, 72–8
  positioning, 89–91
  professional profile, 65, 79–84
  profile definition, 87–8
  retirement visualization, 69
  selecting and prioritizing, 85–7
pronouns, 204, 205, 206
proof, 67–8, 121, 164, 179, 209
proofreading, 198
punctuation, 206
purpose, 103–4

qualifiers, 201
quality of experience, 41

quantitative orientation, 16, 24
questions
  behavioral, 65, 160
  essay questions
    archetypal *see* archetypal essay questions
    mapping your message to, 93–4, 146–9
  interview questions, 158–60, 162
  shadowing-the-question structure, 182–3
  your questions at the end of the interview,
    165–7
quotations, 190

raising the pace, 207
rankings of business schools, 21, 44–5
rapport, 161, 165
reach school (dream school), 47
reader
  adjunct application readers, 10, 52
  attention as a finite resource, 172–5
  fatigue, 174
  half-life of diminishing reader interest,
    189, 191
  managing the reader's experience, 67, 86,
    171–81
  what readers skip, 174
reading the application file, 52–5
recommendations, 32–8, 54
  dangers of self-written, 38
  guide form for, 34–7
recommenders, 32–8, 54
  fatigue, 38
  priming, 37
  selecting, 33–4
recruitability, 20, 24, 41
recruiters, 13, 44, 45
'red flags', 24–5
redundant phrases, 199–200
redundant points, 199
redundant words, 200
reflective writing, 12–13, 122
relevance, 151, 173–4
repetition of material, 151
reputation of business school, 43, 44–5
research
  on the interviewer, 157
  on the school/program, 8–9, 26, 42–50,
    106
    analysis of your own needs, 42–3
    due diligence and fit, 48–50
    essay question, 142
    evaluating business schools, 44–7

resume, 31–2, 161, 179
retirement visualization, 69
reuse of essay material, 197
revised mapping, 147–8
rewriting and revising essays, 196
role models, 75, 82, 131–4

safety needs, 70–1
safety school, 47
sales pitches, 92–3
scale, 68
scandals, business, 18, 124–5
selecting profile information, 85–6, 87–8
selection, fine-tuning, 98
self-actualization needs, 70–1
self-compromise, 8
self-knowledge, 63–4, 66, 122, 208–9
self-promotion, 109
self-reflection, 12–13, 122
self-review essay, 141
sensemaking, 99
sentence construction, 199–207
    avoiding ambiguity, 205–6
    brevity, 199–201, 207
    conjunctions and pronouns, 204–5
    subject, object and verb, 203
    verbs, 203–4
shadowing-the-question structure, 182–3
signposting, 186–7
simplicity, 181
sincerity, 180–1
skills, 74, 80–1
smart applying, 2, 26–7
'so what?' test, 173–4
social contribution, 18, 24
    essay, 139–41
social media, 49–50
    managing material about oneself, 50
soft skills, 21
Soros, G., 29, 111–12, 115
speakers, 45
specialties, 43, 46
specific, writing and the, 178–9
spellchecker, 198
spoken outline, 186
sports, 129
stakeholders, 13–14
standing out, 123
Stanford GSB, 12, 40, 195
starting salaries, 44–5
staying on message, 92

stereotypes, 8
    breaking, 150–1
sticky messages, 181
stories, 66, 67, 181, 209
    choosing and the 'carry freight' principle,
        176
    finding and developing, 67–9
    personal profile, 72–8
    professional profile, 79–84
    self-evaluation and telling one's own story,
        64
    tips for thinking of good stories, 68–9
    writing human-interest stories, 175–9
strengths, 165
    archetypal essay question, 101, 107–10
    profile development, 74, 80–1
structure
    persuasive argument, 171–2
    of a program, 46–7
    writing, 182–7, 193
        classic structures, 182–4
        outline, 184–6
        signposting, 186–7
student discussion forums, 49–50
student profiles, 46
student visa, 58
students, current, 10, 13, 48–9, 49–50, 52
subject (of a sentence), 203
subjective reality, 69
subordinate clauses, 203
success
    archetypal essay question, 101, 107–10
    track record 16, 24, 209
sucking up, 149, 209
supervisor, current, 33
support, acknowledging, 165
surprise, 181

'take-home' message, 194
tautologies, 200
team roles, 129, 130
teamwork skills, 18–19, 24, 89
    archetypal essay question, 101, 128–30,
        144
technology, 137–8
template structures, 182–4
tenacity, 109
thank-you note, 167
'that', avoiding, 201
themes, 87–91, 193
    choosing, 89–91

developing, 88
  essay writing, 148
thesis statement, 187, 188
time, 68
  right time for an MBA, 40, 41, 106–7
  as structure, 182–3
timing of application, 56–9
tone, 115, 180–1
toughness, mental, 17
transitions, 192
triple-archetype questions, 143–5
truth, 149
tumbling strategy, 159–60
Turner, T., 29
tweets, for essays, 148–9

UCLA-Anderson School Director of MBA
  Admissions, 11
uniqueness, 83, 110, 150, 210
  apparent lack of distinctiveness, 121–3
  essay question, 101, 120–4, 135, 144
  themes of, 89–90
unsubstantiated claims, 152

value
  communicating your value, 14
  delivering in the interview, 163–4
  essays and adding value, 99–100
values, 18, 24
  archetypal essay question, 101, 124–8
  profile development, 77, 83–4
verbs
  avoiding overuse of the verb 'to be', 201
  keeping subject, object and verb close
    together, 203
  using more and better, 203–4
vision, 118
visiting the business school, 49
visual outline, 184–5
visual presentation, 138–9
vulnerability, 149–50

waitlisting, 57, 58–9
weaknesses, 26, 158–9
  archetypal essay question, 101, 110–16,
    144

managing, 24–5, 141
  optional essay and dealing with, 143
  profile development, 74–5, 81–2
websites, 48
Welch, J., 29
Wharton *Student-2-Student* discussion forum,
  49–50
whistle-blowing, 126, 127
'why an MBA' essay question, 100–7, 144
words, 199–207
  avoiding imprecise use of, 206
  conjunctions, 204–5
  empty qualifiers, 201
  modifiers, 201, 206
  nouns, 204, 205
  pronouns, 204, 205, 206
  redundant, 200
  verbs, 201, 203–4
  word limits, 194–5
writing the essays, 3, 171–207, 208
  active voice, 202–3
  body of text, 188, 191–2
  brevity, 199–201, 207
  conclusion, 189, 192–4
  cooling period, 195
  drafts, 188, 194, 195, 196
  editing, 195, 196
  everyday language, 175, 201–2
  freshness, 179–80
  introduction, 188–90, 193
  managing the reader's experience, 171–81
  outline, 149, 184–6
  persuasive, 171–2
  proofreading, 198
  raising the pace, 207
  reusing material for other applications, 197
  revising and rewriting, 196
  signposting, 186–7
  structure, 182–7, 193
  thesis statement, 187, 188
  tone, 115, 180–1
  word limits, 194–5
  word and sentence strategies, 199–207
written word, the, 174–5

younger applicants, 40–1, 41

Related books from Open University Press

Purchase from www.openup.co.uk or order through your local bookseller

---

ON LEADERSHIP: DEFINITIVE WRITINGS ON POWER, AUTHORITY AND INFLUENCE

Barbara Kellerman

Indispensable advice for business professionals and students - from history's wisest leaders

A highly regarded scholar of leadership and the qualities shared by outstanding leaders, Barbara Kellerman provides expert analysis of the works of history's greatest authorities on leadership - theorists and practitioners alike.

On Leadership contains writings from some of history's most influential figures, ranging from Lincoln to Lenin, Hobbes to Havel, and Machiavelli to Marx. Kellerman chose her entries based on their contemporary significance regarding power, authority, and influence, and she clearly explains how today's business leaders can put the words of the masters to practical use.

Providing a remarkably wide scope of perspectives from the fields of history, psychology, philosophy and government, *On Leadership* is an eminently instructive book for any leader in any field.

Contents

Part I: Contemplating Leadership – Lao Tzu – Confucius – Plato – Plutarch – Machiavelli – Hobbes – Locke – Carlyle – Spencer – James – Tolstoy – Weber – Freud – Follett – Barnard – Drucker – Burns – Milgram – Arendt – Part II: Exercising Leadership – Wollstonecraft – Paine – Marx and Engels – Stanton – Stowe – Lenin – DuBois – Hitler – Alinsky – Fanon – Carson – Friedan – Kramer – Singer – Part III: Leaders – Julius Caesar (Shakespeare) – Hamilton – Madison – Lincoln – Mao – Gandhi – F. D. Roosevelt – Churchill – King – J. F. Kennedy – Mandela – Havel.

May 2010   352pp   £24.99   €26.99
978–0–071–63384–0 (Hardback)

THE HIGH-VELOCITY EDGE
HOW MARKET LEADERS LEVERAGE OPERATIONAL EXCELLENCE TO BEAT THE COMPETITION

Steven J. Spear

Spear has dazzled readers with his insights,

Harvard Business Review

What do Toyota, Aloca and other world-class organizations share in common? As Steven Spear reveals in *The High-Velocity Edge*, they all manage their complex internal systems so skillfully that they generate constant, almost automatic operational self-improvements at rates faster, durations longer and breadths wider than the competition.

Excellence in operational management is not merely the realm of a select group of geniuses. It depends on core competencies that can be taught, practiced, and applied to an organisation, and Spear helps readers do just that in *The High-Velocity Edge*. The book puts readers on the fast track to operational excellence, regardless of the type of company they operate. Spear explains how to:

- Build a system of "dynamic discovery" that reveals operational problems and weaknesses
- Attack and solve problems at the time and in the place where they occur, converting weaknesses into strengths
- Disseminate knowledge gained from solving local problems throughout the company as a whole
- Create managers invested in the process of continual innovation

Contents
Chapter 1: Getting to the Front of the Pack – Chapter 2: Complexity: The Good News and the Bad News – Chapter 3: How Complex Systems Fail – Chapter 4: How Complex Systems Succeed – Chapter 5: High Velocity Under the Sea, In the Air and On the Web – Chapter 6: Capability 1: System Design and Operation – Chapter 7: Capability 2: Problem Solving and Improvement – Chapter 8: Capability 3: Knowledge Sharing – Chapter 9: Capability 4: Developing High-Velocity Skills in Others – Chapter 10: High-Velocity Crisis Recovery – Chapter 11: Creating High-Velocity Health-Care Organizations – Chapter 12: Conclusion.

June 2010 416pp £20.99 €22.99
978–0–071–74141–5 (Hardback)

The *McGraw·Hill* Companies

What's new from Open University Press?

Education... Media, Film & Cultural Studies

Health, Nursing & Social Welfare... Higher Education

Psychology, Counselling & Psychotherapy... Study Skills

Keep up with what's buzzing
at Open University Press
by signing up to receive
regular title information at
www.openup.co.uk/elert

Sociology

OPEN UNIVERSITY PRESS

McGraw - Hill Education